"Nolo's home page is wortl  W9-CYV-632
—WALL STREET JOURNAL

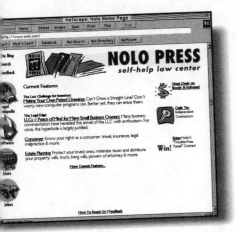

LEGAL INFORMATION ONLINE

www.nolo.com

 24 HOURS A DAY

AT THE NOLO PRESS SELF-HELP LAW CENTER ON THE WEB, YOU'LL FIND:

○ Nolo's comprehensive Legal Encyclopedia, with links to other online resources

Downloadable demos of Nolo software and sample chapters of many Nolo books

○ An online law store with a secure online ordering system

○ Our ever-popular lawyer jokes

○ Discounts and other good deals,
our hilarious SHARK TALK game

THE NOLO NEWS

Stay on top of important legal changes with Nolo's quarterly magazine, *The Nolo News*. Start your free one-year subscription by filling out and mailing the response card in the back of this book. With each issue, you'll get legal news about topics that affect you every day, reviews of legal books by other publishers, the latest Nolo catalog, scintillating advice from Auntie Nolo and a fresh batch of our famous lawyer jokes.

National Seventh Edition

EVERYBODY'S
GUIDE TO

SMALL
CLAIMS
COURT

by Attorney Ralph Warner

NOLO PRESS BERKELEY

Your Responsibility When Using a Self-help Law Book

We've done our best to give you useful and accurate information in this book. But laws and procedures change frequently and are subject to differing interpretations. If you want legal advice backed by a guarantee, see a lawyer. If you use this book, it's your responsibility to make sure that the facts and general advice contained in it are applicable to your situation.

Keeping Up-to-Date

To keep its books up to date, Nolo Press issues new printings and new editions periodically. New printings reflect minor legal changes and technical corrections. New editions contain major legal changes, major text additions or major reorganizations. To find out if a later printing or edition of any Nolo book is available, call Nolo Press at 510-549-1976 or check the catalog in the *Nolo News,* our quarterly newspaper. You can also contact Nolo Press on the Internet at www.nolo.com.

To stay current, follow the "Update" service in the *Nolo News.* You can get a free one-year subscription by sending us the registration card in the back of the book. In another effort to help you use Nolo's latest materials, we offer a 25% discount off the purchase of the new edition of your Nolo book when you turn in the cover of an earlier edition. For details, see the back of this book. This book was last revised in: October 1997

Seventh Edition	October 1997
Legal Editing	Stanley Jacobsen, Lisa Guerin and Beth Lawrence
Illustrations	Linda Allison
Production	Susan Cornell and Amy Ihara
Proofreading	Sheryl Rose
Index	Sayre Van Young
Printing	Bertelsmann Industry Services, Inc.

Warner, Ralph E.
 Everybody's guide to small claims court / by Ralph Warner. —
National 7th ed.
     p. cm.
   Includes index.
   ISBN 0-87337-400-2
   1. Small claims courts—United States—States. I. Title.
KF8769.Z95W37   1997
347.73'04—dc21

                                                           97-29742
                                                               CIP

Quantity sales: For information on bulk purchases or corporate premium sales, please contact the Special Sales Department. For academic sales or textbook adoptions, ask for Academic Sales. 800-955-44775, Nolo Press, Inc., 950 Parker St., Berkeley, CA, 94710.Special Sales department. For academic sales or textbook adoptions, please ask for Academic Sales. 800-955-4775, Nolo Press, 950 Parker St., Berkeley, CA 94710.

To Our Readers

This book can be of great help to you and your family. The advice it offers about Small Claims Court is as sound as I have been able to make it, after much study of, and experience in, the area. A number of knowledgeable people have reviewed these materials and many of their suggestions for change and clarification have been included. Hundreds of readers have taken the time to give me the benefit of their insights and experience—resulting in my fine-tuning and improving the text.

But advice—no matter how sound—will not always work. Like well-meaning recommendations of all kinds, some of the advice I present here may not be helpful. So here are some qualifications. If you have access to a lawyer's advice and it is contrary to that given here, follow your lawyer's advice; the individual characteristics of your problem can better be considered by someone in possession of all the facts. Laws and procedures vary considerably from one state to the next and it's impossible to guarantee that every bit of information and advice contained here will be accurate. It is your responsibility to get a copy of the rules governing your local Small Claims Court and to make sure that the facts and general advice contained in this book are applicable in your state and to your situation. Small Claims Court rules and regulations change constantly, and you should check with your Small Claims Court clerk to make sure that information printed here is still current. And finally, please pay attention to this general disclaimer: Of necessity, neither the author nor the publisher of this book makes any guarantees regarding the outcome of the uses to which this material is put. Thank you, and good luck!

R.W.
Berkeley, California

Thank You

A number of talented friends have read the manuscript of this book and made helpful suggestions for improvement. With enough help, even a tarnished penny can be made to shine. Thanks to Leslie Ihara Armistead, Steve Elias and, especially, Stephanie Harolde and Susan Cornell, who have labored hard to round up many errant thoughts. Thanks, too, to Judge Roderic Duncan, Mary Alice Coleman of the California State Department of Consumer Affairs and Jeanne Stott—San Francisco's pre-eminent Small Claims Court Legal Advisor; they don't always agree with what I write, but are nonetheless unfailingly helpful.

Lisa Guerin, Stanley Jacobsen and Beth Lawrence compiled the research for all material appearing in the Appendix. Their thorough, patient and dedicated work has made this a better book.

Linda Allison's wonderful drawings speak for themselves. Working with her is like catching the first ray of sunshine on a clear morning.

For Toni,

the light, the heart, and the love of my life

Contents

Introduction

Here is a practical book on how to use Small Claims Court. It is a tool that will help you answer such questions as:

"How does Small Claims Court work?"

"Do I have a case worth pursuing or defending?"

"How do I prepare my case to maximum advantage?"

"What witnesses and other evidence should I present?"

"What do I say in court?"

"Can I appeal if I lose?"

"How do I collect my judgment?"

Proper preparation and presentation of your Small Claims action can often mean the difference between receiving a check and writing one. This isn't to say that I can tell you how to take a hopeless case and turn it into a blue ribbon winner. It does mean that with the information you will learn here and your own creativity and common sense, you will be able to develop your position in the best possible way. It does mean that I can show you how a case with a slight limp can be improved and set on four good legs.

Just as important as knowing when and how to bring your Small Claims action is knowing when not to. You don't want to waste time and energy dragging a hopeless case to court. Here I will teach you to understand the difference between winners and losers, and hopefully to keep the losers at home.

The goal of this book is to give both people bringing a case and those defending one all the step-by-step information necessary to make the best possible use of Small Claims Court. From deciding whether you have a case, through gathering evidence, arranging for witnesses, planning your courtroom presentation, and collecting your money, you will find everything you need here.

Certain arbitrary decisions have had to be made as to order and depth of coverage. For example, the question of whether an oral contract is valid is discussed in Chapter 2, but not again in Chapter 16 on automobile repairs, where you may need it. So please take the time to read, or at least skim, the entire book before you focus on the chapters that interest you most. A good way to get an overview of the entire Small Claims process is by carefully reading the Table of Contents. Also, be sure to examine the detailed rules (in the Appendix) for your state.

Chapter 24 is the last part of this book designed to help you win your case and collect your money. Chapter 25 is devoted to a different cause—how our court system must be changed to deliver more justice and less frustration. In many ways this material is intensely personal in that it reflects my own experience with our formal, lawyer-dominated legal delivery system. It springs from my own painful realization that neither law, nor justice, nor the resolution of disputes is what our courts are presently about. We have allowed them to become instead the private fiefdom of lawyers, judges and other professionals, and it is their selfish interests rather than the common good that are being served.

I have included this material because I believe that it will be of interest to all of you who have become involved in the resolution of your own disputes in Small Claims Court. You have had the courage to take responsibility for solving your own problems. Given the opportunity, you can do a great deal more. It is past time that you are allowed to participate in your own legal system. It is past time that you are made welcome in your own courthouses. It is past time that all of us realize that a society whose legal system is run by and for lawyers can't long survive.

Now a few words about two potentially sensitive subjects. First, when grappling with the ever tricky personal pronoun, I have decided to simply take turns rather than using the cumbersome "he or she" and "his or her" every time both men and women could be involved.

Second, I want to say a few words about the many referrals to other Nolo Press self-help law books you will find sprinkled throughout this one. At first glance it may appear that I am trying to sell you another book on every third page. In my own defense, however, I would like to make three points. First, Nolo Press is by far the largest and most comprehensive publisher of self-help law materials in the United States. As a result, there are many legal areas where Nolo publishes the only materials aimed at nonlawyers. Second, I simply don't have the space in this already chunky book to repeat all the information in Nolo's fifty or so other volumes. Third, as Nolo's books are available at most libraries (public or law) in the United States, it shouldn't be hard to read any other Nolo volumes pertinent to your problem at no cost.

Icons Used in This Book

Look for these icons to alert you to certain kinds of information.

 Warning: A caution to slow down and consider potential problems.

 Fast Track: Lets you know when you may skip reading some material that is not relevant to your situation.

 Tip: Gives practical suggestions for handling a legal or procedural issue that may come up.

 Recommended Reading: Suggests references for additional information.

CHAPTER

In the Beginning

A. First Things

Small Claims procedures are established by state law. This means there are differences in the operating rules of Small Claims Courts from state to state, including the maximum amount for which you can sue, who can sue, and what papers must be filed where and when. There are even differences among names used for Small Claims Court (or its equivalent) in the different states, with "Justice," "District," "Municipal," "City," "County" and "Magistrates" court among the names commonly used.

    While the details of using Small Claims Courts vary from state to state, the basic approach necessary to prepare and present a case properly is remarkably similar everywhere. But details are important, and you will wish to do two things to make sure you understand how Small Claims Court works in your state:

1) Look up your state in the 50-state Appendix towards the back of this book. It includes much key information you'll need.

2) Obtain your local Small Claims rules from your Small Claims Court Clerk's office.

The purpose of Small Claims Court is to hear disputes involving modest amounts of money, without long delays and formal rules of evidence. Disputes are normally presented by the people involved. Lawyers are prohibited in some states, including Michigan and California (except when involved in their own disputes), but are allowed in most. However, the limited dollar amounts involved usually make it uneconomical for people to hire them. The maximum amount of money for which you can sue (in legal jargon, this is called the "jurisdictional amount") is $5,000 in the District of Columbia, $3,000 in New York and $7,500 in Minnesota. These amounts are typical, although there is considerable variation. Some states allow Small Claims Court cases up to $10,000, while others limit cases to no more than $2,000. (See Appendix.)

In recent years, the maximum amount for which suits can be brought has been on the rise almost everywhere. Don't rely on your memory, or what a friend tells you, or even what you read here. Call the local Small Claims Court clerk and find out exactly how much you can sue for. You may be pleasantly surprised to find that the maximum is more than you thought.

There are three great advantages of Small Claims Court:

- First, you get to prepare and present your own case without having to pay a lawyer more than your claim is worth.

- Second, bringing a dispute to Small Claims Court is simple. The gobbledygook of complicated legal forms and language prevalent in other courts is kept to a minimum. To start your case, you need only fill out a few lines on a simple form—for example, "Honest Al's Used Chariots owes me $5,000 because the 1995 Neon they sold me in supposedly 'excellent condition' died less than a mile from the car lot." When you get to court, you can talk to the judge without a whole lot of "res ipsa loquiturs" and "pendente lites." If you have documents or witnesses, you may present them for what they are worth, with no requirement that you comply with the thousand years' accumulation of rusty, musty procedures, habits and so-called rules of evidence of which the legal profession is so proud.

- Third, and perhaps most important, Small Claims Court doesn't take long. Most disputes are heard in court within a month or two from the time the complaint is filed. The hearing itself seldom takes more than 15 minutes. The judge announces her decision either right there in the courtroom, or mails it out within a few days.

But before you decide that Small Claims Court sounds like just the place to bring your case, you will want to answer a basic question. Are the results you are likely to achieve in proportion to, or greater than, the effort you will have to expend? This must be answered by looking at each dispute individually. It is all too easy to get so involved in a particular dispute that you lose sight of the fact that the time, trouble and expense of bringing it to court may be way out of balance with any likely return.

In order to clearly assess whether your case is worth the effort of bringing it to court, you will want to understand the details of how Small Claims Court works—who can sue, where and for how much, is a good start. You will also want to learn a little law—are you entitled to relief? how much? and how do you compute the exact amount? Finally, and most importantly, comes the detail so many people overlook, to their later dismay. Assuming you prepare and present your case brilliantly and get a judgment for everything you request, can you collect? The ability to get paid seems a silly thing to space out, doesn't it? Unfortunately, many plaintiffs commonly go through the entire Small Claims procedure with no chance of collecting a dime because they have sued a person who has neither money nor any reasonable prospect of getting any.

The purpose of the first dozen chapters of this book is to help you decide whether or not you have a case worth pursuing. These are not the chapters where grand strategies are brilliantly unrolled to baffle and confound the opposition—that comes later. Here we are more concerned with such mundane tasks as locating the person you want to sue, suing in the right court, filling out the necessary forms and getting them properly served. Perhaps it will disappoint those of you with a dramatic turn of mind, but most cases are won or lost before anyone enters the courtroom.

Here and there we reproduce forms used in California and New York. Forms used elsewhere will often look quite different, but you will find that the differences are usually more a matter of graphics than of substance. The basic information requested—who is suing whom about what—is very similar everywhere. Blank copies of all forms are available at your local Small Claims clerk's office.

B. Checklist of Things to Think Out Before Initiating or Defending Your Case

Here is a preliminary checklist of things you will want to think about at this initial stage. As you read further, we will go into each of these areas in more detail. But let me remind you again, if you haven't already gotten a copy of your local Small Claims Court rules, do it now. It's silly to come to bat with two out in the ninth and the bases loaded and not know if you are supposed to run to first or third.

PLAINTIFFS' (FILERS') CHECKLIST

☐ 1.	Do you have a good case? That is, can you establish or prove all key elements necessary to win your legal action? (See Chapter 2 for a discussion of what is needed to win contract, debt, property damage and other common types of cases.)
☐ 2.	How many dollars is your claim for? If it is for more than the Small Claims maximum, do you wish to waive the excess and still use Small Claims Court? (See Chapter 4.)
☐ 3.	Have you made a reasonable effort to contact the other party to offer a compromise? (See Chapter 6.)
☐ 4.	Is your suit brought within the proper time period? (See Chapter 5.)
☐ 5.	Which Small Claims Court should you bring your suit in? (See Chapter 9.)
☐ 6.	Whom do you sue and how do you identify this person or business on your court papers? In some types of cases, especially those involving businesses and automobiles, this can be a little more technical and tricky than you might have guessed. (See Chapter 8.)
☐ 7.	If mediation is offered or required by your Small Claims Court, do you understand how it works and how best to use it? (See Chapter 6.)
☐ 8.	Can you prove your case? That is, do you understand what evidence you need to bring to court to convince a judge you are in the right? (See Chapters 14 through 22.)
☐ 9.	Can you make a convincing courtroom presentation? The key here is practice, practice, practice. (See Chapter 15.)
☐ 10.	And again, the most important question—assuming that you can win, is there a reasonable chance you can collect? (See Chapters 3 and 24.)

DEFENDANTS' CHECKLIST

☐ 1.	Do you have legal grounds for a countersuit against the plaintiff? Or put another way, does the plaintiff really owe you money? (See Chapters 10 and 12.)
☐ 2.	Do you have a partial or complete legal defense against the claim of the plaintiff? Or put another way, has the plaintiff filed a bogus lawsuit? (See Chapters 2 and 12.)
☐ 3.	Has the plaintiff sued for a reasonable or an excessive amount? (See Chapter 4.)
☐ 4.	Has the plaintiff brought his suit within the proper time limit? (See Chapter 5.)
☐ 5.	Has the plaintiff followed reasonably correct procedures in bringing suit and serving you with the court papers? (See Chapters 11 and 12.)
☐ 6.	If mediation is offered or required by your Small Claims Court, do you understand how it works and how to use it? (See Chapter 6.)
☐ 7.	Have you made a reasonable effort to contact the plaintiff in order to arrive at a compromise settlement? (See Chapters 6 and 12.)
☐ 8.	Assuming you'll contest the case in court, you'll normally need proof that your version of events is correct. Can you collect evidence and witnesses to accomplish this? (See Chapters 13 through 16.)
☐ 9.	Are you prepared to present your side of the case convincingly in court? (See Chapter 15.)

C. Legal Jargon Defined

Mercifully, there is not a great deal of technical language used in Small Claims Courts. But there are a few terms that may be new to you and with which you will have to become familiar. Don't try to learn all of these terms now. Refer back to these definitions when you need them. Here we give you the most widely used version of most terms. In some states, jargon may vary slightly, but the substance will be remarkably similar everywhere.

Abstract of Judgment: An official document you get from the Small Claims Court clerk's office which indicates that you have a money judgment against another person. Filing it with the County Recorder places a lien on real property owned by the judgment debtor. Some states may use slightly different terminology.

Appeal: Some states only allow a defendant to appeal; others allow appeals based only on law—not facts. Many require a bond to be posted. (See Chapter 23 and Appendix.)

Arbitration: A voluntary system under which a case is heard by arbitrators rather than in a court setting. Not available in most states, but used widely in New York City night courts. Ask your court clerk for local rules, if any.

Calendar: List of cases to be heard by a Small Claims Court on a particular day. A case taken off calendar is removed from the list. This usually occurs because the defendant has not been served or because the parties jointly request that it be heard on another day.

Civil Code (CC) and Code of Civil Procedure (CCP): The Civil Code contains much of a state's substantive law. The Code of Civil Procedure contains its legal procedures. These books are available at all public libraries and at law libraries. (Law libraries are located at the county courthouse and are open to the public.) A number of states call these legal codes by other names, such as "Revised Statutes," "Rules of Civil Procedure" (RCP) and "Rules of Court." Ask the law librarian for help if you have trouble finding the right book.

Claim of Defendant: A claim by a defendant that the plaintiff owes him money. A Claim of Defendant, also called a "Defendant's Claim," is filed as part of the same Small Claims action that the plaintiff has started.

Claim of Exemption: A procedure by which a "judgment debtor" can claim that, under federal and/or state law, certain of his money or other property is exempt from being grabbed to satisfy a debt.

Commissioner: A court employee designated to hear Small Claims cases in certain states, such as California. Usually a commissioner has the same powers to hear and decide cases as does a judge.

Continuance: A court order that a hearing be postponed to a later date.

Counterclaim: Basically the same as a Claim of Defendant or a Cross Complaint. Different states use different names.

Default Judgment: A court decision given to the plaintiff (the person filing suit) when the defendant fails to show up (that is, defaults).

Defendant: The person being sued.

Dismissed Case: A dismissal usually occurs when a case is dropped by the plaintiff. If the defendant has not filed a claim, the plaintiff simply files a written request for dismissal. If the defendant has filed a claim, both plaintiff and defendant must agree in writing before a dismissal will be allowed. If a plaintiff does not show up in court on the appointed day, the judge may dismiss the case.

Equity: The value of a particular piece of property that you actually own. For example, if a car has a fair market value of $2,000 and you owe a bank $750 on it, your equity is $1,250.

Formal Court: As used here, this term refers to the regular "lawyer-dominated" state courts. The states call their trial courts by all sorts of names (municipal, superior, district, circuit, supreme, civil, etc.). For example, in California, claims of up to $25,000 that are not eligible for Small Claims Court are heard in Municipal Court, and claims over that amount are heard in Superior Court. All of these courts require a knowledge of confusing language and procedure, and you will want to avoid them if possible.

Garnish: To attach (legally take) money—usually wages, or commissions or a bank account—for payment of a debt.

Hearing: The court trial.

Homestead: Homestead laws allow homeowners to protect the equity in their homes up to a certain amount from attachment and sale to satisfy most debts. Homestead laws can work in one of two ways. In some states, the homeowner must file a paper called a "Declaration of Homestead." In other states, simply owning a home (and having the deed recorded) is enough to entitle the homeowner to homestead protection.

Judge: In many states Small Claims cases are heard by full-time judges who also hear cases in other courts.

Judge Pro Tem: A lawyer who pinch hits for a regular judge on a temporary basis. Since this person isn't a real judge, she can only hear your case with your written consent.

Judgment: The decision rendered by the court.

Judgment Creditor: A person to whom money is owed under a court decision.

Judgment Debtor: A person who owes money under a court decision.

Jurisdiction: Jurisdiction generally refers to the authority a court has to hear a case. A Small Claims Court has jurisdiction to hear cases involving money damages up to a certain amount—for example, $5,000 in Alaska, $1,000 in Kansas. (This is often called the "jurisdictional amount.") Some Small Claims Courts also have jurisdiction over certain types of nonmoney cases, such as unlawful detainer (eviction) actions, and some may award nonmoney remedies, including rescission, restitution, reformation and specific performance, as discussed in Chapter 4.

Law: A synonym for Statute.

Levy: A legal method to seize property or money for unpaid debts under court order. For example, a sheriff can levy on (sell) your automobile if you refuse to pay a judgment.

Lien: A legal right to an interest in the real estate of another for payment of a debt. To get a lien, you first must get a court judgment and then take proper steps to have the court enter an "Abstract of Judgment." To establish the lien, you then take the Abstract to the county office where property deeds are recorded in a county where the judgment debtor has real estate.

Magistrate: A synonym for Judge.

Mediation: Many Small Claims Courts recommend or require parties to meet with a neutral third party (called "the Mediator") to try to voluntarily agree on a settlement. Mediation sessions often last an hour or two and take place in a conference room at the courthouse or other public building. If no settlement is mutually agreed to (mediators have no power to impose a decision), the case is heard in Small Claims Court.

Motion to Vacate a Judgment: The motion the defendant must file to reopen a proceeding because she did not appear in court to defend a case on the proper date and the judge has entered a Default Judgment. See Chapter 10.

Order of Examination: A court procedure allowing a judgment creditor to question a debtor about the extent and location of his assets. It is very common in California, and other states have similar procedures, but names may vary somewhat. Often it is referred to as "Supplemental Proceedings."

Ordinance: A law or statute adopted by a local government, such as a city or county.

Plaintiff: The person who starts a lawsuit.

Process Server: The person who delivers court papers to a party or witness. See Chapter 11.

Recorder (Office of the County Recorder): The person employed by the county to make and record documents. The County Recorder's office is usually located in the main county courthouse.

Satisfaction of Judgment: A written statement filed by the judgment creditor when the judgment is paid. See Chapter 23.

Statute: A law adopted by a state or the federal government. In Small Claims Court, state law is applicable in almost all situations. (See Section D of this chapter for information on how to look up the law.)

Statute of Limitations: The time period in which you must file your lawsuit. It is normally figured from the date the act or omission giving rise to the lawsuit occurs, and varies depending on the type of suit. See Chapter 5.

Stay of Enforcement: When a Small Claims Court judgment is appealed by a defendant, enforcement (collection) of the judgment is stayed (stopped) until the time for appeal has expired.

Stipulation: An agreement to compromise a case, which is entered into by the parties and then presented to the judge.

Submission: When a judge wants to delay decision on a case until a later time, she "takes it under submission." Some judges announce their decision as to who won and who lost right in the courtroom. More often, they take cases under submission and mail out decisions later.

Subpoena: A court order requiring a witness to appear in court. It must be served on the person subpoenaed to be valid. See Chapter 14.

Subpoena Duces Tecum: A court order requiring that certain documents be produced in court.

Substituted Service: A method by which court papers may be served on a defendant who is difficult to serve by other means. See Chapter 11.

Transfer: The procedure by which the defendant can have a Small Claims case transferred to a "formal court." In most states this can be done when the defendant has a claim against the plaintiff for an amount more than the Small Claims maximum. In a few states, it can also be done because the defendant simply doesn't want to be in Small Claims Court. In many states, a defendant who wants a jury trial can also transfer to formal court. See Appendix for details.

Trial De Novo: The rehearing of a Small Claims case from scratch when an appeal has been taken by a defendant. In this situation, the previous decision by the Small Claims judge has no effect and the appeal takes the form of a new trial (trial de novo). This is allowed only in some states. Check the Appendix.

Unlawful Detainer (known as "summary dispossess" and "forcible entry and detainer" in some states): Legalese for "eviction." Unlawful detainers may be brought in Small Claims Court in some states. Check the Appendix.

Venue: This basically refers to the proper location (court) to bring a suit, and is discussed in detail in Chapter 9. If a suit is brought in the wrong place, it can be transferred to the right court or dismissed, in which case the plaintiff must refile in the right court.

Wage Garnishment: After a judgment has been issued (and the defendant's time to appeal, if any, has elapsed), the Small Claims Court clerk will issue a writ of execution upon request. This may be turned over to a sheriff, marshal or constable with orders to collect (garnish) a portion of the judgment debtor's wages directly from his employer.

Writ of Execution: An order by a court to the sheriff, marshal or constable of a specific area (in most states, this is either a city or county) to collect a specific amount of money due.

D. Legal Research

As part of using Small Claims Court, you may need to look up a state law or city or county ordinance. In many states, laws are roughly divided by subject matter, often into sets of books that are usually called "codes" or "statutes." Thus, there will be a Civil Code, Probate Code, Penal Code, Vehicle Code and many more. Other states follow a somewhat different organizational system under which all laws are lumped together in one seemingly endless numerical sequence. In either case, a subject index (often in the last volume) will be available.

You can get access to state laws at any large public library, publicly funded law school library or county law library (which, in many states, are located in the main county courthouse and often in larger branch courthouses), which are open to the public. (See Box, "Law Online.")

Ordinances are passed by cities and counties and have the force of law in that municipality. Among other things, ordinances often include zoning rules, building codes, leash laws, parking restrictions, view and tree-cutting rules and often minor vehicle violations. Usually, you can get copies of local ordinances from city or county offices. Collected sets are commonly available at the public library and, for more populous cities and counties, increasingly available online.

If you do your research at a law library, you may have an opportunity to look up state laws in the annotated codes. In addition to the basic laws, these codes also list relevant court decisions (called "cases") interpreting each law. If you find a court case that seems to fit your situation, you may want to read it. If it seems relevant to your case, point it out to the judge as part of your Small Claims presentation. (See Chapter 23, Section D, for an example of an appropriate written presentation.)

For a more thorough exploration of how to use the law library, see one or both of the following resources, which are available at most libraries:

*   *Legal Research: How to Find and Understand the Law,* by Stephen Elias and Susan Levinkind (Nolo Press), an easy-to-read book that provides step-by-step instructions on how to find legal information, including much key information on how to do legal research on the Internet.

- *Legal Research Made Easy,* a 2½ hour video tape, hosted by Robert Berring, an experienced law librarian and legal research professor, that clearly explains what resources to use and how to go about efficiently researching a legal problem.

Law Online

A majority of states and an increasing number of cities and counties make their laws available online. Nolo publishes a very useful book, *Government on the Net,* by James Evans, which explains how to find local, state and federal statutes online. Here is a list of the online sites for all states which currently make their statutes available.

STATE CODES AND STATUTES

Alaska	http://www.legis.state.ak.us/folio.pgi/stattx96?
	http://info.alaska.edu:70/1s/Alaska/crime/akstatute
	http://www.touchngo.com/lglcntr/akstats/statutes.htm
Arizona	http://www.azleg.state.az.us/ars/ars.htm
Arkansas	http://www.uark.edu/~govinfo/PAGES/WAIS-SEARCH/acts.cgi
California	http://www.leginfo.ca.gov/calaw.html
Colorado	http://crs.aescon.com/
Connecticut	http://www.cslnet.ctstateu.edu/statutes/index.htm
Florida	http://www.scri.fsu.edu/fla-leg/statutes/
Idaho	http://www.idwr.state.id.us/idstat/TOC/idstTOC.html
	Search by Keyword or Section Number: http://www.idwr.state.id.us/legislat/idstat.html
Indiana	State Code: http://www.law.indiana.edu/codes/in/incode.html
	Administrative Code: http://www.ai.org/legislative/iac/
Iowa	http://www2.legis.state.ia.us/Code.html
Kentucky	http://www.lrc.state.ky.us/statrev/frontpg.htm
	State Administrative Code: http://www.lrc.state.ky.us/kar/TITLES.HTM
	http://www.lrc.state.ky.us/kar/frntpage.htm
Louisiana	http://www.state.la.us/osr/lac/lac.htm
Michigan	http://www.icle.org/leg-sums/leglist.htm
Minnesota	http://www.revisor.leg.state.mn.us/stats/
	http://www.leg.state.mn.us/leg/statutes.htm
Mississippi	http://www.mscode.com/

Missouri	http://www.house.state.mo.us/homestat.htm
Montana	http://www.nfoweb.com/folio.pgi/MTCODE/doc?
Nebraska	http://unicam1.lcs.state.ne.us/folio.pgi/statutes.nfo?
Nevada	http://venus.optimis.com/nrs.htm
New Jersey	http://www.njleg.state.nj.us/folio.pgi/STATUTES.NFO?
	http://www.njleg.state.nj.us/folio.pgi/stdobject/buttonc5.gif/
	statutes.nfo/query=*/toc/@1?127,19
New York	gopher://lbdc.senate.state.ny.us/
Oklahoma	http://www.onenet.net/oklegal/statutes.basic.html
Oregon	http://www.efn.org/%7Ebobl/index4.html
South Carolina	http://www.lpitr.state.sc.us/newlaws.htm
Texas	http://www.sos.state.tx.us/tac/index.html
Utah	http://www.le.state.ut.us/~code/code.htm
Vermont	http://www.leg.state.vt.us/statutes/statutes.htm
Virginia	http://leg1.state.va.us/000/src.htm
Washington	http://leginfo.leg.wa.gov/www/rcw.htm
Wisconsin	http://badger.state.wi.us/agencies/wilis/Statutes.html
Wyoming	http://legisweb.state.wy.us/titles/statutes.htm ■

Do You Have a Good Case?

A. Stating Your Legal Claim in Court Papers

One of the often advertised advantages of Small Claims Court is that you don't plead theories of law—you state facts and rely on the wise judge to fit them into one or another legal theory of recovery. In short, even if you are not sure that what happened qualifies as a valid legal claim, it's fine to bring your case anyway. All you really need to know to file a Small Claims case is that you have suffered real monetary damage and that the person or business you are suing caused your loss.

To illustrate how this works, let's jump ahead to Chapter 10 and take a look at the form you will fill out when you file your case (the form in your state will differ slightly). Look at Line 5 of the Plaintiff's Statement. As you can see, there is no space to state a lengthy legal argument. Indeed, there is barely room to describe your dispute. Depending on the facts of your case, you should use this space to describe your dispute more or less like this:

- "I took my coat to John's Dry Cleaners and it was returned in a severely damaged (shrunken) condition."

- "Defendant's dog bit me on the corner of Rose and Peach Streets in Dover, Pennsylvania, with the result that I needed ten stitches and other medical care."

- "The car repairs that Joe's Garage did on my car were done wrong, resulting in an engine fire. Joe's Garage has refused to fix or replace the engine."

- "Defendant refused to return the cleaning deposit when I moved out of my apartment even though I left it clean and gave 30 days' notice."

- "The used car I purchased from Robert Yee was not in 'excellent condition' as promised. In fact, the engine blew a gasket the day after I bought it."

- "The $5,000 I lent defendant has not been repaid by July 12, ____, as promised."

Don't try to argue your case until you get to court. When you state your case on the court papers, your goal is to notify the other party and the court as to the broad outline of your dispute. You don't need or want to try to list your evidence or otherwise try to convince anyone that you are in the right or that the law is on your side. Your chance to do this will come later in court.

Time to Get Organized

Even before you file your case, you should set up a good system to safeguard key records and evidence. It's no secret that more than one case has been won (or lost) because of good (or bad) record keeping. One excellent approach is to get a couple of manila envelopes or file folders and label them with the name of your dispute (Lincoln vs. Williams Ford). One folder or envelope can be used to store all documentary evidence, such as receipts, letters, names and addresses of potential witnesses and photographs. The other is for your court papers. Once organized, make sure you conscientiously store your folders in a safe place.

B. But Is My Case Really Any Good?

If you have read the little pamphlets Small Claims Court Clerks hand out, you will have learned pretty much what I have outlined in Section A of this chapter. Almost always you will be advised to briefly state the nature of your dispute, organize any evidence and witnesses you think may help, come to court when told to and let the judge decide.

At a very primitive level this can be seen as good advice—you expend little effort or thought letting the judge do all the heavy lifting. The only problem is that the little pamphlet never tells you that the judge will not simply be deciding who is "right" or "wrong," but will be applying exactly the same laws and legal rules to your case as would be done if your dispute was heard in a formal court. And because you don't know this, chances are good that you won't prepare your case to fit one of the legal categories (lawyers call them "causes of action") that the judge will apply.

Obviously there are a number of problems with this "stay ignorant and trust us" approach. Among them, these are most significant:

* Since you don't know the legal rules which will decide your case, you run the risk of wasting time and energy bringing a losing case.

* Because you don't understand the legal realities that underlie your case, you probably won't prepare as sensibly as you otherwise would—you may not even understand the key legal requirements necessary to have a judgment entered in your favor.

* If you win—and especially if you lose—you won't know why.

If none of this sounds good to you, perhaps you are open to considering a different approach. This consists of learning enough law to be able to come up with a pretty decent answer to the fundamental question the judge will ask: Do you have a winning case?

If you are game, start by reading the rest of this chapter. It contains a discussion of the legal theories most commonly used to establish legal liability. In many instances this information will be all you need to understand how to properly prepare your case. But occasionally you will want to do additional legal research, as would be true if the exact wording of a statute or key court decision has a direct bearing on your case.

Below I list the most common legal theories (causes of action) and the requirements (lawyers call them elements) you need to prove to establish each. In the rest of this chapter, I'll review each in detail, so you can see if the facts of your loss fit the requirements of at least one of them:

* *Breach of Contract:* One or more terms of a valid contract (written, oral or implied) has been broken by the person you are suing. As a result, you have suffered a monetary loss. (See Section C below.)

- *Bad Debt:* A type of contract case. To prevail, you need to prove the debt exists, its amount, when payment was due, and that the person you are suing hasn't paid it or has only partially paid it.

- *Failure to Return a Security Deposit:* Another variety of contract case that commonly arises between tenants and landlords. As discussed in more detail in Chapter 20, for a tenant to prevail, you need to prove a deposit was made, it was not returned or only partially returned, and that the premises were sufficiently clean and undamaged when you left that the landlord owes you some or all of the amount withheld. (In most states you may also be eligible for additional—punitive—damages if the landlord had no good reason for withholding your deposit or followed improper procedure.)

- *Negligence:* The careless behavior of the person you are suing has caused you to suffer a personal injury or property damage resulting in a monetary loss. (Negligence that results in damage to property is covered in Section D1 below. Negligence resulting in a personal injury is covered in Section E below.)

- *Intentional Harm:* The intentional behavior of the person you are suing has caused you to suffer personal injury or property damage resulting in a monetary loss. (See Section D2 for cases involving property damage and Section E for those involving personal injury.)

- *Personal Injury:* The negligent or intentional behavior of the person you are suing has caused you to suffer personal injury. (See Section E.)

- *Product Liability:* You or your property were injured by a defective product and you qualify for recovery under the doctrine of "strict liability," which holds the manufacturer responsible for the damages you suffered, without your having to prove negligence. (See Section F.)

- *Breach of Warranty:* A written or implied warranty extended to you by a merchant has been breached and, as a result, you have suffered a monetary loss—for example, a new car suffers mechanical problems while still covered by warranty. (See Section G.)

- *Violation of a Statute:* A right created by statute has been violated and, as a result, you have suffered a monetary loss. This would be the case if a consumer protection law was violated, resulting in your being out some money. (See Section H.)

- *Professional Malpractice:* A lawyer, doctor or other professional's failure to use the ordinary skills of members of that profession has resulted in your suffering a monetary loss. (See Section I.)

- *Public and Private Nuisance:* Someone creates a health or safety hazard affecting you (and perhaps other neighbors or nearby property owners), or does something that interferes with your ability to use and enjoy your property—for example, a factory is so noisy that you and other nearby residents are kept awake all night. (See Section J.)

⚠ Other legal theories exist. Because the legal theories (lawyers call them "causes of action") listed above make up the basis of well over 95% of Small Claims cases, and because it's not required to state a formal legal theory to file a Small Claims case in the first place, I do not list the technical legal requirements for more obscure types of lawsuits—for example, libel and slander. However, if your case isn't covered here, you may sensibly want to do some additional research to determine whether your case qualifies (contains the correct "legal elements" or criteria) under a different legal theory (cause of action).

Now, before we consider each of these legal theories individually, here is an example of why it's so important to establish not only that you have suffered a loss, but that someone is legally liable to make it good.

Example 1: One night someone entered the garage in Sue's apartment complex, smashed her car window and stole a fancy AM-FM radio and tape deck worth $500. Upon discovery of the theft, and after reporting it to the police, Sue promptly filed suit against the landlord in Small Claims Court. As part of preparing for her day in court, Sue got several witnesses to the fact that her car had been vandalized, and obtained a copy of the police investigation report. She also got several estimates as to the cost of repairing the damage to the car window and replacing the tape deck.

    Sue only overlooked one thing. Unfortunately for her, it was an important one. Under the circumstances the building owner wasn't liable. He had never promised (agreed by contract, either orally or in writing) to keep the garage locked. In addition, he had never locked the garage or otherwise led Sue to believe that he would do so. Once the judge determined that all the tenants were reasonably on notice that it was easy to gain access to the garage either from inside or outside the building and that there had been no previous crimes committed there, he concluded that in failing to lock the garage the building owner was neither in violation of a contract nor guilty of any negligent behavior. As he explained to Sue when he ruled for the landlord, the legal situation she faced was little different than it would have been if her car had been damaged on the street.

Example 2: Now let's take this same situation, but change a few facts. Let's assume the lease contract signed by the landlord and tenant stated that the tenant would be assigned a parking place in a "secure garage." Let's also assume that the garage had always been locked until the lock broke seven days before the theft occurred. Finally, let's assume that Sue and other tenants had asked the owner to fix the lock the day after it broke, but that he hadn't "gotten around to it." In this situation, Sue should win. The landlord made certain contractual promises to the tenants (to keep the garage locked) and then failed to keep them in a situation where he had ample opportunity to do so. The failure presumably allowed the thief access to the car.

C. How to Approach a Breach of Contract Case

A contract is any agreement between identifiable parties where one side agrees to do something for the other in exchange for something in return. The agreement can be written, oral or implied from the circumstances. Contracts made by minors can be disaffirmed (rejected) if it's done prior to the minor turning 18. However, in most states, if a contract is honored by a person after she turns 18, the contract is valid and can no longer be annulled.

Not all oral contracts are valid. Most oral contracts are valid and enforce-able But there are major exceptions to this rule. Generally speaking, contracts that 1) can't be completely performed within a year or 2) are for the sale of real estate or 3) involve the sale of goods (personal property) worth more than $500 (see Chapter 22) must be in writing. However, because the great majority of consumer-type con-tracts can be performed in a year (even if it actually takes longer) and involve services, most oral contracts are enforceable in court—assuming, of course, they can be proven.

Here are some examples that should help you understand when a valid contract does and does not exist.

Example 3: Marcia tells Steve she is in a bad way financially, and Steve promises to give Marcia $750 on January 1. Later Steve changes his mind because he decides he doesn't like Marcia. Can Marcia go to court and sue Steve for the $750? No. This is not a contract, because Marcia has promised to do nothing for Steve in return for his promise to make a loan. Steve has only indicated that he will give Marcia a gift in the future. A promise to make a gift is not enforceable as a contract.

Example 4: Steve promises to pay Marcia $750 on January 31 in exchange for Marcia's promise to pay it back with interest or to either thoroughly clean Steve's office or tutor Steve's oldest son. This is a valid contract, since each person has promised to do something for the other. If Steve fails to pay Marcia on January 31, Marcia can go to court and get a judgment for the $750, claiming breach of contract.

Example 5: Paul asks Barbara if she wants her house painted. Barbara says "yes." Paul paints Barbara's house but Barbara refuses to pay, claiming that since they never agreed on a price, there was no contract. Barbara is wrong. A court will use the traditional doctrine of "quantum meruit" (as much as is deserved for labor) to rule that when one person does work for another in circumstances where payment is normally expected, and the second person accepts it (consent can be implied, as would be the case if Barbara simply watches Paul paint her house), a contract exists. In other words, even though one or more technical parts of a contract are missing, the law will require that a person who knowingly benefits from another person's work pay for it.

1. Unpaid Debts

Often the contract that has not been honored involves a failure to pay money. Hardly a day goes by when someone isn't sued for failing to pay the phone company, the local hospital, a friend (former, probably) or relative, or even late fines to the public library. (See Chapter 18 for more on Small Claims suits where money is owed.) Normally, winning this type of case is easy. As a plaintiff, you must prove:

- the identity of the debtor;
- the existence of a contract with the debtor;
- if the contract is in writing, bring it to court. If it's oral, be prepared to prove its existence. Be creative—if you lent money to a debtor using a check, bring a copy. Along with your own testimony, that should be all you need;
- the fact that the debt hasn't been paid. From a defendant's point of view you'll want to be prepared to prove any amounts you have already paid. In many situations, getting a judgment for an unpaid debt involves no more than stating that the defendant committed himself to buy certain goods and services, that they were, in fact, provided and that a legitimate bill for X dollars has not been paid.

2. Failure to Perform a Contract

Sometimes a breach of contract suit results, not from a simple refusal to pay a bill, but because one party has performed his duties under the contract badly, late or not at all, and the other person has been damaged as a result. Such would be the case if:

- an apartment owner accepted a deposit and agreed to rent an apartment to a tenant and then rented it to someone else. (Leases and rental agreements are discussed in more detail in Chapter 20.)

- a caterer showed up with the food and drink for an important party four hours late.

- a wedding photographer used the wrong film, with the result that all the photos were badly overexposed.

- a freelance writer agreed to produce a history of a business organization for an annual report but gets so many key facts wrong, his work is worthless.

Damages resulting from a breach of contract are normally not difficult to prove. You must first show that the contract existed. If it is written, the document itself (or several documents, as would be the case where there is a written offer and later acceptance) should be presented to the court. If the contract is oral, or implied from the circumstances, the facts necessary to establish it should be stated and proved. You must then testify as to the circumstances of the other person's breach of the contract and the amount of damages you have suffered as a result.

> **Example 6:** Justine and Bob planned a June wedding. Since the families of both prospective spouses were widely dispersed, this was to be a combination family reunion and wedding. As a result, the couple planned a large reception with a meal and arranged to have it catered by Top Drawer Deli. An order listing food and drink was prepared by the Deli and signed by Justine. When the big day arrived, everything went swimmingly, until the 200 guests arrived at the reception to find that, while the band was playing cheerfully, Top Drawer had not shown up with the food and bubbly. Fortunately, the best man hopped into his station wagon, drove to the nearest liquor store and in less than 20 minutes was back with 10 cases of champagne. (Clearly there was a reason he was picked as best man.) Someone else had the presence of mind to order 30 pizzas.
>
> Two hours later, Top Drawer showed up full of apologies. (A key employee called in sick and their van broke down.) Justine and Bob accepted the cake and turned down the rest. When the bill came, they paid for the cake and told Top Drawer to eat the rest. Top Drawer sued for $4,000 for breach of contract. Bob and Justine countersued for $5,000 for emotional distress. The judge ruled that by being two hours late to a time-sensitive event, the caterer had breached its contract and that Bob and Justine owned her nothing. The judge then dismissed the emotional distress claim after remarking that the reception obviously turned into an unforgettable party.

The fact that many contract cases are easy to win doesn't mean that all result in victory. In fact, I have seen a good number of plaintiffs lose what to them seemed to be open and shut cases. Why? Usually because they:

- failed to show that a contract existed (see Examples 1 and 7);
- failed to sue the right person (again, see Example 7); or
- failed to show that a valid contract was broken (see Example 8).

Example 7: Ben, a landlord, sued John, the parent of one of his tenants, for damages the roommates had caused John's daughter's apartment. John was sued because he had co-signed his daughter's lease. Ben easily convinced the judge that the damage had, in fact, occurred, and the judge seemed disposed toward giving him a judgment for the $980 requested, until John presented his defense. He showed that the lease between his daughter and the landlord had been rewritten three times after he originally co-signed it and that he had not added his signature to any of the revised versions, one of which involved replacing several of his daughter's original roommates with others. The judge agreed that because John had not co-signed any of the subsequent leases (contracts), he wasn't liable. The reason was simple: There was no longer a contract between Ben and John. (Leases and rental agreements, including a detailed discussion of the rights and responsibilities of co-signers, are discussed in more detail in *Every Landlord's Legal Guide,* by Marcia Stewart and Attorneys Ralph Warner and Janet Portman (Nolo Press).)

Example 8: Sid sued Acme Dry Cleaners for $650, the cost of replacing a pigskin suede jacket that was ruined (it shrunk dramatically) by Acme. Sid established that he had taken the jacket to Acme for cleaning, and had agreed to pay Acme $80. Since Acme, by accepting the jacket, clearly implied it would properly clean the jacket, there was no question that a contract existed. Sid was very sure of his loss. He stood in the courtroom and slowly tried to wriggle into the jacket. The whole courtroom burst out laughing—including the judge, who almost choked trying to keep a straight face. The sleeves barely came to Sid's elbows, and the coat itself didn't reach to his waist. By putting on the shrunken jacket, Sid had made his point more effectively than he could have with ten minutes of testimony.

Unfortunately for Sid, he had overlooked two key things—one obvious and one not so obvious. As you have probably guessed, Sid's obvious oversight involved his asking for the full $650 replacement value of a jacket that was eight months old and had been worn a good bit. Valuation is a common problem in clothing cases. (I discuss it in detail in Chapters 4 and 21.) Let's just say here that the jacket was worth no more than $400 in its used condition and that, in any situation where your property is damaged or destroyed, the amount of your recovery will be limited to the fair market value of the goods at the time the damage occurred—not their replacement value.

Now let's look at Sid's less obvious mistake. Vijay, Acme Dry Cleaner's owner, testified that when he saw the jacket after cleaning, he was amazed. His cleaning shop specialized in leather goods, and the cleaning process used should have resulted in no such shrinkage. What's more, he testified that he had examined a number of other items in the same cleaning batch and found no similar problem. To determine what happened, he sent the jacket to an "independent testing laboratory." Their report, which he presented to the court, stated that it was the jacket itself, not the cleaning, that was the problem. According to the report, this was because the leather had been severely overstretched prior to assembly and shrank when placed in the cleaning fluid.

What happened? The judge was convinced by the testing lab report and felt that Acme had breached no contract as far as the cleaning was concerned. However, the judge also felt that Acme, as a leather cleaning specialist, had some responsibility to notify Sid that the jacket should not have been cleaned in the first place. Therefore, the judge held mostly for Acme, but did award Sid $100. He also suggested that Sid might want to consider suing the store that sold the jacket, claiming that, by selling clothing containing seriously defective material, the store had breached an implied warranty that the goods sold were reasonably fit for the purpose they were designed to fulfill. For information on breach of warranty actions, see Section G, below.

 More material affecting contracts:

- How much you should sue for in breach of contract cases (how to value your damages) is discussed in Chapter 4, Section C1.
- Breach of warranty—based on a written or oral contract—is covered in Section G, below.
- Material on how the violation of a state or federal law can make a contract unenforceable is covered in Section H, below.
- Material involving leases and rental agreements—a specialized type of contract—is covered in Chapter 20.
- How to collect on contracts involving unpaid bills is covered in Chapter 18.
- If your contract involves fraud, undue influence or a simple mistake ($2,000 was mistakenly written as $20,000), you may have a right to have the contract ended or rewritten or to get your goods back, under the legal doctrine of "equitable relief." See Section H, below.

D. How to Approach a Case Where Your Property Has Been Damaged by the Negligent or Intentional Acts of Someone Else

After cases involving breach of contract, the most common disputes that come to Small Claims Court involve damage to property claimed to be caused by the defendant's negligent actions. Less often, the plaintiff claims that he suffered loss because the defendant intended to damage his belongings.

1. Negligence

A technical definition of negligence could—and does—fill entire law texts. But I don't recommend your reading one, since I remember thinking in law school that the more scholarly professors wrote about the subject, the more mixed up they got. Like good taste or bad wine, negligence seems to be easy to recognize, but hard to define.

So I'll breeze right past the "ifs," "ands" and "wherefores" and give you the sort of peasant's definition that always made the most sense to me: If, as a result of another person's conduct, your property is injured, and that person didn't act with reasonable care under the circumstances, you have a valid legal claim based on his or her negligence. In addition, negligence can occur when a person who has a duty or responsibility to act fails to do so. For example, a car mechanic who fails to check your brakes after you tell him they have been working poorly and he promises to do so would be negligent.

> **Example:** Jake knows the brakes on his ancient Saab are in serious need of repair, but does nothing about it. One night, when the car is parked on a hill, the brakes fail and the car rolls across the street and destroys Keija's persimmon tree. Keija sues Jake for $225, the reasonable value of the tree. Jake will lose because he did not act with reasonable care under the circumstances.

Another obvious situation involving negligence would be one where a car or bus swerves into your driving lane and sideswipes your fender. The driver of the offending vehicle has a duty to operate it in such a way as to not harm you. By swerving into your lane, it is extremely likely that he has failed to do so. A situation where negligence could be difficult to show, however, might involve your neighbor's tree that falls on your car, properly parked in your driveway. Here you have to be ready to prove that, for some reason (such as age, disease or an obviously bad root system), the tree was in a weakened condition, and the neighbor was negligent in failing to do something about it. If the tree had looked to be in good health, you probably could not prove that your neighbor was negligent in not cutting it down or propping it up, since there is no duty to remove or care for healthy trees. Here are some additional examples where a person or business failed to act with reasonable care and as a result was negligent:

- While playing with his kids in his small back yard, Kevin hits a ball over the fence, smashing a neighbor's overlooking window.
- While upgrading Eddie's computer, Bill carelessly installs the wrong chip, which crashes Eddie's hard drive and ruins his computer.
- RapidMail Inc., a local courier service, loses several time-sensitive messages and fails to notify the sender of the problem.

Compound negligence exists where more than one person is responsible for the damages you suffer—for example, if you are injured because you fall down a staircase with no hand railing after someone who is paying attention to where she is going runs into you. When dealing with any situation in which more than one person may have contributed to your loss, Rule #1 is to sue them all.

Example 1: Sandy comes home from work one day to find her new fence knocked over and Fred's Chevy Blazer in the middle of her front lawn. Fred admits his vehicle knocked over the fence when his brakes failed. To Sandy, this may at first seem like a simple case involving filing suit against Fred, but what if Fred had just picked up his car from Atomic Auto Repair, where he had his brakes worked on? Fred's liability may range from minimal (Atomic is only 50 feet away; he just left the shop with the assurance that the brakes were fixed) to extensive (Atomic is located across town and at the last two stop signs, Fred's brakes acted "funny" but he continued to drive anyway). Sandy would be well advised to sue both Fred and Atomic and let the judge sort out who is most at fault.

Example 2: Now suppose that Fred's brakes are fine, but he claims he was rear-ended at the stop sign by Dana, whose pickup truck pushed his vehicle through Sandy's fence. Again, Fred's liability may be minimal (Dana was drunk and speeding) or it may be extensive (Fred ran a stop sign while turning and was rear-ended by Dana, who had the right of way). Again, Sandy would be wise to sue both parties and let the judge decide who was most at fault.

Negligence concepts are tricky: Don't try to be a judge. There is often no foolproof way to determine in advance if someone is or is not negligent. It's often a close legal question that lawyers regularly get wrong. If you have suffered a real loss and think someone else caused it, bring your case and let the judge decide. After all, he or she gets paid (by you, the taxpayer) to do it.

Here are a couple of questions, the answers to which may help you make a decision as to whether you have a good case based on someone else's negligence.

- Did the person whose act (or failure to act) injured you behave in a reasonable way? Or to put it another way, would you have behaved differently if you were in her shoes?

- Did your conduct significantly contribute to the injury?

If you believe the person who caused you to suffer a monetary loss behaved in an unreasonable way (ran a red light when drunk) and that you were acting sensibly (driving at 30 mph in the proper lane), you probably have a good case. If you were a little at fault (slightly negligent), but the other fellow was much more at fault (very negligent), you can still recover most of your losses, since courts follow a legal doctrine called "comparative negligence." This involves subtracting the percentage of your negligence from 100 percent to find out how legally responsible the other party is. Thus, if a judge finds that one person (drunk and speeding) was 80 percent at fault, and the other (slightly inattentive) was 20 percent at fault, the slightly inattentive party can recover 80 percent of her loss.

More Information About Negligence: If, despite my advice to keep it simple, you want to get into the gory details of negligence theory, go to your nearest law library and get any recent hardbound legal text on "torts" (wrongful acts or injuries). Or, even easier, if you are near a law bookstore, buy a copy of one of the several competing paperback course summaries covering torts that law students actually rely on to get through their torts exam. (For example, *The Gilbert Law Summary of Torts* is available for $18.95 from Nolo's bookstore, at 950 Parker Street, Berkeley, CA 94710, tel. (800) 992-6656.)

2. Intentional Acts

Not all injuries to people or property are accidents. You also have the right to recover money damages if you or your personal property have been intentionally damaged by someone. (I cover personal injuries in Section E, below.)

Example: Basil and Shirley are neighbors who can't stand the sight of each other, despite, or perhaps because of, the fact that both are prize-winning rose growers. When Basil took first place in the local garden club contest for his exotic roses. Shirley, who was angry, frustrated and jealous, intentionally left her hose running and drowned all of Basil's roses. Basil should be able to recover the value of his roses from Shirley.

In theory, at least, it is also possible to recover punitive damages if you are damaged by the malicious conduct of someone else. However, in part because public sentiment is running strongly against punitive damage awards, they are seldom awarded in most states. Nevertheless, Basil, in the above example, might be tempted to sue Shirley for more than the cost of replacing the roses, based on her bad conduct. Unfortunately, for two reasons, it's rarely possible to effectively bring actions requesting punitive damages in Small Claims Court:

- About half the states simply don't allow claims for punitive damages to be initiated in Small Claims Court;
- Low dollar limits in Small Claims Court mean that even in states where punitive damages can, in theory, be awarded, there is little realistic ability for the judge to do so. In short, if you believe you really might recover punitive damages, you should almost always file your case in a formal court, asking for lots more money than the Small Claims limit.

But suppose you are convinced you deserve punitive damages and want to sue for an extra few thousand dollars (assuming the Small Claims limit in your state is high enough). First, check your local court rules. If you find no prohibition, go ahead. The worst the judge will do is to allow you actual damages, while denying your claim for punitives.

 More material affecting property damage:

- To determine how much to sue for, see Chapter 4, Section C2.

E. How to Approach a Personal Injury (and Mental Distress) Case

I treat personal injury cases in this separate section because so many people look at them as being a different kind of lawsuit. In fact, most personal injury cases are based on a claim that someone has been negligent (and a few are based on claims of intentional injury). The legal theories involved are the same as set out in Section D, above. To prevail, you must show that your injury was caused by someone's negligent or intentional behavior (unless your case qualifies as one of the very few where the law applies the doctrine of strict liability—see Section F, below).

Start by understanding that most personal injury cases involve amounts of money that are clearly over the Small Claims maximum and should therefore be pursued in formal courts. However, occasionally a minor personal injury case will be appropriate for Small Claims.

> **Example 1:** Jenny and Karen are playing softball in a picnic area of a park, where many families are picnicking in the sun. Jenny, never a star fielder, misses a batted ball that hits seven-year-old Willie in the face and chips his tooth. Assuming Willie (with the help of his parents) sues Jenny and Karen for the $500 it will cost to fix his tooth, is he likely to win? Probably. Since Willie was in a picnic area where he had a right to be, we can safely assume that Jenny and Karen were careless (negligent). Why? Because as a society, we have decided that picnic areas are for picnickers—not ballplayers—and since Jenny and Karen's game was inappropriate and dangerous to others, they are going to have to pay for their negligence.

> **Example 2:** Now assume that Jenny and Karen have moved over to a ball field. Their skills still haven't improved and Karen again misses the ball, which again hits Willie, who has escaped his parents and wandered onto the field unobserved. Are Jenny and Karen liable? Probably not. Jenny and Karen took reasonable precautions to avoid hitting picnickers by playing on the ball field. While they may have a responsibility to get little Willie off the field if they spot him, they are probably not legally responsible—that is, negligent—in a situation where he wanders onto the field unnoticed. So this time a Small Claims judge is likely to award nothing to Willie.

Consider not only your loss, but whether the other party acted reasonably under the circumstances. Before you sue someone for injury, consider whether it was really caused by their negligence. If so, the person is legally liable to make good your loss. If not (you trip and fall down a perfectly safe set of stairs), you have no right to recover, no matter what your injury, unless your case involves an injury suffered because of a defective product. (See Section F, below.) If in doubt, go ahead and sue, but be prepared to deal with the liability question, as well as simply showing the extent of your injury. In Chapters 14 and 15, I give you some practical advice as to how to prove your case.

As discussed in more detail in Chapter 4, you do not have to suffer a physical injury to successfully recover in court as a result of someone else's negligent or intentionally obnoxious behavior. Invasion of privacy and the intentional infliction of mental distress are but two of the types of lawsuits that can be based on nonphysical injuries.

Example: Suppose your landlord enters your apartment several times without notice, permission or good legal reason. You make it clear that this behavior is highly upsetting and ask her to cease invading your privacy. She nevertheless persists in entering your apartment with no good reason, causing you to become genuinely upset and anxious. You file a Small Claims case based on the intentional infliction of mental distress. Assuming you can convince the judge that you were truly and seriously upset, your chances of winning are good.

Obviously, not every instance of antisocial behavior that makes you mad qualifies as being serious enough to bring a successful lawsuit. Generally, to recover, the other person's actions must:

- be truly obnoxious;
- violate a state law or local ordinance (the invasion of a tenant's privacy qualifies, since statutes in most states prohibit a landlord from entering without notice or permission, except in an emergency);
- continue after you have asked the person to stop (it's best to do this in writing and to do it more than once).

In addition, you must be able to convince a judge that you have genuinely suffered mental distress as a result of the other person's conduct. (Therapy bills or loss of weight would be evidence to present to the judge, if that were your situation.)

 Damages for pain and suffering are not allowed in many states. As discussed in Chapter 4, "How Much Can You Sue For?," Small Claims Courts in some states do not have the power to award damages for "pain and suffering." In these states, actions to recover this type of damage must be filed in formal court.

➡️ **More material affecting personal injuries:**

- To figure out how much to sue for in personal injury cases, see Chapter 4, Section C4.

F. How to Approach a Case When You Are Injured by a Defective Product (Doctrine of Strict Liability)

Under a legal concept called "strict liability," there is usually no need to prove negligence when an injury occurs as a result of something going wrong with the defendant's product. (This legal area is often referred to as "product liability.") The point is, if your vacuum cleaner, hair dryer, steam iron, lawnmower, car or other product malfunctions and you are injured as a result, you are entitled to recover from the manufacturer or other defendant (usually the person you bought or rented the product from) without having to prove negligence. Appropriately, because of the large sums of money often involved, most product liability cases will end up in formal court, but now and then a defect in a product will cause an injury small enough that the damage caused falls within the Small Claims Court maximum.

G. How to Approach a Breach of Warranty Case

First you need to understand that warranty law is extremely confusing, even to lawyers. A principal reason is that, in every state, at least two separate and distinct warranty statutes can apply to the retail sale of goods (see Sidebar). The sad result is that, short of presenting you with a major treatise, it's impossible to thoroughly explain the warranty law of all 50 states. The best I can do in the short space I have here is to give you several basic rules:

1. If a new or used product comes with a written warranty, you have the right to rely on it.

2. If a seller makes written or oral statements describing a product's features (for example, "these tires will last at least 25,000 miles") or what it will do ("it will work for two years"), and you rely on these statements as part of your decision to purchase the product, these statements constitute an express warranty that you have a right to rely on. It is important to understand that this is true even though the written warranty printed on the package states there are no other warranties.

3. In most situations, an implied warranty of general fitness for the intended use or "merchantability" is also present (for example, that a lawnmower will cut grass, a tire will hold air and a calculator will subtract). This warranty exists in addition to the written and express warranties discussed just above. Again, it's important to understand that it applies even though there is a statement (often called a "warranty disclaimer") printed on the product or packaging saying no warranties exist beyond the express written warranty, or that no warranty exists at all, or that all implied warranties are specifically disclaimed.

Warranty Law: Where Does It Come From

The Magnuson-Moss Consumer Warranty Act (15 USC 2302) is a federal law that applies in every state. In addition, every state has adopted a "commercial code," which includes other warranty protections for consumers. Some states have enacted separate consumer protection laws that go beyond the Magnuson-Moss Act and the Commercial Code. For example, California has the Song-Beverly Credit Card Act (Civil Code Secs. 1747–1748.5). To find your state's warranty law, look up the word warranty in the index to your state's statutes. See Chapter 1, Section D, for more on how to do this.

See Chapter 17 for a discussion of warranties as they apply to new and used car purchases.

If a warranty is breached—for example, a TV set with a six-month warranty on parts and labor breaks the day after purchase—you should notify the seller and manufacturer in writing, keeping copies of both letters. Give them a reasonable chance to make necessary repairs or replace the defective product. Thirty days to accomplish this is usually considered to be reasonable. If they fail to do so, it's time to think about filing in Small Claims.

In considering whether and how to pursue a breach of warranty case, you should realize that many Small Claims Court judges evaluate warranty disputes based on their own broad view of what is fair under the circumstances. In other words, if you purchase goods that are clearly defective or do not accomplish the task the seller claimed they would accomplish (either in an advertisement or a personal statement to you), and you have made and documented a good faith effort to have the seller or manufacturer either fix or replace the goods or refund your money, file in Small Claims Court and let the judge worry about the details of warranty law. But do be prepared to document the statement (warranty) of the seller that you relied on.

Example: Alan purchases a computer and some expensive accounting software from ABC Computer. He explains his high-end bookkeeping needs to the salesperson in detail and is assured that the computer and software will do the job. The computer contains a written warranty against defects in parts and labor for 90 days. The warranty statement says that all implied warranties are disclaimed. The software contains no written warranty statement. It is apparent to Alan after a couple of days' work that the software simply is not sophisticated enough to meet his bookkeeping needs as explained to the salesperson and that the salesperson didn't know what he was talking about when he said it was "perfect for the job."

Two days later the computer breaks. Alan calls ABC and asks for the computer to be fixed or replaced and for his money back on the software. As to recovering for the computer, Alan should have no problem—it failed within the written warranty period.

The software raises a different problem. In asking for his money back, Alan claims the seller breached an express warranty (the salesperson's statement that it would meet his needs), as well as the implied warranty of general fitness or merchantability (Alan must show the software really does fall below the reasonable standard for sophisticated small business accounting packages). However, this latter claim might be hard to prove—especially if the software is adequate to accomplish most accounting tasks, just not sophisticated enough for Alan's special needs. In court, Alan will be smart to focus on trying to prove that he relied on the salesperson's express statements that the software would meet his specific bookkeeping needs as part of his decision to purchase it.

How should he do this? If Alan had given the salesperson written specifications as to his accounting needs and had a copy, or if he had a witness to the salesperson's overly optimistic promises, he would be in good shape. Otherwise, it might come down to his word against the salesperson's, with the judge left to decide who appears to be telling the truth.

H. How to Approach a Case When Your Rights Under State Law Have Been Breached

There are thousands of laws designed to protect consumers. Everything from the construction of home swimming pools, to regulation of retail sales, to the moving of household goods, to the types of contracts that you can be offered by health clubs are covered. These laws are too extensive to outline here; however, you should be aware that if a provider of goods or services has violated one of these laws, you may be able to cancel your deal with no obligation to pay.

One of the most routine consumer complaints (for which specific laws exist providing remedies for consumers) is false or deceptive advertising. In general, these laws provide that private parties may recover the money they spent for goods or services advertised falsely. The point is simple: If you believe that the person you have a claim against has violated a state law and this violation is directly related to the monetary damage you have suffered, call the judge's attention to the law in question as part of your oral presentation in Small Claims Court.

Another common type of consumer protection law involves a cooling-off period, usually a three- to five-day period, during which you can cancel a purchase agreement. For example, the Federal Trade Commission imposes a three-day cancellation period for door-to-door sales for more than $25. You must be given notice of your right to cancel and a cancellation form when you sign the purchase contract. If you don't get the form, your cancellation right extends until the seller sends it to you, even if it takes months.

Most states have adopted laws that also provide consumers' cancellation rights for a number of other types of contracts, often including health club memberships, discount buying clubs and time-share properties. If you have not been properly notified of your right to cancel, you can raise this as a defense in Small Claims Court.

In addition to the specific consumer protection rights embedded in literally thousands of state laws, there are several general legal rules you should know about. One of the most important of these deals with fraud. Generally speaking, if fraud is present as part of a transaction, the deal can be canceled. Fraud can take the form of intentional misrepresentation, negligent misrepresentation (a positive assertion without adequate information that it is true), fraudulent concealment (hiding a key fact), a false promise (a promise with no intention to perform) or any other act designed to deceive. If you think you have been defrauded, make sure the judge knows about your claim. The judge has the power to "rescind" the sale or other contract that involves fraudulent conduct and order that your money be refunded, along with any damages you have suffered as a result of the fraud.

Not all Small Claims Courts will allow actions for fraud or requests to rescind contracts. Check your state's Small Claims Court rules. In some states, you have to file actions based on fraud in a formal court.

Money Troubles: Legal Strategies to Cope with Your Debts, by Attorney Robin Leonard (Nolo Press), includes a comprehensive list of state laws that allow consumers to cancel contracts.

I. Professional Malpractice

An increasing number of Small Claims cases are being filed against doctors, lawyers, accountants and other professionals. The main reason is that it can be difficult or impossible to get lawyers to represent you and take these cases to a formal court. (Lawyers accept only one in 20 medical malpractice cases, according to one study.) As a result, the injured person must decide to either file without a lawyer in formal court or scale down the dollar amount of her claim to fit into Small Claims Court.

As with all lawsuits (legal claims), to succeed with a malpractice claim, you must establish all its required legal elements as part of your Small Claims case. These normally consist of:

- *Duty:* The professional owed you a duty of care. This one is automatically taken care of as long as you really were a patient or a client.
- *Carelessness:* The professional failed to use at least ordinary professional skills in carrying out the task (unless he claimed to be a specialist, in which case the standard is higher). This one can be tougher to prove, since unless the mistake is breathtakingly obvious, you'll normally need to get the opinion of one or more people (experts) in the same profession that the professional screwed up. In theory, you can do this via a letter, but since the professional you are suing will almost surely be in court denying all wrongdoing, far better to have your expert witness testify in person.
- *Causation:* The professional's carelessness directly caused the harm or injury you suffered. For many types of malpractice, showing that the professional caused your injury isn't a problem. But in the legal field, the causation issue can be tricky where a failed lawsuit is involved, since you typically will need to show not only that the lawyer's mistake caused you to lose, but that you would have won if no mistake had been made. In other words, you need to convince the judge your underlying lawsuit was a winner.

- *Damages:* The harm you suffered at the hands of the professional resulted in actual economic loss to you.

Example: You consult a lawyer about an injury you suffered falling downstairs at a store. The lawyer says he will file a case on your behalf, but forgets to do so before the one-year Statute of Limitations runs out. Several lawyers you consult won't take your malpractice case because your injuries were fairly minor and they aren't sure it will be possible to prove that the store was at fault. (In other words, you might not have been harmed by not being able to proceed with your case, and if you were, the dollar amount you lost wasn't great.) You sue your lawyer in Small Claims Court. His failure to file your case on time is clearly an act of carelessness (a lawyer using ordinary legal skills would have filed on time), but to win you'll also have to show that your lawyer's careless act resulted in harm to you. This means convincing the judge that, in fact, your case against the store was a winner and that your injuries were serious enough to qualify for the amount of money you are requesting.

 Further reading:

- *Mad at Your Lawyer*, by Attorney Tanya Starnes (Nolo Press). Contains an extensive discussion about what is involved in suing an attorney for malpractice.
- *Represent Yourself in Court: How to Prepare and Try a Winning Case*, by Attorneys Paul Bergman and Sara J. Berman-Barrett (Nolo Press). Explores how to bring a malpractice case in formal court.

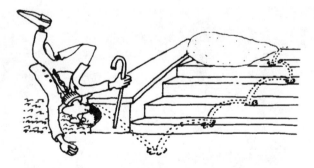

J. How to Prove a Nuisance Case

Sorry to use arcane terminology like "nuisance," but when you deal with legal theories (causes of action), gobbledygook often comes with the territory. Start by understanding that a private nuisance occurs when someone prevents or disturbs your use or enjoyment of your property. For example, if your neighbor lets his dog bark all night, preventing you from sleeping, that's a private nuisance. If it persists and causes you real discomfort, you can sue.

A public nuisance, by contrast, consists of someone's act that causes a group of people (residents of a particular neighborhood, for example) to suffer a health or safety hazard or lose the peaceful enjoyment of their property—for example, if planes suddenly begin flying low over a neighborhood or a chemical plant lets toxic fumes drift over neighboring property, causing people to become ill. Public nuisance suits are often initiated by groups of individuals all filing suits at more or less the same time. One fairly common example of this involves multiple Small Claims lawsuits against neighbors, or their landlords, who sell drugs. (See Chapter 7, Section C, for more about these so-called class actions.) If you want to know more about the law of nuisance generally, locate one of the several law student's course summaries on the field of torts. These are available at specialty law book stores. Or, you can order *The Gilbert Law Summary of Torts*, for $18.95 plus postage, from Nolo Press's bookstore, at (800) 992-6656.

Try mediation before filing a lawsuit against a neighbor. It is very difficult to put a dollar value on lawsuits against neighbors for antisocial acts, no matter how annoying. In addition, filing suit usually makes long-term relationships worse. For these reasons, I believe disputing neighbors should always try mediation before turning to Small Claims Court. (See Chapter 6 for more on mediation.) ■

Can You Recover
If You Win?

This is the shortest chapter and the most important. In it, I ask all of you who are thinking of filing a Small Claims suit to focus on a very simple question—can you collect if you win? This is important because whenever a dispute develops, it is all too easy to get caught up in thinking and arguing about who is wrong—so easy that perspective is often lost and the problems of collecting after you win are forgotten. I emphasize this because I have so often observed people bringing good cases to court in which there was never a hope of collecting.

Collecting from solvent individuals or businesses isn't usually a problem, since they will routinely pay any judgments entered against them. Unfortunately, a goodly number of judgment debtors are either broke (lawyers say "judgment proof") or so adept at hiding their assets that collecting your winnings is likely to prove impossible. Nolo Press publishes *Money Troubles: Legal Strategies to Cope With Your Debts,* by Robin Leonard, which contains information for people who are over their heads in legal debts and don't know how they are going to keep the roof over their heads and clothes on their kids' backs. The message of the book is that there are many legal ways for a debtor to protect a long list of assets from creditors armed with court judgments. For example, because of the existence of debtor protection laws in every state, a creditor who has not been paid can't seize many types of property, usually including the food from the debtor's table, or the TV from his living room, or even, in many cases, the car from his driveway. For example, many states exempt about $1,000–$3,000 of equity in a motor vehicle from being attached to pay debts.

What do these facts mean to you? Again, that many people who are not completely without money are nevertheless "judgment proof." You can sue and get judgments against them until red cows dance on the yellow moon, but you can't collect a dime. Unfortunately, just this sort of frustrating thing happens every day—people go to lots of trouble to win cases only to realize that the judgment is uncollectible. This, of course, compounds the misery. Not only has the person suing lost the money from the original debt or injury, but also the time, trouble and expense of the Small Claims suit. As my grandmother used to say, "No one ever got to live in the big house on the hill by throwing a good quarter after a bad dime."

So a big key to deciding whether to file a Small Claims case should be figuring out whether you can collect any judgment you win. How can you tell ahead of time? In most situations, it's not hard. The first thing you should consider is whether or not the defendant is working. That is because if a person fails to voluntarily pay a judgment, the easiest way to collect it is to garnish his wages. It follows, if the person sued has a job, there is an excellent chance of collecting if payment is not made voluntarily. But you can't garnish a welfare, Social Security, unemployment, pension or disability check. So, if the person sued gets most of his income from one of these sources, red flags should definitely be flying.

But what about other assets? Can't a judgment be collected from sources other than wages that are not protected by state debtor-protection laws? Sure—bank accounts, stocks and bonds, motor vehicles and real estate are other common collection sources. And where a business is the judgment debtor, you can often collect by ordering the sheriff or marshal to take the amount of the judgment right out of the debtor's cash register. But remember, as stated above, many types of personal property are exempt from attachment. In New York, for example, among a long list of exemptions, we find "all stoves kept for use in the judgment debtor's dwelling house," a "pew occupied by the judgment debtor in a place of public worship" and a TV set. Even more significant, the laws of many states say that a portion, or all, of the equity in a debtor's home is exempt. In California, a creditor can't effectively get at the equity in a family house unless it exceeds $75,000 ($100,000 if owner is disabled or over 65). In Arizona, the amount is $100,000. And in Massachusetts, it's $100,000 ($200,000 if over 65 or disabled).

The Law of Wage Garnishments

In most states a creditor with a judgment can't take more than 25% of a judgment debtor's net earnings, or the amount by which the debtor's net earnings exceed 30 times the federal minimum wage, whichever is less. (Net earnings are total earnings less all mandatory deductions for such items as withheld income taxes and unemployment tax.)

A few states offer greater protections for judgment debtors, including Texas, which forbids all wage garnishments, Delaware, which limits a judgment creditor to taking no more than 15% of a debtor's pay and New York, which allows a judgment creditor to take only 10% of a debtor's wages.

The sheriff or marshal's office in your area can supply you with your state's rules.

What does all this boil down to? Simply this. Before you file your Small Claims papers, ask yourself a few questions:

1. Does the person you wish to sue voluntarily pay debts, or are you dealing with a person who will make it as difficult as possible to collect if you win?

2. If the defendant may not pay voluntarily, does he have a job or is he likely to get one in the not too distant future, as might be the case with a student? (Most states allow a judgment to be collected for from five to 20 years from the date it is entered , and usually a persistent creditor may renew this right for a longer period (see Chapter 24, Section E).)

3. If you have your doubts about voluntary payment and the person you are suing doesn't have a job, can you identify some nonexempt assets that you can attach, such as a bank account, or real property other than the place where the person lives (in many states the equity in a dwelling place is exempt from attachment up to a fairly hefty amount)?

4. If a business is involved, is it solvent and does it have a good reputation for paying debts? If the answer is no, is there a readily available cash source you can reach, such as a cash register, or does the business own assets such as valuable office equipment which you can order attached and sold?

Beware of Bankruptcy. If a person or a business declares a straight bankruptcy (under Chapter 7 of the Federal Bankruptcy Act) and lists you as a creditor, your right to recover a Small Claims Court judgment is cut off, just as if you were any other creditor (but if your judgment was based on a secured loan, you do have the right to recover the property pledged as security). But an exception to this general rule exists if the judgment was obtained because you or your property were injured by the malicious behavior of the person declaring bankruptcy. In this situation, your right to collect your judgment should survive the bankruptcy. An example of malicious behavior would be someone getting drunk and then attacking and injuring you.

In Chapter 24, we deal in considerable detail with the mechanics of collecting after you get your judgment. If you think that collection may pose a problem, carefully read this chapter now and, if necessary, do a little research into your opponent's financial affairs. But remember what my canny old grandmother said about bad dimes and good quarters and don't waste your time chasing people who have no money. ∎

How Much Can You Sue For?

The maximum amount for which you can sue in Small Claims Court varies from state to state. For example, it's $7,500 in Minnesota, $1,500 in Kentucky, $3,000 in New York and $5,000 in Texas. You'll find the limits for other states in the Appendix, but because these are increased periodically, you'll always want to check by calling your local Small Claims Court clerk or, better yet, obtaining a copy of your local court rules. With some exceptions, Small Claims Court does not hear cases unless they are for money damages. Thus, you can't use Small Claims Court to get a divorce, stop ("enjoin") the city from cutting down your favorite oak tree, change your name, or do any of the thousands of other things that require a solution other than one side paying money to the other.

One exception to the "money only" rule involves equitable relief, which is available in some states. This is legal speak for a court's power to order a party to perform a specific act, such as return a uniquely valuable piece of property or change a contract that contains an obvious mistake. Often called by their centuries-old names, such as rescission, restitution, reformation and specific performance, these remedies are discussed in Section E of this chapter. Another exception to the money-only rule involves evictions. In some states, a landlord can use Small Claims Court to evict tenants in certain situations. See Chapter 20 and the Appendix for more information.

A. Cutting Down a Claim That's Over the Limit to Fit Into Small Claims Court

It is legal to reduce an excessive claim so that it will fit into Small Claims Court. Thus, you could take a $2,800 debt in Oregon (where the dollar limit is $2,500) and bring it into Small Claims Court, asking for only $2,500. (Costs for filing and serving papers are recoverable in addition to the dollar limit in most states.) But if you do this, you forever waive the $300 difference between $2,800 and $2,500. In legal parlance, this is called "waiving the excess." Why might you want to do this? Because the alternative to Small Claims Court involves filing your suit in a formal court with dozens of complicated rules and the likelihood that you'll need to hire a lawyer, who will surely charge considerably more than $300 to represent you. It is possible to represent yourself in formal court, but doing so requires a good bit of homework and the fortitude to walk into an unfamiliar and sometimes hostile arena. If you do plan to go it alone, see Recommended Reading, just below.

Check out the court just above Small Claims. In most states, there are several levels of courts, with different monetary limits. A case that doesn't fit into Small Claims Court may be appropriately filed in an intermediate level court (possibly called "municipal," "justice" or "county" court, depending on the state). In recent years, these courts, which typically hear cases worth between $10,000 and $25,000, have gradually begun to be "delawyered" as more and more people represent themselves (appear in pro per).

By far the best book ever published on handling your own case is *Represent Yourself in Court*, by Paul Bergman and Sara Berman-Barrett (Nolo Press). It explains in detail what papers to file, how to conduct pretrial discovery and what to do when you finally get your day in court.

B. Splitting Small Claims Court Cases

It is not legal to split one over-the-limit claim into two or more pieces to fit each into Small Claims Court. Taking the $2,800 figure we used above, this means that you can't sue the same person separately for $1,200 and $1,600 based on the same claim.

(Defendants' claims that are over the Small Claims limit are discussed in Chapters 10 and 12.) As with most rules, however, a little creative thought can sometimes point the way to an exception. Start by understanding that it's perfectly okay to bring multiple suits against the same person as long as they are based on different claims, and that there is often a large gray area in which it is genuinely difficult to differentiate between one divided claim and several independent ones. This, of course, is where the creativity comes in. If you can reasonably argue that a $2,800 case actually involves two or more separate contracts or injuries to your person or property, you may as well try dividing it. The worst that will happen is that a judge will disagree and tell you to make a choice between taking your entire case to a formal court, or waiving any claim for money in excess of the Small Claims dollar limit.

> **Example 1:** One morning, a man in the private telephone business came into Small Claims Court with three separate lawsuits against the same defendant, for a combined total of $8,000, in a state where the Small Claims Court maximum is $5,000. One claim, he said, was for failure to pay for phone installation, another was for failure to pay for phone maintenance and the third was for failure to pay for moving several phones to a different location. The man claimed that each suit was based on the breach of a separate contract. The judge, after asking a few questions, told the man that he was on the borderline between one divided (not acceptable) and several separate (acceptable) claims, but decided to give him the benefit of the doubt and allowed him to present each case. The man won all three and got two judgments for $2,000 and a third for $4,000.

> **Example 2:** Another morning in Small Claims Court in the same state, a woman alleged that she had lent a business acquaintance $3,000 on two separate occasions and was therefore bringing two separate suits, each for $3,000. The defendant objected, claiming that she had borrowed $6,000, to be repaid in two installments. A different judge, after briefly listening to each side of the argument, agreed with the defendant and told the plaintiff that only one claim was involved and that if she didn't want to waive all money over $5,000, she should go to Municipal Court, which had a top dollar limit of $25,000.

Think twice before filing separate but related claims on the same day. If you split an over-the-limit claim, you may want to file your two or more separate claims a few weeks apart, since this will result in their being heard on different days, and, in most metropolitan areas, probably by different judges. Unless the defendant shows up and argues that you have split one claim, you will likely get your judgments without difficulty. There is, however, one possible drawback to this approach. If you bring your claims to court on the same day and the judge rules they are really only one claim, he will normally give you a choice as to whether to waive the excess over the Small Claims maximum in your state or go to a formal court. However, if you go to court on different days and the question of split claims is raised on the second or third day, you may have a problem. If the judge decides that your action in splitting the claims was improper, he may throw the second and third claims out of Small Claims Court without giving you the opportunity to refile in a formal court. This is because you have already sued and won, and you are not entitled to sue the same person twice for the same claim.

C. How to Compute the Exact Amount of Your Claim

The exact dollar amount to sue for is often easy to determine, but at times, it can be tricky. Before we get to the tricky part, let's start with rule number one: When in doubt, always bring your suit a little on the high side. Why? Because the court has the power to award you less than you request, but can't give you more, even if the judge feels you are entitled to it. But don't go overboard—if you sue for $4,500 on a $2,000 claim, you are likely to spur your opponent to furious opposition, ruin any chance for an out-of-court compromise and lose the respect of the judge.

Ask to amend your claim if you belatedly discover you should have requested more. If you find yourself in court and belatedly realize you have asked for too little, request that the judge allow you to amend your claim. Some judges will do this and, at the same time, offer the defendant extra time to prepare to defend against the higher claim. Other judges will allow you to dismiss your original case and start over, which is fine as long as your time to file hasn't run out. (See Chapter 5.)

1. Computing the Exact Amount—Contract Cases

To arrive at the exact figure to sue on in contract cases, compute the difference between the amount you were supposed to receive under the contract and what you actually received. For example, if Jeannie Goodday agrees to pay Homer Brightspot $2,200 to paint her house, but then only pays him $1,800, Homer has a claim for $400 plus the cost of filing suit and serving Jeannie with the papers. (Court costs are discussed in more detail in Chapter 15.) The fact that Jeannie and Homer made their agreement orally does not bar Homer from suing. As discussed in Chapter 2, Section C, oral contracts are generally legal as long as they can be carried out in a year and don't involve either the sale of real estate or of goods (personal property) worth $500 or more. (See Chapter 22 for a discussion of the relatively relaxed written contract requirements for the sale of goods.) Of course, since people tend to remember the oral contracts they've made differently, they can be hard to prove.

Unfortunately, some claims based on breach of contract are hard to reduce to a dollar amount. This is due to a legal doctrine known as "mitigation of damages." Don't let the fancy term throw you. As with so much of law, the concept behind the mumbo jumbo is simple. "Mitigation of damages" simply means that the person bringing suit for breach of contract must, himself, take all reasonable steps to limit the amount of damages he suffers. Let's take an example from the landlord-tenant field. Tillie the tenant moves out three months before the end of her lease (remember, a lease is a contract). Her monthly rent is $700. Can Larry the landlord recover the full $2,100 ($700 x 3 months) from Tillie in Small Claims Court? Maybe not. In many states, the law requires Larry to try to limit (or mitigate) his damages by taking reasonable steps to attempt to find a new tenant. If Larry can immediately rerent the apartment to someone else for $700 or more per month, he has suffered little or no damage (he has fulfilled his responsibility to "mitigate damages"). More typically, it might take Larry several weeks or months (unless he had plenty of advance notice, or Tillie herself found a new tenant) to find a suitable new tenant. For example, if it took Larry two months to rerent Tillie's unit, plus $75 worth of newspaper ads, he could recover approximately $1,475 from Tillie.

⚠ Landlords are not required to mitigate damages in every state. In a few states, landlords have no duty to mitigate a tenant's damages by promptly rerenting. In other states, case law on this issue is unclear. For more information and a state-by-state chart, see *Every Tenant's Legal Guide*, by Attorney Janet Portman and Marcia Stewart (Nolo Press).

The mitigation of damages concept applies to contracts in which the person damaged can take reasonable steps to limit her losses. In the earlier house painting example, if Jeannie Goodday had agreed to pay Homer Brightspot $300 per day for seven days to paint her house and then had canceled after the first day, Homer would be eligible to sue her for the remaining $1,800, based on Jeannie's breach of the contract. However, in court, Homer likely would be asked whether he had earned any other money during the six days. If he had, it would be subtracted from the $1,800. But what if Homer refused other work and slept in his hammock all week? If Jeannie could show he had turned down other jobs, or had refused to make reasonable efforts to seek available work, the judge would likely consider this a failure to mitigate damages and reduce Homer's recovery.

a.   Loan Contracts

Assume now you lent money to a person who promised to repay it but failed to do so. You'll want to bring suit for the total you are currently owed, plus any unpaid interest (assuming it doesn't result in your claim exceeding the Small Claims maximum). I have seen several disappointed people sue for the exact amount of the debt (say $500) and not include interest (say $50), thinking they could have the judge add the interest when they got to court. This normally can't be done—in most states, the judge doesn't have the power to make an award larger than the amount you request.

Don't invent interest if none was provided as part of the loan. As a general rule, you can only recover interest when it is called for in a written or oral contract. For example, if you loaned a friend $100, but never mentioned interest, you can sue only for the return of the $100.

Understand special rules for installment loans. If you are owed money under the terms of a promissory note (contract) that calls for repayment to be made in installments, you are normally only entitled to recover the amount of the payments that have already been missed and not those that aren't yet due, even if you are sure they will never be paid. But there is an important exception to this rule: You can sue for the entire loan amount plus any interest if your installment contract contains an "acceleration clause"—language which states that the entire amount of the loan is due if one payment is missed.

b. Extra Damages for Bad Checks

There are several major exceptions to the information on how to compute the amount of your contract claim set out just above. These involve situations where a statute establishes the right to receive extra damages, over and above the amount of the financial loss. The most common of these involves bad checks, where you receive a bad check (or a check on which the writer stops payment in bad faith) and the person giving it to you does not make it good within the time period allowed by the statute—usually within 30 days of your written demand to do so.

Most states have bad-check laws, including Oregon, Arizona, Colorado, California, Montana, Illinois and Texas. In general, these laws allow you to recover the amount of the check plus a penalty of two or three times the amount of the check, up to a certain maximum. (California and Oregon allow a maximum penalty of $500.) In some states, such as California, this law is mandatory—the judge must award the penalty.

In addition, there are usually some minimum and maximum penalties allowed:

1. You can usually sue for some minimum amount in damages, no matter how small the bad check. Thus, in California and Oregon, which both have minimum penalties of $100, if you get a $25 bad check, you can sue for $125.

2. There is usually a top limit on the damages you can sue for, no matter how large the check. Thus, in California, where the maximum penalty is $500, for a $400 bad check, the most you can sue for is $900 (the amount of the check plus the $500 maximum).

 Further Reading:
* *Money Troubles: Legal Strategies to Cope with Your Debts*, by Robin Leonard (Nolo Press). Contains the details of every state's bad check law.

2. Computing the Exact Amount—Property Damage Cases

When your property has been damaged by the negligent or intentional act of someone else, you usually have the right to recover the amount of money it would take to fix the damaged item.

Example: John Quickstop plows into Melissa Caretaker's new Dodge, crushing the left rear fender. How much can Melissa recover? Melissa is entitled to recover the amount it would cost to fix, or if necessary, replace, the damaged part of her car if John won't pay voluntarily. Melissa should get several estimates from responsible body and fender shops and sue for the amount of the lowest one. (See Chapter 19.)

There is, however, a big exception to this rule. This occurs when the cost to fix the item exceeds its market value. Simply put, you are not entitled to a new or better object—only to have your loss made good. Had Melissa Caretaker been driving a 1987 Dodge, the cost to fix the fender might well have exceeded the current market value of her car. If this was the case, she would be entitled to the value of the Dodge, not what it would cost to repair it.

To repeat this important point, in any situation where the value of the repair exceeds the value of the object, you are limited to the fair market value of the object (the amount you could have sold it for) a minute before the damage occurred. From this figure, you have to subtract the scrap value, if any, of the object after the injury.

Give yourself the benefit of the doubt when putting a value on property. No one knows exactly how much any used item is worth. Recognizing that reasonable minds can differ, it makes sense to place a fairly aggressive value on property that has been destroyed. But don't be ridiculous, or you'll likely offend the judge and weaken your case.

> **Example:** Let's return to Melissa from our last example. If several used car price guides indicated her 1987 Dodge was worth $1,200 and the fender would cost $1,400 to replace, she would be limited to a $1,200 recovery, less what the car could be sold for in its damaged state. If this was $150 for scrap, she would be entitled to $1,050. However, if Melissa had recently gotten a new engine and transmission, she might legitimately argue that the car was worth $1,700 and, if the judge agreed, she would legally be entitled to recover the entire $1,400 needed to get her Dodge fixed.

Replacement costs aren't relevant when figuring how much you are owed when property is destroyed. Many people insist on believing they can recover the cost of getting a replacement object when theirs has been totaled. As you should now understand, this isn't necessarily true. If Melissa's $1,200 car was totaled and she claimed she simply couldn't get another decent car for less than $2,000, she would still be limited to recovering $1,200. To recover a judgment for $2,000, she would have to show her car had a sale value of that much just before the accident. This rule can cause you a real hardship when an older object that is in great shape is destroyed. The fair market value may be low, while the cost of replacement high.

Knowing what something is worth and proving it are quite different. A car you are sure is worth $2,500 may look like it's only worth $1,900 to someone else. In court, you will want to be prepared to show your piece of property is worth every bit of the $2,500. The best way to do this is to get some estimates (opinions) from experts in the field (a used car dealer if your car was totaled). One way to present this type of evidence is to have the expert come to court and testify, but in most Small Claims courts, it can also be efficiently accomplished by having the expert prepare a written estimate, which you then present to the judge (see sample letter in Chapter 14, Section D). Depending on the type of property involved, you may also want to check newspaper and flea market ads for the prices asked for comparable goods and submit these to the judge. And of course, there may be other creative ways to establish the dollar amount of the damage you have suffered. We talk more about proving your case in court in Chapters 16–21.

3. Computing the Exact Amount—Cases Involving Damage to Clothing

Clothing is property, so why am I treating it separately? Two reasons: Cases involving clothing are common in Small Claims Court, and judges often apply a logic to them that they apply to no other property damage cases. The reason for this is that clothing is personal to its owner and often has little value to anyone else even though it may be in good condition. It follows that if the rules we just learned (that is, you can recover the repair cost of a damaged item unless this would be more than its market value before the damage occurred, in which case you are limited to recovering its total value) were strictly applied to clothing, there would often be little or no recovery. Fortunately, they usually aren't. Instead, most judges value damaged clothing based on the item's original cost and how long it had been worn.

When suing for damage to new or almost new clothing, it follows that you should sue for the amount you paid. If the damaged item has already been worn for some time, sue for the percentage of its original cost that reflects how worn it was when the damage occurred. For example, if your two-year-old suit that cost $900 new was destroyed, sue for about $450 if you feel the suit would have lasted another two years.

To summarize, in clothing cases, most judges want answers to these questions:

• How much did the clothing cost originally?

• How much of its useful life was consumed at the time the damage occurred?

• Does the damaged item still have some value to the owner, or has it been ruined?

Example 1: Wendy took her new $250 coat to Rudolph, a tailor, to have alterations made. Rudolph cut part of the back of the coat in the wrong place and ruined it. How much should Wendy sue for? $250—as the coat was almost new. She could probably expect to recover close to this amount.

Example 2: The same facts as just above, but the coat was two years old and had been well worn, although it was still in good condition. Here Wendy would be wise to sue for about $175 and hope to recover between $100 and $150.

Example 3: This time let's return Wendy's coat to its almost new condition, but have Rudolph only slightly deface the back. I would still advise Wendy to sue for the full $250. Whether she could recover that much would depend on the judge. Most would probably award her a little less on the theory that the coat retained some value. Were I Wendy, however, I would strongly argue that I didn't buy the coat with the expectation I could only wear it in a closet and that, as far as I was concerned, the coat was ruined.

4. Computing the Exact Amount—Personal Injury Cases

Lawyers quickly take over the great majority of cases where someone is injured. These claims are routinely inflated (a painfully sprained neck might be worth $15,000–$25,000 or more), at least in part because it is in many people's selfish interest to place a high value on injuries. Perhaps surprisingly, insurance company adjusters and lawyers are sometimes as much a part of this something-for-nothing syndrome as are the plaintiff's attorneys, who customarily receive a hefty percentage of the total recovery. This makes sense if you consider that if there weren't lots of claims, lots of lawsuits, lots of depositions and negotiations, it wouldn't take lots of people making lots of money to represent insurance companies. Even in states with so-called "no-fault" automobile insurance, the dispute resolution bureaucracy has managed to exploit loopholes in the law to protect itself very well.

Another reason why personal injury cases are usually filed in formal court is that, in many states, a Small Claims judge can only award an injured party the dollar amount of her out-of-pocket losses (doctors' bills, lost time from work), but doesn't have the power to award an additional amount to cover the injury victim's pain and suffering, no matter how legitimate. So before filing even a minor personal injury case in Small Claims Court, be sure you check your local rules.

Try to settle or mediate your personal injury claims. If you are seriously injured, you'll almost always want greater compensation than the Small Claims maximum. But to gain a significant recovery, it's not always necessary to sue in formal court. Many people successfully negotiate or mediate a satisfactory settlement with an insurance company.

Despite the potential drawbacks, some small personal injury cases do end up in Small Claims Court. Dog bite cases are one common example. To determine how much to sue for, add up the dollar amount of the following losses:

- Out-of-pocket medical costs, including
  medical care providers   _____
- Loss of pay or vacation time
  for missing work   _____
- Pain and suffering (assuming it is
  allowed in your state)   _____
- Damage to property   _____

   TOTAL   _____

Now let's look at each of these categories in a little more detail.

Medical/Hospital. The amount of the medical and hospital bills, including transportation to and from the doctor, are routinely recoverable as long as you have established that the person you are suing is at fault. However, if you are covered by health insurance and the insurance company has already paid your medical costs, you will find that your policy says that any money you recover for these costs must be turned over to the company. Often, insurance companies don't make much effort to keep track of, or recover, Small Claims Court judgments as the amounts of money involved don't make it worthwhile. Knowing this, many judges are reluctant to grant judgments for medical bills unless the individual can show he is personally out-of-pocket for the money.

Loss of pay. Loss of pay or vacation time as a result of an injury is viewed in a similar way. If the cocker spaniel down the block lies in wait for you behind a hedge and grabs a piece of your derriere for breakfast, and as a result you miss a day of work getting yourself patched up, you are entitled to recover your loss of pay, commissions or vacation time. However, if your job offers unlimited paid sick time, so you suffer no loss for missing work, you have nothing to recover.

Pain and suffering. The third area of recovery is for what is euphemistically known as "pain and suffering." When you read about big dollar settlements, a good chunk of the recovery routinely falls into the category of compensating the victim for the physical and sometimes mental pain he has suffered. As noted, in many states, Small Claims judges don't have the power to make awards for pain and suffering. But since in most instances, cases involving serious pain and suffering are worth far too much to be brought in Small Claims Court in the first place, this usually isn't a significant limiting factor.

But suppose you are in a state that allows recovery for pain and suffering and you have suffered a minor, but painful, injury that you do want to file in Small Claims—how much should you ask for? There is no one right answer. When valuing a client's pain and suffering, a lawyer will typically sue for three to five times the amount of the out-of-pocket damages (medical bills and loss of work). Therefore, if you were out of pocket $500, you might wish to ask for $1,500, the overage being for "pain and suffering." Under this approach, if you have no medical bills, it follows that you will find it difficult to recover anything for "pain and suffering." This is why lawyers routinely encourage their clients to get as much medical attention as reasonably possible.

Example 1: Mary Tendertummy is drinking a bottle of soda pop when a mouse foot floats to the surface. She is immediately nauseated, loses her lunch and goes to the doctor for medication. As a result, she incurs a medical bill of $150 and loses an afternoon's pay of an additional $150. She sues the soda pop company for $900, claiming that the extra amount is to compensate her for pain and suffering. This will probably be considered reasonable and, depending on the judge, she will probably recover most of this amount.

Example 2: The same thing happens to Roy Toughguy. But instead of losing his lunch, he just tosses the soda pop away in disgust and goes back to work. A few weeks later he hears about Mary's recovery and decides that he, too, could use $900. How much is he likely to recover? Probably not much more than the price of the soda pop—he apparently suffered little or no injury.

For information on how to negotiate with an insurance company without being skinned and how to decide how much to sue for if negotiations prove unsuccessful, I recommend *How to Win Your Personal Injury Claim,* by Attorney Joseph L. Matthews (Nolo Press). This book thoroughly discusses how to put a dollar value on injuries in the context of developing a strategy to successfully negotiate with an insurance company.

Don't Count on Recovering Punitive Damages in Small Claims Court

Formal trial courts have the power to award extra damages (over and above out-of-pocket losses and pain and suffering) in rare situations when an injury is caused by the malicious or willful misconduct (often a fraudulent or criminal act) of the defendant. When the defendant is wealthy, these damages—which are designed to punish the defendant—can run into the millions. About half of the states do not allow punitive damages (sometimes called "exemplary damages") to be awarded in Small Claims. But even in those states where it is theoretically possible to receive punitive damages, Small Claims Court's low dollar limit largely rules them out—except in a few instances where specific dollar amounts are established for bad checks (see Section C1, above) and failure to return a tenant's security deposit on time (see Chapter 20). If you believe you have been injured by conduct wretched enough to support a claim for punitive damages, see a lawyer.

---

5. Computing the Exact Amount—Emotional or Mental Distress

As noted in Chapter 2, in our increasingly crowded urban environment, there are all sorts of ways we can cause one another real pain without making physical contact. For example, if I live in the apartment above you and pound on my floor (your ceiling) for an hour at 6:00 a.m. every day, I will probably quickly reduce you to the status of a raving maniac. What can you do about it besides slashing my tires? One remedy is for you to sue me in Small Claims Court based on the fact that my actions constitute the intentional infliction of emotional distress. But how much should you sue for? Unfortunately, it's impossible to provide a formula. It depends on how obnoxious my behavior is, how long it has gone on, and how clearly you have asked me to cease it (this should be done several times in writing). And if this isn't vague enough, it will also depend greatly on the personality of the judge, who may be very skeptical of all neighbor disputes, thinking they don't belong in court in the first place. At the very least, you'll need to convince the judge you are an extremely reasonable person and your neighbor is a true boor, before you will be eligible for any recovery.

One way to help try to convince the judge you aren't a hypersensitive complainer is to sue for a reasonable amount. Thus, if you are in a state that permits Small Claims cases up to $5,000, I would normally advise against suing for any amount over $3,000, unless the other person's behavior clearly makes him out to be first cousin to Attila the Hun.

Try mediation first when neighbors are involved. As discussed in Chapter 6, the process of filing, preparing and arguing a lawsuit tends to make people madder than they were before. This may be fine if you are suing a large company, or someone you are never likely to interact with again, but given a neighbor's ability to retaliate in the future, it's usually best to try to amicably settle your case through mediation before going to court.

D. Computing an Exact Amount—Malpractice Cases

In theory most malpractice cases are worth far more than can be sued for in Small Claims Court. But because rules are usually tilted to favor professionals and these cases are expensive to bring, it's often hard to find a lawyer to represent you on a contingency fee (the lawyer doesn't charge you upfront but takes a percentage of the settlement), so many end up being scaled down to fit into Small Claims Court.

For most types of malpractice you simply need to prove that the dollar value of harm caused you was at least equal to the amount you have sued for (usually the Small Claims maximum). Thus if a doctor negligently misdiagnosed an illness and as a result you experienced horrendous problems, you would present the court with

- all medical, hospital and drug bills you paid that occurred after the misdiagnosis which you claim could have been avoided;

- an estimate for your pain and suffering (but first check with your court clerk to be sure pain and suffering damages can be awarded in Small Claims Court); and

- loss of any pay or vacation time.

Special rules for legal malpractice: As discussed in Chapter 2, Section I, if your suit is based on a lawyer's having failed to handle your case properly, you have to be able to prove that you would have won a recovery if the lawyer had not been a bungler and that if you had, your recovery would have been at least as much as you are suing for in Small Claims Court.

E. Equitable Relief (Or Money Can't Always Solve the Problem)

Nearly half the states allow judges to grant relief (provided you ask for it) in ways that do not involve the payment of money, if equity (fairness) demands it. "Equitable relief" is usually limited to one or more of four categories: "rescission," "restitution," "reformation," and "specific performance." Let's translate these into English.

You may need to do more research. If you think you may want to sue "in equity," where the payment of money just isn't enough, start by looking in the Appendix for your state. For example, Alabama, Arizona, California, Louisiana, Maine and Nebraska expressly allow equitable relief in Small Claims Court. If the law says recovery is limited to "payment of money only," or similar words, equitable relief isn't allowed. If you can't tell whether your state offers this relief, your next step will be to look up your state's Small Claims Court law. (You'll find the citation in the Appendix.)

Rescission: This is a remedy that is used to wipe out a grossly unfair or fraudulent contract under any of the following conditions:

- it was based on a mistake as to an important fact, or
- it was induced by duress or undue influence, or
- one party simply didn't receive what was promised, through the fault of the other.

Example: If a merchant sued you for failure to pay for aluminum siding you contended had been seriously misrepresented, you could ask that the contract be rescinded, and any money you paid be returned to you.

Restitution: This is an important remedy. It gives a judge the power to order that a particular piece of property be transferred to its original owner when fairness requires the contracting parties be restored to their original positions. It can be used in the common situation in which one person sells another a piece of property (say a motor scooter) and the other fails to pay. Instead of simply giving the seller a money judgment that might be hard to collect, the judge has the power to order the scooter restored to its original owner. Where money has been paid under a contract that is rescinded, the judge can order it to be returned, plus damages. Thus, if a used car purchase was rescinded based on the fraud of the seller, the buyer could get a judgment for the amount paid for the car, plus money spent for repairs and alternate transportation.

Reformation: This remedy is somewhat unusual. It has to do with changing (reform-ing) a contract to meet the original intent of the parties in a situation where some term or condition agreed to by the parties has been left out or misstated and where fairness dictates the contract be reformed. Reformation is commonly used when an oral agreement is written down incorrectly.

Example: Arthur the Author and Peter the Publisher orally agree that Peter will publish Arthur's 200-page book. They then write a contract, inadvertently leaving out the number of pages. If Arthur showed up with a 3,000-page manuscript and demanded that it be published in its entirety, a court would very likely "reform" the contract to include the 200-page provision, assuming the judge was convinced that it should have been included in the first place.

Specific Performance: This is an important remedy that comes into play where a contract involving an unusual or "one-of-a-kind" object has not been carried out. Say you agree to buy a unique antique jade ring for your mother's birthday that is exactly like the one she lost years before, and then the seller refuses to go through with the deal. A court could cite the doctrine of "specific performance" to order that the ring be turned over to you. "Specific performance" will only be ordered in situations where the payment of money will not adequately compensate the person bringing suit.

The Small Claims dollar maximum applies to cases involving equitable relief. In filling out your court papers, you will still be required to indicate that the value of the item for which you want equitable relief is under the Small Claims maximum (see Appendix). Thus, you might describe the nature of your claim (Chapter 10, Step 1) as follows: "I want the delivery of a 'one-of-a-kind' antique jade ring worth approximately $700 according to my contract with defendant."

Conditional Judgments: In California and in some other states, it's common for judges to issue conditional judgments in cases involving equitable relief. That is, they can order a party to perform, or stop, a certain act or else pay a money judgment. For example, you agree to sell your baby grand piano for $1,000. The buyer fails to pay, and you sue. The judge orders the buyer to either return the piano or fork over the $1,000. If this doesn't occur within a short period, the money judgment may be enforced. (See Chapter 24.) ■

Is the Suit Brought Within the Proper Time Limits (Statute of Limitations)?

Each state has time limits within which lawsuits must be filed. These are called statutes of limitations. Time limits are different for different types of cases. If you wait too long, your right to sue will be barred by these statutes. Why have a statute of limitations? Because it has been found that disputes are best settled relatively soon after they develop. Unlike wine, lawsuits don't improve with age. Memories fade and witnesses die or move away, and once-clear details tend to become blurred. Statutes of limitations are almost never less than one year, so if you file promptly, you should have little to worry about.

Act Fast for Claims Against Government Entities. To sue a city, county, state or governmental agency (for example, a school district), you first must promptly file a claim with the people in charge (the School Board, County Board of Supervisors, City Council). Once it's rejected—and it usually will be—you can file in Small Claims Court. Often your administrative claim must be filed within three to six months after your loss occurred or you are out of luck.

Typically, cases filed in Small Claims Court are brought promptly, so the question of whether the person suing has waited too long usually doesn't come up. If your case is one of the rare ones in which the statute of limitations is, or may be, an issue, you will want to check out your state's time limit. Check your state's laws under the headings "Limitations" or "Statute of Limitations." Read the material carefully—the time periods in which a suit must be brought will vary, depending on the type of suit (for example, oral contract, written contract, personal injury, etc.).

A. Statute of Limitations Periods—California and Texas

I include here statute of limitation periods for two of our largest states. While broadly similar, time limits for starting legal actions in other states will vary slightly, meaning you should always check the rules that apply to you for information on legal research. You will find a set of your state's laws at a public library, a law library and, for most states, online. See Chapter 1, Section D for more on how to do legal research.

California

Personal Injury: One year from the injury, or, if the injury is not immediately discovered, one year from the date it is discovered.

Oral Contracts: Two years from the day the contract is broken.

Written Contracts: Four years from the day the contract is broken.

Damage to Personal or Real Property: Three years from the date the damage occurs. The statute of limitations is ten years for property damage that results from latent defects in the planning, construction or improvement of real property.

Fraud: Three years from the date of the discovery of the fraud.

Professional Negligence Against Health Care Providers: Three years after the date of the injury or one year from its discovery. (See Sidebar, "How the Discovery Rule Works.")

Suits Against Public Agencies: Before you can sue a city, county or the state government, you must file an administrative claim form. The time period in which this must be done is usually short—often three to six months. This is not precisely a statute of limitations, but it has the same effect. (See Chapter 8 for a more complete discussion of how to sue governments in Small Claims Court.)

Texas

Libel and Slander: One year from the date of the libel or slander.

Evictions (Forcible Entry and Detainer): Two years.

Oral Contracts: Two years from the day the contract was broken.

Personal Injuries: Two years from the injury or, if the injury was not immediately discovered, two years from the date of discovery.

Written Contracts: Four years from the day the contract was broken (but the limitation period for actions upon stated or open accounts is only two years).

Most contracts are in writing. Some contracts that you assume to be oral may actually be written. People often forget that they signed papers when they first arranged for goods or services. For example, your charge accounts, telephone service and insurance policies, as well as most major purchases of goods and services, involve a written contract, even though you haven't signed any papers for years. And another thing—to have a written contract, you need not have signed a document full of "whereas's" and "therefores." Any signed writing can be a contract, even if it's written on toilet paper with lipstick. When you go to a car repair shop and they make out a work order and you sign it—that's a contract. (See Chapter 2, Section C, for more about contracts.)

How the Discovery Rule Works

With some types of cases, such as medical malpractice, the limitations period starts from the date the harm was discovered or reasonably should have been discovered. This rule protects people who don't know they have a problem until well after it has occurred.

Example: During an operation a doctor leaves a small clamp in your abdomen. It isn't until a year later that you experience extreme pain and see a different doctor who orders an x-ray which shows the clamp. In most states the statute of limitations for suits based on medical malpractice (often three years) begins from the date you learn of the problem, not the date of the original operation. However, if you walked around in pain for several years before seeing a second doctor and getting an x-ray, chances are a court would rule that the limitations period would start before actual discovery, based on the theory that you should have discovered the problem sooner.

B. Computing the Statute of Limitations

Okay, now let's assume you have found out what the relevant limitations period is. How do you know what date to start your counting from? That's easy. Start with the day the injury to your person or property occurred, or, if a contract is involved, start with the day that the failure to perform under the terms of the contract occurred. Where a contract to pay in installments is involved, the limitation's period for each installment is normally calculated from the date that payment was missed. (See Sidebar, "Tricky Rules for Installment Contracts.")

Example: Doolittle owes Crabapple $500, payable in five monthly installments of $100. Both live in San Jose, California. They never wrote down any of the terms of their agreement. Doolittle misses his third monthly payment, which was due on January 1, 1997. Crabapple should compute his statute of limitations period from that date, assuming, of course, that Doolittle doesn't later catch up on his payments. Since the statute of limitations for oral contracts in California is two years, this means that Crabapple has until December 31, 1999 to file his suit. If a written contract had been involved, Crabapple could file until December 31, 2001, as the statute of limitations on written contracts in California is four years.

Tricky Rules for Installment Contracts

The statute of limitations normally applies to each installment of a contract separately. To understand how this works, assume you agree to pay $5,000 in five installments commencing January 1, 1997, and continuing on January 1 of each succeeding year and that the statute of limitations for written contracts in your state is four years. It follows that you can defend against the creditor's lawsuit to collect the first installment of the loan (in legalese, it is often said his suit is "barred") on the basis that the statute of limitations has expired only if it is filed on or after January 2, 2001. But the creditor's lawsuit for your second payment will not be barred by the statute of limitations until January 2, 2002, and so on.

However, there is one big exception to the rule that the statute of limitations applies separately to each installment. When a contract contains an "acceleration clause" stating that if one payment is missed, all are immediately payable, the statute of limitations for all payments is normally figured from the date the first payment period is missed.

1. Voluntary Payment After Statute Has Run Out

I am frequently asked to explain the legal implications of the following situation: After the statute of limitations runs out (say two years on an oral contract to pay for having a fence painted), the debtor commences voluntarily to make payments. Does the voluntary payment have the effect of creating a new two-year statute of limitations period, allowing the person who is owed the money to sue if the debtor again stops paying? In most states, including California, simply starting to pay on an obligation barred by the statute of limitations doesn't create a new period for suit. (California Code of Civil Procedure, Section 360.) All the creditor can do is to keep his toes crossed and hope that the debtor's belated streak of honesty continues. However, if the debtor signs a written agreement promising to make the payments, this does create a new statute of limitations period. In legal slang, this is called "reaffirming the debt."

Example: Back to the drama of Doolittle and Crabapple. Let's assume that in February 1993, Doolittle experiences a burst of energy, gets a job and decides to pay off all of his old debts. He sends Crabapple $50. A week later, suffering terrible strain from getting up before noon, he quits his job and reverts to his old ways of sleeping in the sun when not reading the racing form. Is the statute of limitations allowing Crabapple to sue reinstated? No. As we learned above, once the limitation period of two years has run out, it can't be revived by simply making a payment. However, if Doolittle had sent Crabapple the $50 and had also included a letter saying that he would pay the remainder of the debt, Crabapple would again be able to sue and get a judgment if he failed to pay. Why? Because a written promise to pay a debt barred by the statute of limitations has the legal effect of reestablishing the debt.

⚠ Debtors Beware of Waiving Statute of Limitations. If a creditor and debtor discuss an unpaid bill and the debtor asks the creditor to give her more time to pay, to lower payments, or make some other accommodation, the creditor, assuming he is willing to agree, will almost always require that the debtor waive the statute of limitations in writing. This means that if the debtor fails to pay, he must wait another statute of limitations period (figured from the date of waiver) before the creditor is prevented from successfully suing.

2. Suspending the Statute of Limitations

In a few situations, the statute of limitations is suspended for a period of time (lawyers say "tolled"). This occurs if the person sued is in prison, living out of the state, insane or a minor. If the statute of limitations is suspended (tolled) by one of these events, it means that it simply isn't counted until the event is over, at which point it starts up again.

Example: Jack borrows money from Tim and signs a note promising repayment. Jack fails to pay the money back on the day required. Six months later, Jack is sentenced to a year in jail. The four-year statute of limitations would be tolled (suspended) during this period and Tim would still have three-and-one-half years after Jack gets out of jail to file suit.

Example: Ed, age 12, stars in a TV series. An accountant for the show tells Ed's family that he hasn't been paid all monies due under his contract. Neither Ed nor his family do anything about it. Eight years later, trying to figure out how to pay for college, Ed wonders if he can still sue the TV production company. The answer is probably yes, as most states would measure Ed's time to sue from his 18th birthday (that is, the statute of limitations period would be suspended or tolled while he was a minor). And since most states have four- or five-year statutes of limitation for disputes based on written contracts, this means that Ed could file suit at least until his 22nd birthday.

C.   Defendant Should Tell the Judge If the Statute of Limitations Has Run Out

What should a defendant do if he believes that the statute of limitations period on the plaintiff's lawsuit has run out? Tell the judge. Do this in court as part of stating your defense or, if your state is one of the few that requires a defendant to file a written request prior to the hearing date (see Appendix), list your claim that the statute of limitations bars plaintiff's lawsuit there. (Sometimes a judge will figure this out without a reminder, but you can't count on it.)   ■

How to Settle Your Dispute

Litigation should be a last, not a first, resort. In addition to being time-consuming and emotionally draining, lawsuits—even the Small Claims variety—tend to polarize disagreements into win-all or lose-all propositions where face (and pocketbook) saving compromise is difficult. It's not difficult to understand how this occurs. Most of us, after all, are terrified of making fools of ourselves in front of strangers. When forced to defend our actions in a public forum, we tend rather regularly to adopt a self-righteous view of our own conduct, and to attribute the vilest of motives to our opponents. Many of us are willing to admit that we have been a bit of a fool in private—especially if the other person does too—but in public, we tend to stonewall, even when it would be to our advantage to appear a little more fallible.

Although I am a strong advocate of Small Claims Court, I have nevertheless witnessed many otherwise sensible people litigate disputes that never should have been filed in the first place. In some instances, the amount of money was too small to bother with. In others, the problem should have been talked out over the back fence. And there were some situations in which the practical importance of maintaining civil personal or business relationships between the parties made fighting over a few thousand dollars look silly.

Let me emphasize this last point: It is almost always wise to look for a noncourt solution when the other party is someone you'll have to deal with in the future. Typically, this would include a neighbor, a former friend or a relative. Similarly, a small business owner will almost always benefit by working out a compromise settlement with another established local business or a long-term customer or client. For example, an orthodontist who depends on referrals for most new customers will want to think twice before suing a patient who has refused to pay a bill in a situation where the patient is genuinely upset (whether rightly or wrongly) about the services she has received. Even if the orthodontist wins in court, he is likely to turn the former patient into a vocal enemy—one who may literally badmouth him from one end of town to the other.

A. Try to Talk Your Dispute Out

Trying to avoid going to court by attempting to negotiate a compromise with the other party is rarely a waste of time. Indeed, you are often *required* to make the attempt. The law in many states requires that a "demand" for payment be made prior to filing a Small Claims Court action. A number of states require this "demand" to be in writing.

But first things first. Before you reach for pen and paper, try to negotiate directly with the person with whom you are having the dispute. The wisdom of trying to talk out a dispute may seem obvious, but it apparently isn't. I am frequently consulted by people with an "insurmountable dispute" who have never once tried to calmly talk it out with the other person. Clearly, many of us have a strong psychological barrier to talking to people we are upset with, especially if we have already exchanged heated words. Perhaps this mind-set would be easier to overcome if we could remember that a willingness to compromise is not a sign of weakness. After all, it was Winston Churchill, one of the twentieth century's greatest warriors, who said, "I would rather jaw, jaw, jaw than war, war, war."

It's important to know that an offer of compromise, made either orally or in writing, does not legally bind the person making it to sue for that amount if the compromise is not accepted. Thus, you could make an oral or written demand for $2,000, then offer to compromise for $1,500, and, if your compromise offer is turned down, still sue for $2,000.

In an effort to help you arrive at a good compromise, here are a few of my personal dispute resolution rules, which, of course, I modify to fit the circumstances:

- If you are the potential plaintiff, start by offering to shave about 20% off your original demand, in exchange for a settlement. Any less and you won't be taken seriously. Any more and you're giving away too much too soon.

- If you are the potential defendant and conclude that the plaintiff probably does have a decent case, start by offering about 50% of what is demanded. This should be enough to start negotiations. Many plaintiffs will ultimately agree to knock as much as one-third off their original demand to save the time and trouble of going to court.

- Money isn't always at the root of the problem. If you pay close attention to the other party's concerns, you may find that the key to arriving at an agreement can be found elsewhere. For example, a print shop might agree to refund a customer $2,000 on a disputed job in exchange for an agreement to continue to work together and speak well of each other in the future.

- The patient negotiator has the edge. Many Americans are in a hurry to arrive at a solution and, in their haste, will concede too much. Take your time. If the other person gets mad and hangs up, you can always wait a few days and call back.

- Good negotiators rarely change their position quickly, even if the other side does. Instead, they raise or lower their offer in small increments. For example, if your opponent counters your original offer of a 20% reduction by offering to pay half of what you ask for, you'll do best by not jumping to accept, but instead countering by reducing your original demand by 30% or 35%. If you do, there is a decent chance your opponent will further improve her offer. And even if she doesn't, you haven't lost anything, since once she has made an offer, she is unlikely to withdraw it.

It's rarely wise to split the difference. Often, an inexperienced negotiator will offer to split the difference or settle a claim for 50¢ on the dollar. It's rarely wise to quickly agree to do this, since, after all, your opponent has already conceded that amount. Better to counter with an amount between your last offer and your opponent's "split the difference" offer.

- Estimate how much money a compromise settlement is worth to you, given the fact it eliminates the time and aggravation of going to court. I do this by putting a dollar value on my time and then multiplying by the number of hours I estimate going to court will take. Also, based on the facts of your case, take into consideration the chances that you might lose, or get less than you ask for. In a recent study of 996 Small Claims cases that actually went to trial, only 32% resulted in the plaintiff receiving 100% of the amount claimed; 22% resulted in the plaintiff getting between 50% and 100% of the amount claimed; 20% resulted in the plaintiff getting less than half; and in 26% of the cases, the plaintiff got nothing at all. ("Small Claims and Traffic Courts," by John Goerdt (National Center for State Courts).)

Example: In a recent dispute my business, Nolo Press, had with a phone company, Nolo originally asked for $5,000. The phone company admitted some liability and offered to compromise. After considering the value of the time and energy Nolo would invest bringing the dispute to court, we were willing to lower our demand to $3,500. And although we were sure we had a strong case, we had to admit that a judge might not agree, so we decided to subtract another $500 and accept a settlement for $3,000. Unfortunately, after several conversations and letters, the phone company wouldn't offer a dime more than $2,000. This was too low, and we decided to go to court. As it happened, the judge awarded us the entire $5,000. But then the phone company appealed and received a new trial (a somewhat unusual feature of California law). After the case was presented over again, the second judge reduced our final award to $3,500. Considering that it was easier to prepare the case the second time, we still came out ahead of the game, as compared to accepting the $2,000, but in truth, given the time needed to prepare for two court presentations, we probably netted only about $500 more.

On several occasions when I have been involved in important negotiations I've gotten help by rereading *Getting to Yes: Negotiating Agreements Without Giving In,* by Roger Fisher and William Ury (Penguin). I also like *Getting Past No: Negotiating Your Way From Confrontation to Cooperation,* by William Ury (Bantam).

Sign a written agreement pronto. If you talk things out with your opponent, write down your agreement as soon as possible. Oral settlement agreements, especially between people who have small confidence in one another, are often not worth the breath used to express them. And writing down an agreement gives each party a chance to see if they really have arrived at a complete understanding. Often one or more details still must be hashed out. (In Section D of this chapter, I show you how to reduce a compromise agreement to writing.)

B. Mediate Your Dispute

Mediation, a procedure in which the disputants meet with a neutral third party who helps them arrive at their own solution, is available in most areas. Depending on your location, trained mediators may be standing by at the Small Claims courthouse or, if not, can usually be found at a local community mediation service. Either way, mediation is often conducted by volunteers at no cost to you. Where fees are charged, they are almost always low. In most areas of the country, mediation of Small Claims disputes is entirely voluntary, but in a few, such as Maine and Washington, D.C., mediation must be attempted before a case can go into the courtroom.

A mediation session, which will typically last anywhere from 30 minutes to three hours, consists of you and all other parties to a dispute sitting down with a mediator whose role is to help you arrive at your own solution. Unlike a judge, a mediator has no power to impose a judgment, with the result that mediation sessions tend to be much more relaxed than a court proceeding.

Many people who find themselves in the middle of a dispute ask why they should waste time mediating with an opponent who they believe is unreasonable. My best answer is that, when the parties to a Small Claims Court case voluntarily agree to mediate, the overwhelming majority of disputes are settled. And even in court systems where everyone is forced to mediate as a mandatory precondition to going to court, about 50% of cases settle. Settlement is especially likely when, deep down, one or both parties realize they have an interest in arriving at a solution at least minimally acceptable to the other party. As noted above, this is particularly common in disputes between neighbors or small business people who live or work in the same geographical area and really don't want the dispute to fester.

It is also of interest that studies have shown that people who agreed to have their cases mediated were more likely to be satisfied with the outcome of the case than litigants who went to trial. Not surprisingly, one reason for this is that people who arrive at a mediated settlement are more likely to pay up than are people who have a judgment imposed on them after losing a contested trial.

Is mediation always a good idea? No. If you are determined to get the total amount you are asking for, and you will have no ongoing relationship with the other party (such as a large corporation or government agency), bypassing mediation and going directly to court (except in the few places where mediation is mandatory) can make sense.

Example: John rented an apartment from Frontier Arms, Inc. When he moved out and left the unit undamaged and spotless, the Frontier Arms manager made up a bogus reason to avoid refunding his deposit. John decided that proposing mediation was a waste of time, since he was pretty sure a judge would enter a judgment for his entire $1,500, plus a $500 penalty, as provided by his state's rental deposit law.

Assuming you do want to mediate, how can you get a reluctant opponent to the table in areas where mediation isn't mandatory? Often you can get help from your local court-sponsored or community mediation program. Typically, as soon as you notify the agency that you have a dispute and would like to try mediation (notification is often automatic with a court-sponsored program), an employee or volunteer with the mediation program will contact the other party or parties and try to arrange a mediation session.

Defendant's Note: Suppose now that you are a defendant in a Small Claims case or have received a letter threatening suit. Should you ask for mediation? The answer is almost always a resounding yes, assuming you have a defense to all or part of the plaintiff's claim or believe that, while the plaintiff may have a decent case, he is asking for too much. Mediation will give you a great opportunity to present your side of the dispute and, hopefully, with the help of the mediator, arrive at an acceptable compromise. It can also allow you to bring up other issues that may be poisoning your relationship, which would not be considered relevant in court.

 People who are well prepared to engage in mediation are likely to achieve better results than those who take a more casual approach. The best source of information on how to mediate successfully is *How to Mediate Your Dispute: Find a Solution Quickly and Cheaply Outside the Courtroom*, by Peter Lovenheim (Nolo Press). I can almost guarantee that if you read it before you mediate, you will achieve better results than would otherwise have been possible.

Arbitration

In addition to mediation, a few states also offer binding arbitration before a volunteer lawyer as an alternative to having a case heard in Small Claims Court. Typically, the lawyer and the parties involved sit down at a table and discuss the case. If the parties don't arrive at their own solution, the arbitrator renders a decision just as a judge would. The only advantage of arbitration over going before a Small Claims judge or a commissioner is that, in some areas, it's faster to meet with the arbitrator. Unfortunately, arbitration comes with a big built-in disadvantage: The arbitrator is likely to be a volunteer lawyer far less knowledgeable about the broad range of laws that apply to consumers and small businesses than a judge. For this reason, I usually recommend against this procedure.

New York Note: In New York state, where volunteer lawyer arbitrators are routinely used, this disadvantage is compounded by the fact that there is no appeal from the decision of an arbitrator as there is from the decision of a regular judge.

Nonbinding Arbitration: In a few areas, a procedure called nonbinding arbitration is available. This is much like mediation, in the sense that both parties must agree to any settlement. The only difference is that, unlike a mediator, who doesn't make a formal recommendation, the arbitrator will recommend—but not compel—a solution. Especially if it's more easily available than mediation, it's often a good idea to try nonbinding arbitration, since the arbitrator's recommendation can be a pretty good guide as to what will happen if the case ends up going to court.

C. Write a Formal "Demand" Letter

If your efforts to talk your problems out fail (or despite my urging you refuse to try) and you decide not to propose or agree to mediation, your next step is to send your adversary a letter. As noted above, many courts require that a "demand" letter be sent. But even where there is no such requirement, it is almost essential that you send one. Why? Two reasons. First, in as many as one-third of all disputes, your "demand" letter will serve as a catalyst to arriving at a settlement. Second, even if no settlement results, setting out your case in a formal letter affords you an excellent opportunity to lay your case before the judge in a carefully organized way. Or, put another way, it allows you to "manufacture" evidence that you will likely be permitted to use in court if your case isn't settled.

You can be sued without first being sent a letter that suit is imminent. Some people believe they can't be sued until they receive a letter asking for payment. This is not necessarily true, even in states where a plaintiff must demand payment as a precondition to suing. A simple past due notice from a creditor, which states that if the account isn't paid promptly, court action will be pursued, usually meets a requirement that a formal demand for payment be made.

A personal note is in order here. In the almost 20 years since I wrote the first edition of *Everybody's Guide to Small Claims Court,* readers have sent in hundreds of Small Claims success stories. One thing has consistently delighted me: Many self-proclaimed winners never had to file their Small Claims case in the first place. These readers took my advice and wrote the other party a clear, concise letter demanding payment. As a result of either the letter itself or conversations it engendered, they received all, or at least a significant part, of what they asked for.

That a simple letter can be so effective may at first seem paradoxical, especially if you have already unsuccessfully argued with your adversary in person or over the phone. To understand why the written word can be so much more effective, think about the times you have found yourself embroiled in a heated consumer dispute. After angry words were exchanged—maybe even including your threat of a lawsuit—what happened next? The answer is often "nothing." For all sorts of reasons, from a death in the family, to the chance to take a vacation, to simply not having enough time, you didn't pursue your verbal threat. And, of course, you aren't the only one who may not have followed up on a verbal threat to bring a lawsuit. In fact, so many people who verbally threaten to sue don't actually do it that many potential defendants don't take such threats seriously.

But things change if you write a letter, laying out the reasons why the other party owes you money and stating that if you fail to get satisfaction, you plan to go to Small Claims Court. Now, instead of being just another cranky face on the other side of the counter or a voice on the phone, you and your dispute assume a sobering realness.

Really for the first time, the other party must confront the likelihood that you won't simply go away, but plan to have your day in court. And they must face the fact that they will have to expend time and energy to publicly defend their position, and that you may win. In short, assuming your position has at least some merit, the chances that the other party will be willing to pay at least a portion of what you ask go way up when you make your case in writing.

1. Writing Your Letter

When writing your demand letter, here are some pointers to keep in mind:

1. *Use a typewriter or computer.*

2. *Start by concisely reviewing the main facts of the dispute.* At first it may seem a bit odd to outline these details; after all, your opponent knows the story. But remember—if you end up in court, the letter will be read by a judge, and you want her to understand what happened.

3. *Be polite.* Absolutely avoid personally attacking your adversary (even one who deserves it). The more annoying you are, the more you invite the other side to respond in a similarly angry vein. This is obviously counterproductive to your goal of getting your opponent to make a businesslike analysis of the dispute and ask themselves such questions as:

- What are my risks of losing?
- How much time will a defense take?
- Do I want the dispute to be decided in public?

4. *Ask for exactly what you want.* For example, if you want $2,000, ask for it. And be sure to set a deadline. Ten days to two weeks is usually best; anything longer and your opponent has less motivation to deal with you right away.

5. *Conclude by stating you will promptly file in Small Claims Court if your demand is not met.*

6. *Keep a copy of all correspondence in your files.*

2. A Real Small Claims Case

Now let's consider a real Small Claims case. The facts (with a little editorial license) were simple. Jennifer moved into Peter's house in August, agreeing to pay $550 per month rent. The house had four bedrooms, each occupied by one person. The kitchen and other common areas were shared. Things went well enough until one chilly evening in October when Jennifer turned on the heat. Peter was right behind her to turn it off, explaining that heat inflamed his allergies.

As the days passed and fall deepened, heat became more and more of an issue, until one cold, late November night when Jennifer returned home from her waitress job to find her room "about the same temperature as the inside of an icicle." After a short cry, she started packing and moved out the next morning. She refused to pay Peter any additional rent, claiming she was within her rights to terminate her month-to-month tenancy without giving notice because the house was uninhabitable. It took Peter one month to find a suitable tenant and to have that person move in. Therefore, he lost rent in the amount of $550.

After calling Jennifer several times and asking her to make good the $550 only to have her slam down the phone in disgust, Peter wrote her the following letter.

January 1, 199x
61 Spring St.
Detroit, MI

Jennifer Tenant
111 Lake St.
Detroit, MI

Dear Jennifer:

You are a real idiot. Actually, you're worse than that: you're malicious—walking out on me before Christmas and leaving me with no tenant when you knew that I needed the money to pay my child support. You know that I promised to get you an electric room heater. Don't think I don't know that the real reason you moved out was to live with your boyfriend.

Please send me the $550 I lost because it took me a month to rerent the place. If you don't, I will sue you.

In aggravation,

Peter Landperson

To which Jennifer replied:

January 4, 199x
111 Lake St.
Detroit, MI

Peter Landperson
61 Spring St.
Detroit, MI

Dear Mr. Landperson:

You nearly froze me to death, you cheap bastard. I am surprised it only took a month to rent that iceberg of a room—you must have found a rich polar bear (ha ha). People like you should be locked up.

I hope you choke on an ice cube.

Jennifer Tenant

As you have no doubt guessed, both Peter and Jennifer made the same mistake. Instead of being businesslike, each deliberately set out to annoy the other, reducing any possible chance of compromise. In addition, they each assumed they were writing only to the other, forgetting that the judge could be privy to their sentiments. Thus, both lost a valuable chance to present the judge with a coherent summary of the facts as they saw them. As evidence in a subsequent court proceeding, both letters were worthless.

Now let's interrupt these proceedings and give Peter and Jennifer another chance to write more sensible letters.

January 1, 199x
61 Spring St.
Detroit, MI

Jennifer Tenant
111 Lake St.
Detroit, MI

Dear Jennifer:

As you will recall, you moved into my house at 61 Spring St., Detroit, Michigan, on August 1, 199x, agreeing to pay me $550 per month rent on the first of each month. On November 29, you suddenly moved out, having given me no advance notice whatsoever.

I realize that you were unhappy that the house was a little on the cool side, but I don't believe that this was a serious problem, as the temperature was at all times over 60 degrees and I had agreed to get you an electric heater for your room by December.

I was unable to get a tenant to replace you (although I tried every way I could and asked you for help) until January 1, 199x. This means that I am short $550 rent for the room you occupied. If necessary, I will take this dispute to court because, as you know, I am on a very tight budget. I hope that this isn't necessary and we can arrive at a sensible compromise.

I am also willing to try to mediate this dispute using the local community mediation service, if you agree. I have tried to call you with no success. Perhaps you can give me a call in the next week to talk this over.

Sincerely,

Peter Landperson

To which our now enlightened Jennifer promptly replied:

January 4, 199x
111 Lake St.
Detroit, MI

Peter Landperson
61 Spring St.
Detroit, MI

Dear Peter:

I just received your letter concerning the rent at 61 Spring St. and am sorry to say that I don't agree either with the facts as you have presented them, or with your demand for back rent.

When I moved in August 1, 199x, you never told me that you had an allergy and that there would be a problem keeping the house at a normal temperature. I would not have moved in had you informed me of this.

From early October, when we had the first cool evenings, all through November (almost two months), I asked that you provide heat. You didn't. Finally, it became unbearable to return from work in the middle of the night to a cold house, which was often below 60 degrees. It is true that I moved out suddenly, but I felt that I was within my rights under Michigan law, which clearly allows tenants to sue landlords for construc- tive eviction when the landlord fails to provide a necessity such as heat. In fact, you are lucky that I am not suing you for damages for constructive eviction.

Since you mentioned the nonexistent electric heater in your letter, let me respond to that. You first promised to get the heater over a month before I moved out, but never produced it. Also, as I pointed out to you on several occasions, the heater was not a complete solution to the problem, as it would have heated only my room and not the kitchen, living room and dining areas. You repeatedly told me that it would be impos- sible to heat these areas.

Peter, I sincerely regret the fact that you feel wronged, but I believe that I have been very fair with you. I am sure that you would have been able to rerent the room promptly if the house had been warm. Since I don't believe that any compromise is possible, mediation does not make sense. If you wish to go to court, I'll be there with several witnesses who will support my position.

Sincerely,

Jennifer Tenant

As you can see, while the second two letters are less fun to read, they are far more informative. In this instance, the goal of reaching an acceptable compromise or agreeing to mediation was not met, but both have prepared a good outline of their positions for the judge. Of course, in court, both Peter and Jennifer will testify, present witnesses and possibly other evidence that will tell much the same story as is set out in the letters. However, court proceedings are often rushed and confused and it's nice to have a written statement for the judge to fall back on. Be sure the judge is given a copy of your demand letter when your case is presented. The judge won't be able to guess that you have it; you will have to let her know and hand it to the clerk. (For more about how to conduct yourself in court, see Chapters 13-15).

3. Sample Demand Letters

Below are letters a consumer might write to an auto repair shop after being victimized by a shoddy repair job and a contractor who botched a remodeling contract.

June 16, 199x
Tucker's Fix-It-Quick Garage
9938 Main St.
Chicago, IL 61390

Dear Mr. Tucker,

On May 21, 199x, I took my car to your garage for servicing. Shortly after picking it up the next day, the engine caught fire because of your failure to properly connect the fuel line to the fuel injector. Fortunately, I was able to douse the fire without injury.

As a direct result of the engine fire, I paid the ABC garage $1,281 for necessary repair work. I enclose a copy of their invoice.

In addition, I was without the use of my car for three days and had to rent a car to get to work. I enclose a copy of an invoice showing the rental cost of $145.

In a recent phone conversation you claimed that the fire wasn't the result of your negligence and would have happened anyway. And even if it was your fault, I should have brought my car back to your garage so you could have fixed it at a lower cost.

As to the first issue, Peter Klein of the ABC Garage is prepared to testify in court that the fire occurred because the fuel line was not properly connected to the fuel injector, the exact part of the car you were working on.

Second, I had no obligation to return the car to you for further repair. I had the damage you caused repaired at a commercially reasonable price and am prepared to prove this by presenting several higher estimates by other garages.

(Continued on next page)

Please send me a check or money order for $1,426 on or before July 15. If I don't receive payment by that date, I'll promptly file this case in Small Claims Court.

You may reach me during the day at 555-2857 or in the evenings until 10 p.m. at 555-8967.

Sincerely,

Marsha Rizzoli

June 6, 199x
Beyond Repair Construction
10 Delaney Avenue
Lincoln, Nebraska

Dear Sirs:

You recently did replacement tile work and other remodeling on my downstairs bathroom at 142 West Pine St., here in Lincoln. As per our written agreement, I paid you $4,175 upon completion of the job on May 17, 199x.

Only two weeks later, on June 1, I noticed that the tile in the north portion of the shower had sunk almost half an inch, with the result that our shower floor was uneven and water pooled in the downhill corner before eventually going down the drain.

In our telephone conversations, you variously claimed that the problem:

- was in my imagination

- was my fault, because the floor was uneven to begin with

- was too minor to bother with.

Sorry, but I paid for a first-class remodeling job and I expect to receive it. Please contact me within 10 days to arrange to pay me $1,200 (the cost of redoing the work per the enclosed invoice from ABC Tile) or to arrange to redo the work yourself. If I don't hear from you by June 15, I will promptly file in Small Claims Court.

Sincerely,

Ben Price

D. Write Down the Terms of Any Settlement

If you and the other party agree to a settlement, either on your own or with the help of a mediator, it's important to promptly write it down. When a mediator is involved, preparing a written agreement is usually the last step in the process. In some areas, this written agreement is then automatically made part of a court order (judgment), while in others it's simply a binding contract. The difference is that if a court order is not obeyed, collection procedures can begin immediately, while in the case of a broken contract, a lawsuit must be filed and a judgment obtained before collection procedures can begin.

If you and your opponent negotiate your own settlement, you'll need to cooperate to reduce it to writing. Lawyers call a contract settling a dispute a "release," because in exchange for some act (often the payment of money), one person gives up or releases her claim against another. For instance, if the paint on John's building is damaged when Joan, a neighboring property owner, spray paints her building on a windy day, John might agree to release Joan from liability (that is, not sue Joan) if Joan agrees to pay $2,000 to have the damaged area of John's building repainted.

As long as a written release is signed voluntarily by both parties, is fair in the sense that neither party was tricked into signing on the basis of a misrepresentation and provides each party with some benefit (if you pay me $500, I won't sue you and I'll keep my dog out of your yard), it is a valid contract. If either party later violates it, the other can file a lawsuit and receive a court judgment for appropriate damages.

It's important to understand that releases are powerful documents. If you release someone who damaged your car for $500, only to later find out that the damage was more extensive, you'll be stuck with the $500 unless your can convincingly claim the other party was guilty of misrepresentation or fraud. Of course, in most situations, where the details of a dispute are all well known, a release can be comfortably signed with the knowledge that the dispute will finally be laid to rest.

Below we provide a sample release adopted from Nolo's book, *101 Law Forms for Personal Use,* by Robin Leonard. That book contains a number of more specialized releases adapted to auto accidents, property damage and personal injuries that I don't have space to reprint here. It also contains mutual release forms for use when both parties are giving up claims. In addition, release forms are often available from office supply stores that carry legal documents and in lawyers' form books, available at law libraries.

No matter where you get your release, it should contain the following information:

1. The names and addresses of the party being released and the party granting the release.

2. A brief description of the "what," "when" and "where" of the dispute or issue to which the release pertains. (The release below provides several blank lines for you to briefly describe the events giving rise to the need for the release.)

3. A statement of what the person giving up a claim is getting in return. As mentioned, for a release to be a valid contract (which it must be to be enforceable), the person signing the release (releasor) must receive something of benefit (called "consideration" by lawyers) in exchange for her agreement to give up her right to sue. The release below provides a space for this "consideration" to be described. Typically, it is money. If so, simply enter the amount. If it is an agreement by the releasee to perform or not perform some act (for example, stop his dog from barking at night), describe the act.

4. A statement that the release applies to all claims arising from the dispute or issue, both those known at the time the release is signed and those that may come along later. This provision is very common in releases; without it they wouldn't be worth much.

5. A statement that the release binds all persons who might otherwise have a legal right to file a claim on behalf of the releasor (for example, the releasor's spouse or heirs).

Although I have included this provision in my releases for caution's sake, it is rare that it will ever prove relevant. In fact, such persons are usually bound by the release anyway. It's important to remember, however, that listing these people in a release does not affect any rights that such persons may otherwise have in their own behalf. Thus, in the community property states of Arizona, California, Idaho, Louisiana, New Mexico, Nevada, Texas, Wisconsin and Washington, where each spouse may independently own a portion of any claim, both spouses should definitely sign every release.

6. The date the release is signed.

7. The signatures of the parties. Legally, only the person granting a release needs to sign it, but we think it is better practice for both parties to do so—after all, this important document contains statements that affect both their rights. In the case of mutual releases, which occur when both parties give up a claim against the other, both must sign.

8. The release below contains a place for the signatures of witnesses. There is no legal requirement for a release to be witnessed, but if you don't trust the other person and think he may later claim "it's not my signature," a witness can be a good idea. If a release involves a lot of money or a potentially large claim, you may want to bolster the chances of its being upheld (should it ever be challenged later) by signing it in front of a witness or two who can later testify, if the issue arises, that the other party was under no duress and appeared to know what he was doing. If your release involves a small claim, it is not necessary to do this. To encourage you to have your release witnessed where appropriate, I have included two lines on each release for witnesses to sign. If you decide to dispense with witnesses, put "N.A." on each of the lines.

GENERAL RELEASE

1.   ___(Person signing release)_____, Releasor, voluntarily and knowingly executes this release with the express intention of eliminating Releasee's liabilities and obligations as described be-low.

2.   Releasor hereby releases ___*(person being released)*___, Releasee, from all claims, known or unknown that have arisen or may arise from the following occurrence: ___*(description of events giving rise to release, including location and date if appropriate)*___

Sample Language:

a. "Repair work incompletely done to Releasor's boat at the Fixemup shipyards on 5/6/87."

b. "Agreement by Releasee made during the week of June 6, 19__ to deliver the fully laid out and pasted-up manuscript for the book <u>Do Your Own Brain Surgery</u> to Releasor's address no later than July 6, 19_, which Releasee failed to keep."

c. "A tree growing on Releasee's property at 1011 Oak St. fell into Releasor's backyard at 1013 Oak St. on August 7, 19_. It damaged Releasor's fence, which had to be replaced. The tree itself had to be removed by ABC Tree Terminators."

---

3.   In exchange for granting this release Releasor has received the following consideration: ___*(amount of money, or description of something else of value which person signing release received from other party)*___

Sample Language:

a. "$150 cash."

b. "a used RCA television set."

c. "an agreement by (Releasee's name) to desist from further activities as described in Clause 3 of this release."

d. "an agreement by (Releasee's name) to repair Releasor's Apple Macintosh computer by January, 19__."

4.   In executing this release Releasor additionally intends to bind his or her spouse, heirs, legal representatives,

assigns and anyone else claiming under him or her. Releasor has not assigned any claim covered by this

release to any other party. Releasor also intends that this release apply to the heirs, personal representatives,

assigns, insurers and successors of Releasee as well as to the Releasee.

This release was executed on _____, 199x at   *(city and state)*_____

Releasor's Signature   Releasee's Signature

Address   Address

Releasor's Spouse's Signature

Witnesses:

Name   Address

Name   Address

If possible, have your settlement made part of a court order. Assuming a Small Claims case has actually been filed, you may have a choice as to whether your agreement is made part of a court order or is simply written as a binding contract between you and the other party. Especially if it's less trouble (sometimes getting a court order involves an extra trip to court), you may be tempted to accept a contract. Generally, I recommend against this. Since a court order is easier to enforce, having your settlement agreement made part of one (assuming it's possible, of course) is definitely worth a little extra effort.

E.   Agreement Just Before Court

Occasionally, disputes are settled while you are waiting for your case to be heard. Even on court day, it is perfectly proper to ask the other person if he or she wishes to step into the hall for a moment to talk the matter over. If you can agree on a last-minute compromise, wait until your case is called by name by the courtroom clerk and then tell the judge the amount you have agreed upon and whether the amount is to be paid all at once, or over time. Typically, the judge will order that the case be dismissed if one person pays the other the agreed-upon amount on the spot, or, if payment is to be made later, will enter a judgment for the amount that you have compromised upon.

Another possibility is that you and your opponent will agree to a last-minute attempt to mediate. If so, you will want to explain this to the judge, who in turn will normally delay ("continue," in legalese) your case until the mediation session takes place. If mediation works and your case settles, you and the other party should jointly notify the court clerk. ■

CHAPTER

Who Can Sue?

Asking who can sue in Small Claims Court is usually an easy question to answer. *You* can, as long as you are an adult (18 in most states) or an emancipated minor and have not been declared mentally incompetent in a judicial proceeding.

Special requirements for some plaintiffs. Some states do not let unlicensed contractors and other business people who work without required licenses to bring suit. Prisoners are allowed to sue in some states, but not others. In states where they can sue, cases must usually be presented in writing. (In a few states, the prisoner can name an adult representative to appear on his behalf.)

The next question is often how do you identify yourself on court papers. Here are the general rules. Your state's requirements may vary slightly, however, so you should check your state's Small Claims guidelines.

1. If you are suing for yourself alone, simply list your full name as plaintiff.

2. If more than one person is bringing suit, list all the names as plaintiffs.

3. If you are filing a claim on behalf of your individually owned business, you (the owner of the business) must do the suing. You should list your name and the business name as plaintiffs, for example, "Jane Poe doing business as ABC Printing." Also, if the business uses a fictitious name (such as Tasty Donut Shop), as opposed to the owner's name, a form stating that the fictitious business name has been properly registered must be completed in many states.

4. If you are a partner filing a claim on behalf of a partnership, list the partnership name as plaintiff (example, Jones & Wood Graphics). Only one of the partners need sign. If the partnership uses a fictitious name, list it and the partners' real names, such as ABC Printing, a partnership, and Jane Poe and Phil Roe, partners.

5. If you are filing a claim on behalf of a corporation, whether profit or nonprofit, list the corporation as plaintiff. In most states, the form must be signed by either:

a. an officer of the corporation, or

b. a person authorized to file claims on behalf of the corporation by the corporation's Board of Directors. If a nonofficer of a corporation is involved, the court clerk may want to see some documentation that the person suing is properly authorized.

6. If you are suing on behalf of a limited liability company (LLC), most states allow any member to sue. But check your local rules, since LLCs are so new procedures are still in flux in many states.

7. If you are filing on behalf of an unincorporated association, do so by listing the name of the association and the name of the officer by whom it is being represented (such as "ABC Society, by Philip Dog, president").

8. When a claim arises out of damage to a motor vehicle, the registered owner(s) of the vehicle must file in Small Claims Court. So, if you are driving someone else's car and get hit by a third party, you can't sue for damage done to the car. The registered owner must do the suing.

9. If you are suing on behalf of a public entity such as a public library, city tax assessor's office or county hospital, you must show the court clerk proper authorization to sue.

Defendants can sometimes challenge a plaintiff's right to sue. As noted above, in certain situations, to qualify to sue in Small Claims Court, specific legal requirements must be met. For example, in some states, contractors must be licensed, and car repair dealers, structural pest control operators, and TV repair people must be registered with the relevant state agency as a condition for using Small Claims Court. And, in some states, anyone doing business under a fictitious name must file and maintain a fictitious business name statement as a precondition to using the courts. If you are being sued by anyone who you feel may not meet these requirements, check your state's rules by asking the court clerk or, better yet, looking up the law. (Your state's Small Claims statute numbers are listed in the Appendix, and Chapter 1, Section D, explains how to look them up.)

A. Participation by Attorneys and Bill Collectors

Attorneys, or other people acting as representatives, cannot normally appear in Small Claims Court in Arkansas (except in rural areas), California, Colorado, Idaho, Kansas, Michigan, Minnesota, Montana (unless all parties have attorneys), Nebraska, Oregon and Washington. Minnesota, Oregon and Washington allow attorneys only if the judge consents. In the majority of states, however, attorneys are permitted. (See Appendix for your state's rules.) Even in states such as California, Colorado and Michigan, in which people filing Small Claims cases can't be represented by a lawyer, attorneys are allowed to sue or defend their own claims. Getting the advice of a lawyer before going to Small Claims Court is perfectly legal in all states, however.

Many states, including California, Michigan, Missouri, Nebraska, New Jersey (except by corporations), New York and Ohio (except by authorized employee or officer of the state to recover taxes), forbid the use of Small Claims Court by "assignees" (a fancy term that usually refers to collection agencies). The majority of states, including Pennsylvania, Massachusetts, Maine and Oregon, still allow suits by collection agencies. Texas and Kentucky seem to be unique in barring lenders of money at interest from using Small Claims Court. New York, on the other hand, bars corporations from suing in Small Claims Court, and in most counties, also bars partnerships. See the Appendix under "Note" for information about your state.

B. Suits by Minors

If you are an unemancipated minor (in all states), or an emancipated minor (in some states), your parent or legal guardian must sue for you. To do this, a form must be filled out and signed by the judge appointing the person in question as your "Guardian Ad Litem." This simply means guardian for the purposes of the lawsuit. Ask the court clerk for the rules in your state.

C. Class Actions

In Small Claims Court there is no such thing as a true class action lawsuit, where a number of people in a similar situation ask a court's permission to join together in one lawsuit. However, a number of community groups have discovered that if a large number of people with a particular grievance (pollution, noise, drug sales) sue the same defendant at the same time, something remarkably like a class action suit is created. This technique was pioneered by a group of determined homeowners living near the San Francisco Airport who, several times, won over 100 Small Claims Court judgments based on excessive noise on the same day. They hired expert witnesses, did research, ran training workshops and paid for legal advice when needed as part of a coordinated effort, while all arguing their own cases. The City of San Francisco maintained that they were, in effect, involved in a class action lawsuit, and such suits are not permitted in Small Claims Court. However, a California Court of Appeals disagreed, saying that, "Numerous 'mass' actions against the City alleging that noise from the City airport constituted a continuing nuisance were neither too 'complex' nor had such 'broad social policy import' that they were outside the jurisdiction of Small Claims Court...." (*City and County of San Francisco v. Small Claims Div.,* San Mateo Co. (1983) 190 Cal. Rptr. 340.)

A similar strategy has been widely used in many cities to shut down drug houses. Neighbors organize to sue landlords who rent to tenants who sell drugs, claiming the legal theory of nuisance (use of property so as to interfere with the rights of others—in this case, the right to be free of emotional and mental distress). Each neighbor sues for the Small Claims maximum. Thus, in a state where it's possible to sue for $7,500, 30 neighbors who coordinate their Small Claims filings can, together, bring what amounts to a $225,000 case. In a number of instances, cases such as these have resulted in large judgments against landlords who rent to dealers, with the result that the problem was quickly cleaned up.

Small Claims "class actions" are exciting; they show that people can change their neighborhood for the better, even in the face of overwhelming power on the other side. However, these suits also carry a negative message. They indicate that normal channels for change have broken down. For example, in the airport case, the residents only sued after prolonged inaction by officials. And in most drug house cases, residents had repeatedly informed police of illegal activities and housing code violations, but to no avail. Although Small Claims Court is a good way to get action on local problems when all else fails, more flexible and effective solutions are needed. One possibility is the creation of a system for community dispute resolution, one that could hear grievances, bring together all interested parties, and if necessary, impose and enforce solutions other than money awards. Such tribunals could be operated in the spirit of Small Claims Court—accessible, inexpensive, quick—with the power to fashion wide-ranging solutions to community problems. For more information on how to use Small Claims Court to close down drug houses, contact Safe Streets, U.S.A., 1221 Broadway (Suite 13), Oakland, CA 94612.

D. Special Rules for Prisoners and Military Personnel Transferred Out of State

Some states have special procedures for prisoners who wish to sue in Small Claims Court. In California, for example, a prisoner can sue in Small Claims Court by filing her papers by mail and then by either waiving personal appearance and submitting testimony in the form of written declarations *or* by having another person (other than a lawyer) appear on her behalf in court (CCP 116.540(g)).

In some states, military personnel who have been transferred out of state are also allowed to bring Small Claims Court cases without the need to appear in court personally. Check your state rules (the index of your state code) for how to do this.

E. Business Owners Who File Claims Do Not Always Have to Appear in Court

It used to be that a legal requirement stating that the owner of a business had to show up in court personally discouraged the owners of many small unincorporated businesses from using Small Claims Court. For example, a dentist who wished to sue on an overdue bill would have had to be in court personally. But today, a number of states are more understanding of business time pressures. If a business (incorporated or unincorporated) wishes to sue on an unpaid bill, it can often send an employee to court to testify about the debt as it is reflected in the written records of the business. For instance, in many states, a landlord suing for unpaid rent can send his or her property manager to court to establish the fact that the rent was unpaid (but see caution about bringing eviction cases in Small Claims Court in Chapter 20). For a business owner to invoke this time-saving procedure, the employee sent to court must be familiar with the company's books and able to testify about how this specific debt was entered in them.

But make sure that anyone who goes to Small Claims Court on behalf of your business has first-hand knowledge as to what is in dispute. For example, if your rug store is suing a customer who refuses to pay because carpet was improperly installed, you will probably lose if you send to court only your bookkeeper, who knows nothing about what happened on the particular job. In this situation, some judges may postpone (continue) the case for a few days to allow the business owner to show up with the carpet installer and present testimony about the quality of the repair, but don't count on it. ■

Who Can Be Sued?

You can sue just about anybody (person, partnership, corporation, state and local government) in Small Claims Court. Indeed, it is more often the "Where can I sue?" question (see Chapter 9), not the "Who can I sue?" question that causes difficulties. For example, you can sue the First National Bank of Vermont, but you will find it very difficult to have the case heard in Billings, Montana, or Emporia, Kansas, unless you can show that the bank does business there, or entered into or agreed to carry out a contract with you there. This doesn't mean you have a problem with suing the bank— you don't. The problem is only with suing in Billings or Emporia. If you go to Vermont, where the bank is located, you can bring your suit with no problem. (See Chapter 9, "Where Can You Sue?," for more information on bringing your suit in the right place.)

No Suits Against the Federal Government. To sue the United States Government, you must file in federal, not state court. Contact the nearest Federal District Court clerk's office for information.

A. Suing One Person

If you are suing an individual, simply name him or her, using the most complete name that you have for that person. If the person calls himself J.R. Smith and you don't know what the J.R. stands for, simply sue him as J.R. Smith. However, if with a little effort you can find out that J stands for James, it's better to sue him as James R. Smith.

What to do if a person has several names. Lots of people change their names by simply using a new name some or all of the time. Thus Jason Graboskawitz may also use J. T. Grab. When in doubt, list the name the person uses most often for business purposes first, followed by the words "also known as" (or "aka") and any other names. Thus you might sue Jason Graboskawitz, a.k.a. Jason Grab.

B. Suing Two or More People

If you are suing more than one person on a claim arising from the same incident or contract, you must list and serve each to bring them properly before the court. (See Chapter 11.) This is also required with a husband and wife. A problem may arise in some states where you can sue a person only in the county or district where he or she lives. What happens when you sue two people who live in different counties or districts? In most states, including California, this type of situation is handled by allowing the plaintiff to sue in either place. But a few states don't make even this exception, so it might actually be impossible to sue both these people in the same court. This possibility is noted in the Appendix where applicable.

Example: J.R. and June Smith, who are married, borrow $1,200 from you to start an avocado pit polishing business. Unfortunately, in the middle of the polishing, the seeds begin to sprout. J.R. and June get so furious that they refuse to repay you. If you wish to sue them and get a judgment, you should list them as James R. Smith and June Smith—not Mr. and Mrs. Smith. But now suppose that J.R. borrowed $1,200 for the avocado pit business in January, June borrowed $1,000 to fix her motorcycle a month later, and neither loan was repaid. In this situation, you would sue each in separate Small Claims Court actions.

C. Suing an Individually Owned Business

Here you list the name of the owner and the name of the business (Ralph C. Smith—doing business as [d.b.a.] Smith's Texaco). Never assume that the name of the business is in fact the same as the name of the owner. Often it is not. Ralph's Garage may be owned by Pablo Garcia Motors, Inc. (See Section E, "Suing a Corporation," below.) If you get a judgment against Ralph's Garage and there is no Ralph, you will find that it's worthless in many states—you can't collect from a nonexistent person. Take the trouble to learn the correct name of the owner of the business before you sue.

Fortunately New York, California and a few other states have liberalized their rules and do not penalize plaintiffs who incorrectly state the business defendant's name. New York allows a plaintiff to sue a defendant under any name used in conducting business if it is impossible to find out the defendant's true name. California allows a plaintiff to correct a defendant's name at the time of the hearing and, in some cases, after judgment, when the defendant is a business person using a fictitious name.

How to Find Out Who Owns a Business: Many states require that all people doing business using a name other than their own file a Fictitious Business Name Statement with the county clerk in the county or counties in which the business operates. This is public information, which you can get from the court clerk. Another way to figure out who owns a business is to check with the Business Tax and License Office in the city in which the business is located. If the business is not in an incorporated area, try the county. The tax and license office will have a list of the owners of all businesses paying taxes. They should be able to tell you, for example, that the Garden of Exotic Delights is owned by Rufus Clod. Once you find this out, you sue Rufus Clod, d.b.a. The Garden of Exotic Delights.

If for some reason the tax and license office and the county clerk can't help, you may want to check with the state. Millions of people, from exterminators to embalmers, must register with one or another state office. So, if your beef is with a teacher, architect, smog control device installer, holder of a beer or wine license, etc., you will very likely be able to learn who and where he is with a letter or phone call. Find the phone book for the capital city of your state (usually available at public libraries or the telephone company) and look under the listings for state offices. When you find an agency that looks like they should have jurisdiction over the type of business you wish to sue, call their public information number and explain your problem. It may take a little persistence, but eventually you should get the help you need.

D. Suing Partnerships

All partners in a business are individually liable for all the acts of the business. It follows that you should list the names of all the business partners, even if your dispute is only with one (Patricia Sun and Farah Moon, d.b.a. Sacramento Gardens). See Section C, just above, for information on how to learn just who owns a particular business.

Example: You go to a local cleaners with your new sky blue suit. They apply too much cleaning fluid, which results in a small gray cloud settling on the right rear shoulder. After unsuccessfully trying to get the cleaners to take responsibility for improving the weather on the back of your suit, you start thinking about a different kind of suit. When you start filling out your court papers (see Chapter 10), you realize that you know only that the store says "Perfection Cleaners" on the front, and that the guy who has been so unpleasant to you is named Bob. You call the city business tax and license people and they tell you that Perfection Cleaners is owned by Robert Johnson and Sal De Benno. You should sue both and also list the name of the business.

Two defendants are better than one. It is wise to get a judgment against more than one person if possible. When it comes to trying to collect, it's always nice to have someone in reserve if one defendant turns out to be an artful dodger.

E. Suing a Corporation or Limited Liability Company (LLC)

Corporations and limited liability companies (LLCs) are legal people. This means that you can sue, and enforce a judgment against, the business entity itself. You should not sue the owners of the corporation or its officers or managers as individuals unless you have a personal claim against them that is separate from their role as part of the corporation. In most situations, the real people who own or operate the corporation aren't themselves liable to pay the corporation's debts. This concept is called "limited liability," and is one reason why many people choose to incorporate or form an LLC.

Be sure to list the full name of the corporation or LLC when you file suit (for example, John's Liquors, Inc., a Corporation). Here again, the name on the door or on the stationery may not be the real name, as corporations and LLCs occasionally use fictitious names. Check with the city or county business license people where the corporation or LLC is headquartered. Information is also usually available from either the Secretary of State or the Corporations Commissioner's Office, located in your state capital. You may sue a corporation or LLC in your state even if its headquarters is in another state, as long as it does business there. (See Chapter 9 for more on where you can sue.)

F. Suing on a Motor Vehicle Accident

Special rules apply in motor vehicle accidents. In most states, if your claim arises from an accident with an automobile, motorcycle, truck or R.V., you should name both the driver of the vehicle and the registered owner as part of your suit. Most of the time, you will have obtained this information at the time of the accident. If a police accident report was made, it will also contain this information. You can get a copy of any police report from the police department for a modest fee. If there was no police report, contact the Department of Motor Vehicles. In most states, for a small fee, they will tell you who owns any vehicle for which you have a license number. In several states, the Department of Motor Vehicles will ask you why you want this information. Simply tell them "to file a lawsuit based on a motor vehicle accident that occurred in (name of city or county) on (date) at (time), involving myself and a car with a license number _____." This is a legitimate reason in most states, and you will get the information you need. However, in some states, the owner of the car will be notified of your request.

Remember, when you sue more than one person (in this case the driver and the owner, if they are different), serve papers on both. When a business owns a vehicle, sue both the driver and the owners of the business.

G. Special Procedures for Suits Against Minors

It is very difficult to successfully sue a minor for breach of contract in most states because minors can disavow (back out of) any contract they sign as long as they do it before they become adults, unless the contract was for a necessity of life—for example, food—in which case the parents are probably responsible. In theory you can sue minors for damage they cause to your person or property, but you must also list a parent or legal guardian on the court papers. Do it like this:

"John Jefferey, a minor, and William Jefferey, his father."

But it is usually not worthwhile to sue children, since it is very difficult to collect from most of them. Of course, there are exceptions to this rule, but most minors are, almost by definition, broke. But what about suing a damage-causing minor's parents? Normally a parent is not legally responsible to pay for damages negligently caused by his children, but there are some exceptions to this rule. In virtually all states, if a child is guilty of "malicious or willful misconduct," a parent may be liable up to a certain dollar amount per act for all property damage ($10,000 in some states; often a lot more if a gun is involved) and sometimes for personal injuries. Parents may also be liable for damage done by their minor children in auto accidents when they authorized the child to drive. (Check the index to your state's laws under "Minors" or "Children" or "Parent and Child" for your rules.)

Example 1: John Johnson, age 17, trips over his shoelace while delivering your newspaper and crashes through your glass door. Can you recover from John's parents? Probably not, as John is not guilty of "malicious or willful misconduct."

Example 2: John shoots out the same glass door with a slingshot after you have repeatedly asked his parents to disarm him. Can you recover from the parents? Probably.

H. Special Rules for Suits Against Government Agencies

As mentioned in Chapter 5, many states have special rules and procedures that must be followed before a suit can be brought against a state or local government entity. Often, you have to act very quickly or you lose your right to sue. Your local Small Claims Court clerk will be able to advise you as to the procedures you must follow and time limits you must meet.

Let's look at the rules of a state we will call Typical. Before you can sue a city because your car was illegally towed away or a city employee who caused you damage, or for any other reason involving personal injury or property damage, you must first file a claim with the city and have it denied. To do this, get a claim form from the city clerk. Your claim must be filed within six months from the date of the incident (in a few states you have even less time to file your claim, so don't delay). The city attorney will review your claim and make a recommendation to the city council. Sometimes the recommendation will be to pay you—most often it will be to deny your claim, no matter how meritorious. Once the city council acts, you will receive a letter. If it's a denial, take it with you when you file your Small Claims action. The clerk will want to see it.

Typical rules for suits against counties and districts (for example, school districts) are basically the same. Get your complaint form from the clerk of the governing legislative body for the county (for example, County Commissions, Board of Supervisors, etc.). Complete and file it within six months of the incident. Within a month or so after filing, you will be told whether your claim is approved or denied. If your claim is denied, you can then proceed to file in Small Claims Court. Claims against the state must also be filed within six months for personal injury and property damage.

No suits against the United States in state court. As noted earlier, suits against the federal government—or a federal employee acting within the scope of her employment—must be brought in federal court.

I.   Special Procedures for Suits Against the Estates of Deceased People

Death does not prevent lawsuits from being brought and judgments collected against the deceased. However, it does present a number of technical legal hurdles that vary somewhat from one state to the next.

Assuming the defendant made a will (or died without a will or other estate planning device such as a living trust), a probate proceeding will be held. All claims against the estate should be promptly made, in writing, to the personal representative (called an executor or administrator in some states) of the deceased person's estate and directly to the court. If you don't know who the personal representative is (usually it's a surviving spouse, adult child or other close relative), check filing records with the court that handles probate proceedings in the county where the defendant died. If the personal representative doesn't honor your claim, you will need to promptly check your state's rules as to where and how to sue.

These days, many people use living trusts and other devices to completely avoid probate. If this is the case, there will be no personal representative and no probate court proceeding; instead, the property of the deceased person is transferred directly to its inheritors. In this situation, you have the right to proceed against these people directly. In most states, you can do this in Small Claims Court. ■

Where Can You Sue?

Small Claims Courts are local. This makes sense, because the amounts involved aren't large enough to make it worthwhile to require people to travel great distances. A Small Claims Court judicial district covers part of a city, an entire city, several cities, or a county. The next city or county will have its own similar, but separate, Small Claims Court. Normally, your dispute will be with a person or business located nearby. If so, all you really need to know is that you can sue in the judicial district in which the defendant resides or, if a corporation is involved, where its main place of business is located.

Occasionally, however, the person or business you want to sue resides at a considerable distance from where you live. How you should proceed in this situation depends primarily as to whether the defendant is located in your state or a different state.

A. Where the Defendant Is Out of State

Because rules as to where you can sue an out-of-state defendant are somewhat different depending on whether your dispute is with an individual or a business, it makes sense to treat these types of defendants separately.

1. Suits Against Individuals

The basic rule is that a state court—including Small Claims Court—only has the power (lawyers call this jurisdiction) to hear cases involving individuals who reside in that state or who are served with court papers while in that state. This means if you want to sue someone who lives in another state and doesn't travel to your state, you will have to sue in the state where he lives, not in the one where you live. Often you can file papers by mail, but normally you'll need to show up in person on court day (a few states allow military persons transferred out of state and occasionally individuals in other categories to present their case in writing).

Out of state drivers can be sued for traffic accidents that occur in your state. Special "motorist laws" allow you to sue people who reside in a different state in the state where you live, for injuries or property damage arising from a traffic accident that occurred on your state's highways. Contact your Small Claims Court clerk for details.

2. Suits Against Businesses

As noted, rules for suing businesses are quite different. You may file suit in your state against any business that is organized (incorporated or established as an LLC) in your state or which has an office, warehouse, retail establishment, restaurant or other facility there, even if they are headquartered or organized elsewhere. For example, if an airline lands at an airport in your state and has a ticketing office there, you can bring suit against the airline company in your state's Small Claims Court.

Even if a business does not maintain a physical facility in your state, you can still sue there if the business has what lawyers refer to as "minimum contacts" with the state. This is a tricky and often litigated legal abstraction, but usually courts will find that "minimum contacts" exist if:

* the business actively sells its goods or services in your state.
* the business employs a sales rep who calls on you personally or by phone to solicit your business.
* the business solicits business in your state by mail—by sending you a catalogue, for example.

- the business solicits your business online, as would be the case with an online store. (But just your accessing an out-of-state business informational site is not enough to give the courts of your state power to hear a lawsuit against that business.)
- the business places advertising in your state's media.
- the business has a franchise or dealership in your state. For example, you can sue Ford in any state where they have an authorized dealer.

What this amounts to is that most large national businesses can be sued in all 50 states, but smaller businesses which operate in one or a few states and don't solicit business elsewhere can only be sued in the states where they operate.

Example 1: On vacation in Vermont, you are injured at a small local restaurant. When you return to Kansas, you file suit in Small Claims Court there. Your case will be tossed out because Kansas courts do not have power (jurisdiction) to hear a case involving a defendant which doesn't operate, advertise or solicit business in that state. The only place you can sue is in Vermont.

Example 2: Same vacation, but this time you are injured at a discount store with branches in all fifty states. Now when you return to Kansas you can sue in Small Claims Court. The fact that the store does business in Kansas gives that state's courts jurisdiction to hear your case.

B. When the Defendant Is in Your State

Assuming that the person or business you want to sue resides or does business in your state, the next question is where?

Of all the aspects of Small Claims Court that differ from state to state, the rule on where to sue seems to be the most variable. Some states let you sue another person only in the district or county where she resides. Others also allow you to choose the place in which an accident occurred, a contract was broken or originally signed, merchandise was purchased, a corporation does business and so on.

On the first page of the first chapter, we asked you to get a copy of the rules for your local Small Claims Court. Refer to them now to determine where to sue (also look at your state's listing in the Appendix). The first things you will wish to understand are the types of political subdivisions (judicial district, precinct, city, county) your state uses to define the geographical boundaries of its Small Claims Courts. Next, you will want to carefully study your local rules in order to understand the criteria used to define which district a particular lawsuit should be brought in (for example, suits can always be brought where a defendant lives). If this information is not set out in the information sheet, call the clerk of the court and ask. Often you may be eligible to sue in more than one judicial district (for example, where a defendant lives and where a traffic accident occurred). If you have a choice, you'll obviously want to pick the court that is most convenient to you.

In a few states you can sue for larger amounts in some areas. Some states, such as Virginia and Tennessee, allow suits to be brought for higher amounts in some areas. Obviously, if yours is a larger claim, you'll want to see if you are eligible to sue at one of these locations. (The rules for all states are set out in the Appendix.)

General Rules as to Where You Can Sue

Depending on the specific rules of your state, you can generally sue in any one of the following counties:

1. In all states, you can sue in the judicial district in which the defendant resides or has a place of business at the commencement of the action.

2. In about half of the states, you can also sue in the judicial district in which the obligation on which the suit is based was contracted to be performed.

3. In about half of the states, you can also sue in the judicial district in which an injury to persons or personal property occurred.

4. In a very few states, including California, you can also sue in the judicial district in which the defendant resided or did business at the time a contract was entered into, in some circumstances.

Now let's consider in more detail typical rules concerning where you can sue within a state.

1. You Can Sue Where a Person Resides/or a Corporation Does Business

It makes good sense that a person can be sued where he or she resides, or a corporation where it does business, doesn't it? If a suit is brought where the defendant is located, she can't complain that it is unduly burdensome to appear. Still, books have been written about the technical definition of residence. Indeed, I remember with horror trying to sort out a problem on a law school exam in which a person with numerous homes and businesses had "contact" with six different judicial districts. The point of the examination was for us students to figure out where he could be sued. Thankfully, you don't have to worry about this sort of nonsense. If you believe a business or individual to be sufficiently present within a particular judicial district so that it would not be a hardship for the business owner to appear in court there, go ahead and file your suit. The worst that can happen—and this is highly unlikely—is that the judge or clerk will tell you to start over someplace else or transfer your case to another judicial district.

Example: Downhill Skier lives in the city, but also owns a mountain cabin at which he spends several months a year. Late one snowy afternoon, Downhill drives his new Porsche from the ski slopes to his ultra-modern, rustic cabin. Turning into his driveway, he skids and does a bad slalom turn right into Woodsey Carpenter's 1957 International Harvester pickup. Where can Woodsey sue? He can sue in the city where Downhill has his permanent address. He can probably also sue in the county where the cabin is located, on the theory that Downhill also lives there. But read on—as you will see below, it might not be necessary for Woodsey to even get into the residence question, because many states would allow Woodsey to sue in the mountain county on the theory that the damage occurred there.

When defendants live in different places: In California, Illinois, Minnesota, New Jersey and the great majority of states, you can sue multiple defendants in any judicial district in which one resides, even though the other(s) live in another part of the state. But in a few states, including New York and Massachusetts, you can sue only in the place in which the defendant resides or does business, and thus can't bring one lawsuit against defendants who reside in different judicial districts. (Check with your court clerk and see the Appendix; if the listing says that you must sue where "*a* defendant resides," you can probably sue them all in one place, but if it says that you must sue where "*the* defendant resides," you probably can't unless you can find another valid reason to do so (such as where the act or omission occurred).)

2. You Can Sue Where a Contract Was Entered Into

Most states assume that where a written contract is signed is the place where it will be carried out. Thus they assume that the place where the contract was signed is the place in which "the act or omission occurred" if a problem develops.

Arizona, California, Indiana and a few other states are more thorough. (See Appendix.) In these states, a suit can be brought either where the contract was signed or where the contract was to be performed. This is good common sense, as the law assumes that, if people enter into a contract to perform something at a certain location, it is probably reasonably convenient to both. If, for example, Downhill gets a telephone installed in his cabin, or has a cesspool put in, or agrees to sit for a portrait in the mountain county, he can be sued there if he fails to keep his part of the bargain, because the contract was (or was to be) performed in the mountain county. Of course, as we learned above, Downhill might also be sued in the city (judicial district) where he resides permanently, or where the contract was entered into.

Example: John Gravenstein lives in Sonoma County, California, where he owns an apple orchard. He signs a contract with Acme Mechanical Apple Picker Co., an international corporation with offices in San Francisco, New York, Paris and Guatemala City. John signs the contract in Sonoma County. The parts are sent to John from San Francisco via U.P.S. They turn out to be defective. After trying and failing to reach a settlement with Acme, John wants to know if he can sue them in Sonoma County. Yes. Even though Acme doesn't have a business office in Sonoma County and they performed no action there in connection with their agreement to sell John the spare parts, the contract was signed there. But what if John was from Bergen County, New Jersey, and signed the contract in New York City (with the goods going through New York City)? Could John sue in Bergen County? No. Acme doesn't reside in Bergen County and performed no action there in connection with their agreement to sell John the spare parts. John would have to bring his claim in New York City.

But now let's assume that John dealt with Acme's Bergen County representative, who came to his orchard to take the order and who later installed the defective machinery. In this case John can sue locally because the contract was to be performed in Bergen County.

Reminder: You should realize by now that there may be several reasons why it can be okay to bring a suit in a particular place. You only need one, but it never hurts to have more. Also, as you should now understand, there may be two, three or more judicial districts in which you can file your case. In this situation, simply choose the one most convenient to you, or at least the one in which it's permissible to bring all the defendants (if there are more than one) into court. But check the Appendix and your local rules to make sure which places are appropriate in your case. If you choose the wrong one, your action will either be transferred or dismissed. If it is dismissed, you can refile in the correct district.

Where to sue in cases involving contracts: It isn't always easy to know where a contract has been "entered into" in a situation where the people making the contract are at different locations. If you enter a contract over the phone, for example, there could be an argument that the contract was entered into either where you are or where the other party is. Rather than trying to learn all the intricacies of contract law, your best bet is to sue in the place most convenient to you. On the other hand, if someone sues you at the wrong end of the state and you believe they have not met any of the requirements set out in the summary above, write the court as soon as you have been served and ask that the case be transferred to a court closer to you. Either way, if in doubt, let the judge decide.

3. In Most (But Not All) States, You Can Sue Where a Personal Injury or Damage to Property Occurred

California, Illinois, Indiana and many other states allow you to sue in the district in which the act or omission occurred (see Appendix). "Act or omission" is a shorthand way of lumping together things like automobile accidents, warranty disputes and landlord-tenant disputes for the purpose of deciding where you're allowed to sue. This means that if you are in a car accident, a dog bites you, a tree falls on your noggin or a neighbor floods your cactus garden, for example, you can sue in the judicial district where the "act" or injury occurred, even if this is a different district from the one in which the defendant resides.

Example: Addison is returning to his home in Indianapolis from Bloomington, Indiana, following an Indiana University basketball game. At the same time, Lenore is rushing to Bloomington from her home in Brown County, Indiana, more than 40 miles west of Bloomington. Lenore jumps a red light and demolishes Addison's Toyota near the Indiana University gym in downtown Bloomington, which is in Monroe County. After parking his car and taking a bus home, Addison tries to figure out where he can sue if he can't work out a fair settlement with Lenore. Unfortunately for him, he can't sue in Indianapolis, as Lenore doesn't reside there and the accident occurred in Bloomington. Addison would have to sue either in Monroe County, where his property was damaged, or in Brown County, where Lenore lives. Luckily for Addison, Monroe County is just an hour from Indianapolis. Had the accident occurred in Gary, Indiana, however, which is much further away, Addison would have been put to a lot more trouble if he wished to sue. (Presumably he would have chosen Brown County, which is much closer to his home than is Gary.) ■

Plaintiffs' and Defendants' Filing Fees, Court Papers and Court Dates

A. How Much Does It Cost?

Fees for filing a case in Small Claims Court are very moderate. It's rare to find a state that charges as much as $50, and some charge less than $10. In some states people with very low incomes can often qualify to have court filing fees waived. Normally, a defendant is not charged at all unless he or she files her own claim against the plaintiff (often called a counterclaim). There is usually an additional fee for serving papers on the opposing party, unless you are in a state that allows personal service to be carried out by a nonprofessional process server and you have a friend who will do it for you without charge. (See Chapter 11.) Most states allow service by certified or registered mail, so service costs are usually low. In a few situations, you may have to hire a professional process server. This will normally cost about $25, but will be higher if the person you are suing is hard to locate. You can get your filing fees and service costs added to the court judgment if you win. (See Chapter 15.)

B.   Filling Out Your Court Papers and Getting Your Court Date

Now let's look at the initial court papers themselves to be sure that you don't trip over a detail. Again, I refer specifically to forms in use in California and also include some New York forms, but you will find that your local forms will require similar information. You should have little trouble filling out your papers by following the examples printed here but, if you do, simply ask the clerk for help. Small Claims Court clerks are required by law in most states to give you as much help as possible, short of practicing law (whatever that is). A friendly, courteous approach to the clerk can often result in securing much helpful information and advice. In a very few Small Claims Courts, such as those in New York City, trained legal assistants will be available to help you.

Step 1. Fill Out the Plaintiff's Statement

To start your case in Small Claims Court, go to the Small Claims Court clerk's office and complete the form entitled "Plaintiff's Statement." (In some states, slightly different terminology is used, such as "General Claim" or "Plaintiff's Claim.") All you need to do is properly name the defendant(s), as discussed in Chapter 8, and briefly state what happened, as outlined in Chapter 2, Section A.

Step 2. Check It with the Court Clerk

When you have completed your Plaintiff's Statement, give it to the court clerk. In some states, the clerk will file your form as is, but often, he or she will type it in a slightly different format and assign it a case number. You will be asked to sign this second form under penalty of perjury. A copy of the "Claim of Plaintiff" will go to the judge, and another must be served on the defendant. (See Chapter 11.)

Step 3. Supplying Documentary Evidence

In most Small Claims Courts, no written evidence need be provided until you get to court, but others, such as Washington, D.C., require that certain types of evidence (such as copies of unpaid bills, contracts or other written instruments on which the claim is based) be provided at the time you file your first papers.

Whether your local rules require written documentation of certain types of claims or not, it is wise to spend a little time thinking about how you will prove your case. We discuss this in detail in the later chapters of this book. You should read ahead and figure out exactly what proof you will need and how you will present it, before you file your first court papers. Being right is one thing—proving it is another.

PLAINTIFF'S STATEMENT

PLAINTIFF'S STATEMENT

1. State your name and residence address, and the name and address of any other person joining with you in this action. If this claim arises from a business transaction, give the name and address of your business and complete a fictitious business name declaration on back of this form if applicable.

    a. Name _Andrew Printer_

    Address _1800 Marilee St_
    Street   Phone No. _(510) 827-7000_

    Fremont   _CA_   _94602_
    City   State   Zip

    b. Name _____

    Address _____ Phone No. _____
    Street

    _____
    City   State   Zip

2. State the name and address of each person or business firm you are suing. See "Information to Plaintiff".

    If you are suing one or more individuals, give full name of each.
    If you are suing a business owned by an individual, give the name of the owner and the name of the business he/she owns. You must state if you want to sue the individual as well as the business.
    If you are suing a partnership, give the name of the partners and the name of the partnership.
    If you are suing a corporation, give the corporations full name, and the name and title of an officer.
    If your claim arises out of a vehicle accident, the driver and the registered owner of the other vehicle must be named.

    a. Name _Acme Illusions, Inc._

    Address _100 Primrose Path_
    Street   Phone No. _(510) 654-1201_

    Oakland   _CA_   _94602_
    City   State   Zip

    b. Name _____

    Address _____ Phone No. _____
    Street

    _____
    City   State   Zip

    c. Name _____

    Address _____ Phone No. _____
    Street

    _____
    City   State   Zip

3. State the amount you are claiming. $ _950 00_

4. Describe briefly the nature of your claim and date it happened:
    Failure to pay for printing & typesetting
    _____

5. ☒ I have asked defendant to pay this money, but it has not been paid.

    ☐ I have NOT asked defendant to pay this money because (explain): _____

6. From venue table on reverse side select the reason why this is the proper court for your case.

    ☐ _A_ Place appropriate letter in box.

    If you select D, E, or F, specify additional facts in this space.
    _____

7. Give address below where obligation was entered into or was to be performed or where injury was incurred, **IF NOT A VEHICLE ACCIDENT.** See #8 for vehicle accident claims.
    100 Primrose Path, Oakland, California
    (Street address)   (City or locality)

8. If your claim **DOES** arise out of a vehicle accident, fill out this section:
    a. Date on which accident occurred: _____, 19 _____.
    b. Street or intersection and city or locality where accident occurred:
    _____

    c. If you are claiming damages to a vehicle, were you on the date of the accident the registered owner of that vehicle?
        ☐ Yes   ☐ No (Place X in one box)

9. I have received and read the form entitled "Information to Plaintiff".

Date _April 27, 19___   Signature _____

Form No. 214-127 (REV. 3/93)

PLAINTIFF'S STATEMENT SMALL CLAIMS
(SEE REVERSE)

PLAINTIFF'S CLAIM

Name and Address of Court: Alameda County Municipal Court
Oakland-Piedmont
600 Washington Street
Oakland, CA 94614

SMALL CLAIMS CASE NO.: 002001

— NOTICE TO DEFENDANT — YOU ARE BEING SUED BY PLAINTIFF	— AVISO AL DEMANDADO — A USTED LO ESTAN DEMANDANDO
To protect your rights, you must appear in this court on the trial date shown in the table below. You may lose the case if you do not appear. The court may award the plaintiff the amount of the claim and the costs. Your wages, money, and property may be taken without further warning from the court.	Para proteger sus derechos, usted debe presentarse ante esta corte en la fecha del juicio indicada en el cuadro que aparece a continuación. Si no se presenta, puede perder el caso. La corte puede decidir en favor del demandante por la cantidad del reclamo y los costos. A usted le pueden quitar su salario, su dinero, y otras cosas de su propiedad, sin aviso adicional por parte de esta corte.

PLAINTIFF/DEMANDANTE (Name, street address, and telephone number of each):

Andrew Printer
1800 Marilee St.
Fremont, CA 94536

Telephone No.:   (510) 555-5555

DEFENDANT/DEMANDADO (Name, street address, and telephone number of each):

Acme Illusions, Inc.
100 Primrose Path
Oakland, CA 94602

Telephone No.:   (510) 555-1212

Telephone No.:
Fict. Bus. Name Stmt. No.   Expires:

Telephone No.:
☐ See attached sheet for additional plaintiffs and defendants.

PLAINTIFF'S CLAIM

1. a. [X] Defendant owes me the sum of $ 950.00   , not including court costs, because (describe claim and date):
He failed to pay for a printing and typesetting job which was completed on March 15, 19__.
   b. ☐ I have had an **arbitration of an attorney-client fee dispute**. (Attach form Attorney-Client Fee Dispute Attachment).
2. ☐ This claim is against a government agency, and I filed a claim with the agency. My claim was denied by the agency, or the agency did not act on my claim before the legal deadline. (See form SC-150.)
3. a. [X] I have asked defendant to pay this money, but it has not been paid.
   b. ☐ I have NOT asked defendant to pay this money because (explain):
4. This court is the proper court for the trial because   [A]   (In the box at the left, insert one of the letters from the list called "Venue Table" on the back of this sheet. If you select D, E, or F, specify additional facts in this space):

5. I ☐ have [X] have not   filed more than one other small claims action anywhere in California during this calendar year in which the amount demanded is more than $2,500.
6. I ☐ have [X] have not   filed more than 12 small claims, including this claim, during the previous 12 months.
7. I understand that
   a. I may talk to an attorney about this claim, but I cannot be represented by an attorney at the trial in the small claims court.
   b. I must appear at the time and place of trial and bring all witnesses, books, receipts, and other papers or things to prove my case.
   c. **I have no right of appeal on my claim**, but I may appeal a claim filed by the defendant in this case.
   d. If I cannot afford to pay the fees for filing or service by a sheriff, marshal, or constable, I may ask that the fees be waived.
8. I have received and read the information sheet explaining some important rights of plaintiffs in the small claims court.
I declare under penalty of perjury under the laws of the State of California that the foregoing is true and correct.
Date: April 27, 19__

                Andrew Printer
....
(TYPE OR PRINT NAME)

▶ *Andrew Printer*
(SIGNATURE OF PLAINTIFF)

ORDER TO DEFENDANT

You must appear in this court on the trial date and at the time LAST SHOWN IN THE BOX BELOW if you do not agree with the plaintiff's claim. Bring all witnesses, books, receipts, and other papers or things with you to support your case.

TRIAL DATE FECHA DEL JUICIO		DATE	DAY	TIME	PLACE	COURT USE
	1.					
	2.					
	3.					

Filed on (date):   Clerk, by_____, Deputy

— The county provides small claims advisor services free of charge. Read the information on the reverse. —

Form Adopted by the
Judicial Council of California
SC-100 [Rev. January 1, 1997]

PLAINTIFF'S CLAIM AND ORDER TO DEFENDANT
(Small Claims)

Cal. Rules of Court, rule 982.7
Code of Civil Procedure, § 116.110 et seq.

Step 4: Getting a Hearing Date

One of the great advantages of Small Claims Court is that disputes are settled quickly. This is important. Many people avoid lawyers and the regular courts primarily because they take forever to get a dispute settled. Business people, for example, increasingly rely on private mediation or arbitration, caring more about resolving a dispute promptly than winning a complete victory. Anyone who has had to wait four years for a case to be heard in one or another constipated state trial court knows, through bitter experience, the truth of the old cliché, "Justice delayed is justice denied."

In New York and some other states, an "early" hearing is required, but no maximum number of days is set. Many other states require that the case be set for trial within a certain number of days.

When you file your papers, you should also arrange with the clerk for a court date. Select a date that is convenient for you. You need not take the first date the clerk suggests. Be sure to leave yourself enough time to get a copy of the "Claim of Plaintiff" or "Notice of Claim" form served on the defendant(s). (See Chapter 11 for service information.) If you fail to properly serve your papers on the defendant in time, there is no big hassle—just notify the clerk, get a new court date and try again.

Small Claims Court cases are most often heard beginning at 9:00 a.m. on working days. Some judicial districts are beginning to hold evening and Saturday sessions. (New York City's sessions are held in the evenings.) Ask the clerk for a schedule. If evening and Saturday sessions aren't available, ask why not.

C. The Defendant's Forms

In most states, no papers need be filed to defend a case in Small Claims Court unless the defendant wants the case transferred to formal court (see your state's transfer rules in the Appendix). However, in a few states, including Alabama, Arkansas, Connecticut, Iowa and Oregon, a defendant must respond in writing. (See Appendix for your state's rules.) In the great majority of states the defendant simply shows up on the date and at the time indicated, ready to tell her side of the story. If you need to get the hearing delayed, see "Changing a Court Date," below. It is proper, and advisable, for a defendant to call or write the plaintiff and see if a fair settlement can be reached without going to court. (See Chapter 6.)

Sometimes, someone you were planning to sue sues you (for example, over a traffic accident in which you each believe the other is at fault). As long as your grievance stems from the same incident, you can file a written "Defendant's Claim" for up to the Small Claims Court maximum and have it heard by a judge at the same time that the plaintiff's claim against you is considered. However, if you believe that the plaintiff owes you money as the result of a different injury or breach of contract, you may have to file your own separate case.

Many states call a Defendant's Claim a "Claim of Defendant" or "Counterclaim." All states have rules stating that any defendant's claim (counterclaim) must be filed in writing within a certain time period after being served with the plaintiff's claim (usually 10–30 days). When you file a Claim of Defendant, you become a plaintiff as far as this claim is concerned. In a few states, such as California, where only the defendant can appeal, this means that if you lose on your Claim of Defendant, you can't appeal that part of the case. Of course, even in these states, if you lose on the original plaintiff's claim, you can normally appeal that portion of the judgment. Appeal rules vary a great deal from state to state and can be complicated. (See Chapter 23 and the Appendix.)

In most states, if a defendant's claim is for more than the Small Claims maximum, the case will be transferred to a formal court, although in some, this is done only at the discretion of a judge, who may inquire if the defendant's claim is made in good faith. (Check your court rules and your state's listing in the Appendix.) A defendant who does not want to cope with a formal court may be wise to scale down her claim to fit under the Small Claims limit (see Chapter 4).

A defendant may be required to file a defendant's claim or lose the right to do so. A defendant who has a claim against a plaintiff arising out of the same incident the plaintiff has just sued on will almost always want to promptly file it. But what if for some reason she doesn't? Can a defendant decide not to file a defendant's claim (counter-claim) as part of a plaintiff's case and instead sue later? The answer is yes in some states where filing a counterclaim is mandatory and no in others where it isn't. If this is an issue for you, check your state's rules.

DEFENDANT'S CLAIM

Name and Address of Court:

Alameda County Municipal
Oakland-Piedmont
600 Washington St.
Oakland, CA

SMALL CLAIMS CASE NO.

— NOTICE TO PLAINTIFF — **YOU ARE BEING SUED BY DEFENDANT** To protect your rights, you must appear in this court on the trial date shown in the table below. You may lose the case if you do not appear. The court may award the defendant the amount of the claim and the costs. Your wages, money, and property may be taken without further warning from the court.	— AVISO AL DEMANDANTE — *A USTED LO ESTA DEMANDANDO EL DEMANDADO* *Para proteger sus derechos, usted debe presentarse ante esta corte en la fecha del juicio indicada en el cuadro que aparece a continuación. Si no se presenta, puede perder el caso. La corte puede decidir en favor del demandado por la cantidad del reclamo y los costos. A usted le pueden quitar su salario, su dinero, y otras cosas de su propiedad, sin aviso adicional por parte de esta corte.*

PLAINTIFF/DEMANDANTE *(Name, address, and telephone number of each)*:

Andrew Printer
1800 Marilee St.
Fremont, California 94536

Telephone No.:

Telephone No.:

☐ See attached sheet for additional plaintiffs and defendants.

DEFENDANT/DEMANDADO *(Name, address, and telephone number of each)*:

Acme Illusions, Inc.
100 Primrose Path
Oakland, California 94602

Telephone No.:

Telephone No.:

Fict. Bus. Name Stmt. No.   Expires:

DEFENDANT'S CLAIM

1. Plaintiff owes me the sum of $300.00   not including court costs, because *(describe claim and date)*:
   of delays and poor workmanship in a printing job he performed for me
   in April of 19__.

2. a. ☐ I have asked plaintiff to pay this money, but it has not been paid.
   b. ☐ I have NOT asked plaintiff to pay this money because *(explain)*:

3. I ☐ have ☐ have not   filed more than one other small claims action anywhere in California during this calendar year in which the amount demanded is more than $2,500.

4. I understand that
   a. I may talk to an attorney about this claim, but I cannot be represented by an attorney at the trial in the small claims court.
   b. I must appear at the time and place of trial and bring all witnesses, books, receipts, and other papers or things to prove my case.
   c. **I have no right of appeal on my claim**, but I may appeal a claim filed by the plaintiff in this case.
   d. If I cannot afford to pay the fees for filing or service by a sheriff, marshal, or constable, I may ask that the fees be waived.

5. I have received and read the information sheet explaining some important rights of defendants in the small claims court.

I declare under penalty of perjury under the laws of the State of California that the foregoing is true and correct.

Date: (fill in date)

Waldo Fergus
(TYPE OR PRINT NAME)

Waldo Fergus, President
(SIGNATURE OF DEFENDANT)

ORDER TO PLAINTIFF

You must appear in this court on the trial date and at the time LAST SHOWN IN THE BOX BELOW if you do not agree with the plaintiff's claim. Bring all witnesses, books, receipts, and other papers or things with you to support your case.

		DATE	DAY	TIME	PLACE	COURT USE
TRIAL DATE	1.					
FECHA DEL JUICIO	2.					
	3.					
	4.					

Filed on *(date)*:   Clerk, by _____ , Deputy

— The county provides small claims advisor services free of charge. (Advisor phone no: ____)—

Form Approved by the
Judicial Council of California
SC-120 [Rev. January 1, 1992]

DEFENDANT'S CLAIM AND ORDER TO PLAINTIFF
(Small Claims)

Rule 982.7

D. Jury Trials

Jury trials are not available in Small Claims Court in the great majority of states, including California, Colorado and Michigan. Plaintiffs know this when they file and can usually opt for a different court if they want trial by jury. Defendants, of course, don't have this upfront choice. To compensate, some states allow a defendant to transfer a case to a formal court in order to be eligible for a jury trial no matter how small her claim. Others, including California and Ohio, only allow transfer when the Claim of Defendant is for a dollar amount above the Small Claims Court maximum. Normally, a defendant must request a jury trial (or a transfer to a court where a jury is permitted) promptly after being served with court papers. And "jury fees" (often ranging from $100 to $500) must typically be paid in advance. Fees are normally recoverable if you win. Asking for a jury trial also tends to delay proceedings, and some people will make the request for this reason.

E. Changing a Court Date

It is sometimes impossible for a defendant to be present on the day ordered by the court for the hearing. It can also happen that the plaintiff will pick a court date and get the defendant served only to find that an unexpected emergency makes it impossible for the plaintiff to be present.

It is normally not difficult to get a case postponed. To arrange this, call the other party and see if you can agree on a mutually convenient date. Don't call the clerk first—he doesn't know what days the other party has free. Sometimes it is difficult to face talking to someone with whom you are involved in a lawsuit, but you will just have to swallow your pride. Once all parties have agreed to a new date, send the court clerk a notice in writing signed by both parties. Here is a sample:

11 South Street
Denver, CO
January 10, 19__

Clerk of the Small Claims Court
Denver, CO
Re: SC 4117 Rodriguez v. McNally

    Mr. Rodriguez and I agree to request that you postpone this case to a date after March 1, 19__.

JOHN MCNALLY

JOHN RODRIGUEZ

If you speak to the other party and find that he is completely uncooperative, put your request for a delay (continuance) in writing, along with the circumstances that make it impossible for you to keep the first date. Send your letter to the clerk of the Small Claims Court.

    Here is a sample:

37 Birdwalk Blvd.
Trenton, NJ
January 10, 19__

Clerk
Small Claims Court
Trenton, NJ

Re: Small Claims No. 374–628

Dear Clerk:

    I have been served with a complaint (No. 374–628) by John's Laundry, Inc. The date set for a hearing, February 15, falls on the day of my son's graduation from Nursing School in Oscaloosa, Oklahoma, which my husband and I plan to attend.

    I called John's Laundry and asked to have the case delayed one week. They just laughed and said they would not give me any cooperation.

    I feel that I have a good defense to this suit. Please delay this case until any date after February 22, except March 13, which is my day for a medical check-up.

Thank you,

Sally Wren

F.   If One Party Doesn't Show Up

If one party to a case doesn't appear in court on the proper day, at the proper time, the case is normally decided in favor of the other. Depending on whether it is the plaintiff or defendant who fails to show up, the terms used by the judge to make her decision are different. If the plaintiff appears, but the defendant doesn't, a "default judgment" is normally entered in favor of the plaintiff. (See Chapters 12 and 15 for more information on defaults.) Occasionally, although it happens far less frequently, it is the plaintiff who fails to show up. In this situation, the judge may normally either dismiss the case or decide it on the basis of the defendant's evidence. The defendant will usually prefer this second result, especially if a Claim of Defendant has been made. If the judge dismisses the case, depending on how it is done and the rules of the particular state, the plaintiff may or may not have the right to begin the case again. If you find yourself in this situation, check with the court clerk.

In some states, if neither party appears, a judge may simply take the case "off calendar," meaning that the plaintiff will get another chance to schedule it for a hearing.

If you are the person who failed to show up (whether defendant or plaintiff) and you still want a chance to argue the case on its merits, you must act immediately or forever hold your peace.

1. Setting Aside a Default (Defendant's Remedy)

Courts are not very sympathetic to setting aside or vacating a default judgment to allow a defense to be made unless you can show that the original papers weren't properly served on you and that you didn't know about the hearing. In some states, this can happen if someone signs your name for a certified letter and then doesn't give it to you. In all states, it can occur because a dishonest process server doesn't serve you, but tells the court he did. As soon as you find out that a default judgment has been entered against you, call the court clerk. It doesn't make any difference if the hearing you missed was months before, as long as you move to set it aside immediately upon learning about it.

If you have had a default judgment entered against you after you were properly served, you will face an uphill struggle to get it set aside. Some judges will accept excuses such as "I forgot," "I was sick," "I got called out of town," etc., and some will not. Generally, judges assume that you could have at least called, or had a friend call, no matter what the emergency. However, if you act promptly and if you have a good excuse, you stand a reasonable chance of getting the judge to set the default aside

To appeal, you must first set aside a default judgment. In most states, you can't appeal a default judgment even if you have a great case. Instead, you must promptly try to get the default set aside or the judgment will be final. To try to set aside a default, go to the Small Claims Court clerk's office and ask for the proper form, which will normally be titled something like "Notice of Motion to Vacate Judgment."

Sometimes a motion to vacate (set aside) a default judgment is not filed by the defendant until after a "writ of execution" to collect the Small Claims judgment has already been entered for the plaintiff. If so, in most states the writ of execution will be recalled (stayed) by the court until a decision on the motion to vacate the default judgment is made. If the writ of execution has already been served as part of an effort to collect, the defendant must file a motion so that the writ of execution is suspended (often called a Motion to Stay or Quash the Writ of Execution), pending the court's decision on whether or not to set aside the default judgment and reopen the case. For more information on how to do this, or to find out the exact rules for your state, consult your Small Claims Court clerk.

NOTICE OF MOTION TO VACATE JUDGMENT

Name and Address of Court:

SMALL CLAIMS CASE NO.

PLAINTIFF/DEMANDANTE *(Name, address, and telephone number of each)*:

DEFENDANT/DEMANDADO *(Name, address, and telephone number of each)*:

Telephone No.:

Telephone No.:

Telephone No.:

Telephone No.:

☐ See attached sheet for additional plaintiffs and defendants.

NOTICE TO *(Name)*:

One of the parties has asked the court to CANCEL the small claims judgment in your case. If you disagree with this request, you should appear in this court on the hearing date shown below. If the request is granted, ANOTHER TRIAL may immediately be held. Bring all witnesses, books, receipts, and other papers or things with you to support your case.	*Una de las partes en el caso le ha solicitado a la corte que DEJE SIN EFECTO la decisión tomada en su caso por la corte para reclamos judiciales menores. Si usted está en desacuerdo con esta solicitud, debe presentarse en esta corte en la fecha de la audiencia indicada a continuación. Si se concede esta solicitud, es posible que se efectúe otro juicio inmediatamente. Traiga a todos sus testigos, libros, recibos, y otros documentos o cosas para presentarlos en apoyo de su caso.*

NOTICE OF MOTION TO VACATE JUDGMENT

1. A hearing will be held in this court at which I will ask the court to **cancel** the judgment entered against me in this case. If you wish to oppose the motion you should appear at the court on

HEARING DATE FECHA DEL JUICIO		DATE	DAY	TIME	PLACE	COURT USE
	1.					
	2.					
	3.					

2. I am asking the court to cancel the judgment for the reasons stated in item 5 below. My request is based on this notice of motion and declaration, the records on file with the court, and any evidence that may be presented at the hearing.

DECLARATION FOR MOTION TO VACATE (CANCEL) JUDGMENT

3. Judgment was entered against me in this case on *(date)*:
4. I first learned of the entry of judgment against me on *(date)*:
5. I am asking the court to cancel the judgment for the following reason:
   a. ☐ I did not appear at the trial of this claim because *(specify facts)*:

   b. ☐ Other *(specify facts)*:

6. I understand that I must bring with me to the hearing on this motion all witnesses, books, receipts, and other papers or things to support my case.

I declare under penalty of perjury under the laws of the State of California that the foregoing is true and correct.

Date:

▶

....
(TYPE OR PRINT NAME)   (SIGNATURE)

CLERK'S CERTIFICATE OF MAILING

I certify that I am not a party to this action. This Notice of Motion to Vacate Judgment was mailed first class, postage prepaid, in a sealed envelope to the responding party at the address shown above. The mailing and this certification occurred

at *(place)*:   California,

on *(date)*:

Clerk, by _____ , Deputy

— **The county provides small claims advisor services free of charge.** —

Form Approved by the
Judicial Council of California
SC-135 (Rev. January 1, 1992)

**NOTICE OF MOTION TO VACATE
JUDGMENT AND DECLARATION**
(Small Claims)

Rule 982.7

2. Vacating a Judgment of Dismissal (Plaintiff's Remedy)

The plaintiff who fails to show up in court at the appointed time and then requests that the judge vacate his decision to dismiss the case will encounter even more difficulty than a no-show defendant who tries to persuade the judge to set aside a default. Why? Because the plaintiff is the one who initiated the case and arranged for the court date. The judge assumes that the plaintiff should be able to show up for his or her own case, or at least call the court clerk prior to the court date and explain why not.

However, now and then emergencies happen, or someone simply makes a mistake about the day. Judges can, and do, vacate dismissals if both of the following circumstances exist:

- The plaintiff moves to have the judgment vacated immediately upon learning of his mistake. "Immediately" is never interpreted to be more than a few weeks, at most, after the day the dismissal was entered, and is thought by most judges to be a much shorter time, and

- the plaintiff has a good explanation as to why he or she was unable to be present or call on the day the case was regularly scheduled. A judge might accept something like this: "I had a flu with a high fever and simply lost track of a couple of days. As soon as I felt better, which was two days after my case was dismissed, I came to the clerk's office to try to get the case rescheduled."

To get a dismissal vacated (when allowed), you must fill out a form similar to the one shown above. ■

Serving Your Papers

After you have filed your Claim of Plaintiff form with the clerk, following the instructions in Chapter 10 under "Filling Out Your Court Papers and Getting Your Court Date," a copy must be served on the person, persons or corporation you are suing. This is called "service of process." Your lawsuit is not complete without it. The reason that you must serve the other side is simple—the person(s) you are suing are entitled to be notified of the general nature of your claim and the day, time and place of the hearing, so that they can show up to defend themselves. The general rules of all states are similar, but details do differ. Refer to your local rules and to the Appendix of this book.

A. Who Must Be Served

All defendants that you list on your Claim of Plaintiff or Notice of Claim should be served. It is not enough to serve one defendant and assume that he will tell the other(s). This is true even if the defendants are married or living together. If you don't serve a particular defendant, the court can't enter a judgment against that person. If you sue more than one person and can serve only one, a judge can only enter a judgment against the person served, in effect dismissing your action against the other defendant(s). Depending on the state, you may be able to refile against these defendants if you wish.

B. Where Can Papers Be Served?

Normally, papers must be served within the state in which your action is brought. Thus, you can't sue someone in a Massachusetts court and serve papers on them in Oklahoma. An exception involves suits having to do with motor vehicle accidents. Many states have a procedure for out-of-state service on this type of claim. Your Small Claims Court clerk will show you how this is handled in your state.

Now let's assume that the person you want to sue resides or does business in your state. In most states, papers can be served anyplace in the state as long as the suit is brought in the correct judicial district. (See Chapter 9, "Where Can You Sue?") But a few states, including New York, require, with some exceptions, that a defendant be served in the same county or judicial district where the suit was filed. (See the Appendix.)

C. How to Serve Your Papers

There are several approved ways to serve papers. All depend on your knowing where the defendant is, lives or does business. If you can't find the defendant and do not know where she lives or works, you can't serve her, and it makes little sense, in that case, to file a lawsuit.

Method 1:   Personal Service

Sheriff, Marshal or Constable: All states allow personal service to be made by law officers, although not all officers will serve civil subpoenas. Adopting this method is often valuable for its sobering effect. Twenty to thirty dollars is the average fee, but you can get it added to your judgment if you win.

Private Process Servers: Many states also allow service by private process servers, whom you will find listed in the Yellow Pages. Fees charged are usually based on how long the service takes. See your state's listing in the Appendix for information as to whether service by private process servers is authorized.

Service by Disinterested Adult: California, Colorado, Ohio and a number of other states (but by no means all—see Appendix) allow service by any person who is 18 years of age or older, except the person bringing a suit. *Any* person means just that—a relative or a friend is fine.

No matter who serves the papers, if this method is used, the Claim of Plaintiff and a summons must be handed to the defendant. You can't simply leave the paper at her job or home or in the mailbox. A person carrying out a service who doesn't know the person involved should make sure that he is serving the right person. If the process server locates the right person, but he or she refuses to take the paper, acts hostile or attempts to run away, the process server should simply put the paper down and leave. Valid service has been accomplished. The process server should never try to use force to get a defendant to take any papers.

Method 2:   By Certified or Registered Mail

In California, New York and the majority of states, you can also serve papers by certified mail. In some states, service by certified (or registered) mail is an option of the plaintiff, while others require that it be attempted first, before any other method of service. (See Appendix.) Normally, the court clerk does the mailing for you and charges a small fee. This is recoverable if you win. (See Chapter 15.) The mail method is both cheap and easy, but in most states depends for its success on the defendant signing for the letter. (In a few states, including Alaska and Arkansas, service is accomplished even though a certified letter is rejected by the defendant.) Most businesses and many individuals routinely sign to accept their mail. However, some people never do, knowing instinctively, or perhaps from past experience, that nothing good ever comes by certified mail. I have asked several court clerks for an estimate as to the percentage of certified mail services that are accepted. The consensus is 50%. If you try using the mail to serve your papers and fail, and end up paying a process server, tell the judge about it as part of your presentation and chances are your costs will be added to the judgment.

Make sure service of process was accomplished. Never show up in court on the day of the court hearing on the assumption that your certified mail service has been accomplished. If the defendant didn't sign for the paper, you will be wasting your time in all but a few states. Call the court clerk a couple of days in advance and find out if the service of process has been completed. This means the certified letter has been signed for by the defendant, not by someone else at the address.

Method 3:   By Regular First-Class Mail

A minority of states, including New York and Connecticut, allow papers to be served by first-class mail. The states differ, however, on what you must do if the defendant doesn't answer your complaint within the time limit. New York, for example, presumes that the defendant received the papers unless the envelope comes back as "undeliverable." Connecticut, on the other hand, requires you to back up unanswered regular mail service with personal service by the sheriff. Check with your court clerk to see if this method is available in your area.

Method 4:   Substituted Service (or "Nail and Mail")

It can be difficult to serve certain individuals. Some people have developed their skill at avoiding process servers into a high art. In some states, this no longer works, as there is now a procedure that allows "substituted service" if you try to serve a defendant and fail. Often the slang for this type of service is "Nail and Mail," because in several states, if you are unable to serve the defendant personally, you do not have to leave the claim with a live person, but can simply tack one copy to the defendant's door and mail the second copy.

In a typical state, substituted service works like this: If a person can't be served with "reasonable diligence," the papers may be served by leaving a copy at the person's dwelling place in the presence of a competent member of the household who is at least 18 years of age and who must be told what the papers are about *and* afterwards mailing a copy by first-class mail to the person served. Service is complete 10 days after mailing. Be sure that all steps are carried out by an adult who is not named in the lawsuit. Because some Small Claims Court clerks interpret the requirement for "reasonable diligence" differently, it is wise to check out the substituted service procedure with your local clerk before trying it. If your suit is against a corporation, the substituted service procedure is easier, as there is normally no requirement that personal service be attempted before using it. Papers may be served by leaving them at the defendant's office with a person apparently in charge of the office during normal business hours, and then mailing another copy to the person to be served at the same address. Service is accomplished 10 days after mailing.

After service is accomplished, you must return a "Proof of Service" form to the court clerk stating that all proper service steps have been completed. (See "Serving a Business," below.)

Method 5:   For Serving Subpoenas Only

In Chapter 14, we discuss subpoenaing witnesses and documents. Subpoenas can't be served by mail. They must be served by personal service. The rules as to who can do the serving, etc., are the same as those set forth above, in Method 1, with one important difference: Any person, including the person bringing the suit, can serve the subpoena. In addition, in many states, the person making the service must be ready to pay the person subpoenaed a witness fee on the spot if it is requested. This is often a flat fee (normally $40–$100), plus a mileage fee based on the distance from the courthouse. If you hire a sheriff or marshal to do the service, he or she will ask you to pay this fee, plus the service fee, in advance. In many states, if the witness doesn't ask for the fee, it will be returned to you.

D. Costs of Personal Service

Professional process servers and law enforcement agencies commonly charge from $20–$50 per service, depending on the time and mileage involved. You can usually get your costs of service added to your judgment if you win, but be sure to remind the judge to do this when you conclude your court presentation. However, a few courts will not give the successful party an award of costs for a process server unless he or she first tried to have the papers served by the cheaper certified mail approach (Method 2, above). Other judicial districts prefer that you don't use the mail approach at all, because they feel that, too often, the mail isn't accepted. Ask the Small Claims Court clerk in your district how she prefers that you accomplish service and how much the judge will allow as a service of process fee.

E. Time Limits in Which Papers Must Be Served

All states have a rule that the defendant is entitled to receive service of the Claim of Plaintiff or Notice of Claim form before the date of the court hearing. Rules as to how many days in advance of the hearing papers must be served vary considerably, with some states requiring as little as five and others requiring as many as 30. Check your local rules for details.

If the defendant is served fewer than the required number of days before the trial date, he can either go ahead with the trial anyway, or request that the case be delayed (continued). If a delay is granted, it is normally in the range of two weeks to a month. If it is impossible to show up in person to ask for a delay, call the court clerk (telegraph if you can't call) and point out that you weren't served in the proper time and that you want the case put over (delayed). The clerk will see that a default judgment is not entered against you. (See Chapter 10, Section E, Changing a Court Date.) But just to be sure, get the clerk's name.

To count the days to see if service has been accomplished in the correct time, in most states you do not count the day the service is accomplished, but do count the day of the court appearance (check your local rules). Also count weekends and holidays. Thus, if Jack served Julie on July 12, in Los Angeles County (where the limit is five days), with a "Declaration and Order" listing a July 17 court date in the same county, service would be proper. This is true even if Saturday and Sunday fell on July 14 and 15. To determine the number of days, you would not count July 12, the day of service, but you would count July 13, 14, 15, 16 and 17, for a total of five days. If you are unable to serve the defendant(s) within the proper time, simply ask the court clerk for a new court date and try again.

How to deal with improper service. If you are improperly served, either because you are not given adequate time, or the papers weren't handed to you personally, or a certified letter wasn't signed for by you, it is still wise for you to call the court clerk or show up in court on the day in question. Why should you have to do this if service was improper? Because the plaintiff may succeed in getting the case heard as a default if you fail to show up. While this is improper, the fact remains that it is often more trouble to get an improper default judgment set aside than to protect yourself from the start. But isn't this a Catch-22? You are entitled to proper service, but if you don't get it, you have to show up in court anyway? Perhaps, but as Catch-22's go, this one is mild. You can call the clerk or show up in court and request that the judge grant you a continuance (delay) to prepare your case. If the original service was in fact improper, your request will be honored. Of course, if you were improperly served and simply want to get the hearing out of the way, you can show up and go ahead with your case.

F. Serving a Business

If you are suing someone who is the sole proprietor of a business, or is a partner in a business, you must serve the person individually, using the rules set out above (although in some states substituted service, as described in Method 4 above, is also allowed).

However, if you are suing a corporation or limited liability company (LLC), the rules are a little different. Although a corporation or limited liability company (LLC) is a legal person for purposes of lawsuits, you will still need to have your papers served on someone who lives and breathes. This is true whether you have the papers served personally or use certified mail. The flesh-and-blood person can be an officer of the corporation (president, vice president, secretary or treasurer) or member of an LLC. Simply call the corporation or LLC and ask who, and where, these people are and when you can serve them. If the business won't cooperate, the city or county business tax and license people should be able to provide you with their names. (See Chapter 8.) If you have trouble getting someone at a large national corporation to accept service, call or write your Secretary of State or Commissioner of Corporations at your state capital. They will be able to tell you who is authorized to accept service for the corporation in your state.

Many states allow you to leave court papers at a business office. As discussed in Method 4: Substituted Service above, it's also usually possible to serve papers on a corporation or limited liability company (LLC) by leaving the summons and plaintiff's statement (complaint) at the defendant's place of business. Check with your court clerk for details.

G. Serving a Public Agency

As discussed in Chapter 8, before you can sue a city, county or other government body, you often must first file a claim against that agency within a specified number of days of the incident that gave rise to your claim. Once your claim is denied, you can sue in Small Claims Court. To serve your papers, call the governmental body in question and ask them who should be served. Then proceed, following the rules set out in Method 1 or 2, above.

H. Notifying the Court That Service Has Been Accomplished ("Proof of Service")

Where certified or registered mail is involved, you need do nothing. The court clerk sends out the certified mail for you, and the signed post office receipt comes back directly to the clerk if service is accomplished. It's as simple as that.

However, a court has no way of knowing whether or not papers have been successfully served by personal service unless you tell them. This is done by filing a piece of paper known as a Proof of Service with the court clerk after the service has been made. The Proof of Service is often a small, perforated tear-off form, or a separate form that you get from the court clerk, and which must be signed by the person actually making the service. A Proof of Service is used both by the plaintiff and by the defendant if he files a Claim of Defendant. It must be returned to the clerk's office before the trial. A Proof of Service is used when any legal documents are served by personal service.

We will refer back to this example several times in future chapters. Frequently there isn't time after a defendant is served for her to properly complete service of a Claim of Defendant. In this situation, the defendant should simply file her Claim of Defendant and bring up the service problem in court. The plaintiff may well waive the time of service requirement and agree to proceed. Or, the plaintiff may request that the judge continue the case to a later date. The judge will normally grant the continuance if there is a good reason. If the papers are served by a law enforcement officer, he or she will prepare and file the Proof of Service automatically. Check your local rules for specific filing requirements.

PROOF OF SERVICE

ATTORNEY OR PARTY WITHOUT ATTORNEY *(Name and Address)*:	TELEPHONE NO.:	FOR COURT USE ONLY

Ref. No. or File No.

ATTORNEY FOR *(Name)*:

Insert name of court and name of judicial district and branch court, if any:

SHORT TITLE OF CASE:

PROOF OF SERVICE **(Summons)**	DATE:	TIME:	DEPT./DIV.:	CASE NUMBER:

1. At the time of service I was at least 18 years of age and not a party to this action, and **I served copies** of the *(specify documents)*:

2. a. Party served *(specify name of party as shown on the documents served)*:

   b. Person served: ☐ party in item 2a ☐ other *(specify name and title or relationship to the party named in item 2a)*:

   c. Address:

3. I served the party named in item 2
   a. ☐ **by personally delivering** the copies   (1) on *(date)*:   (2) at *(time)*:
   b. ☐ **by leaving** the copies with or in the presence of *(name and title or relationship to person indicated in item 2b)*:

   (1) ☐ **(business)** a person at least 18 years of age apparently in charge at the office or usual place of business of the person served. I informed him or her of the general nature of the papers.
   (2) ☐ **(home)** a competent member of the household (at least 18 years of age) at the dwelling house or usual place of abode of the person served. I informed him or her of the general nature of the papers.
   (3) on *(date)*:   (4) at *(time)*:
   (5) ☐ **A declaration of diligence** is attached. *(Substituted service on natural person, minor, conservatee, or candidate.)*
   c. ☐ **by mailing** the copies to the person served, addressed as shown in item 2c, by first-class mail, postage prepaid,
   (1) ☐ on *(date)*:   (2) ☐ from *(city)*:
   (3) ☐ with two copies of the Notice and Acknowledgment of Receipt and a postage-paid return envelope addressed to me.
   (4) ☐ to an address outside California with return receipt requested.   ◄ *(Attach completed form.)* ►
   d. ☐ **by causing** copies to be mailed. A declaration of mailing is attached.
   e. ☐ **other** *(specify other manner of service and authorizing code section)*:

4. The "Notice to the Person Served" (on the summons) was completed as follows:
   a. ☐ as an individual defendant.
   b. ☐ as the person sued under the fictitious name of *(specify)*:
   c. ☐ on behalf of *(specify)*:
      under: ☐ CCP 416.10 (corporation)   ☐ CCP 416.60 (minor)   ☐ other:
             ☐ CCP 416.20 (defunct corporation)   ☐ CCP 416.70 (conservatee)
             ☐ CCP 416.40 (association or partnership) ☐ CCP 416.90 (individual)

5. **Person serving** *(name, address, and telephone No.)*:   a. **Fee** for service: $
                                                                      b. ☐ Not a registered California process server.
                                                                      c. ☐ Exempt from registration under B&P § 22350(b).
                                                                      d. ☐ Registered California process server.
                                                                         (1) ☐ Employee or independent contractor.
                                                                         (2) Registration No.:
                                                                         (3) County:

6. ☐ **I declare** under penalty of perjury under the laws of the State of California that the foregoing is true and correct.
7. ☐ **I am a California sheriff, marshal, or constable** and I certify that the foregoing is true and correct.

Date:

                                                                      ► _____
                                                                              (SIGNATURE)

I. Serving a Claim of Defendant

As you will remember from our discussion in Chapter 10, a Claim of Defendant (or counterclaim) is the form the defendant files when he wishes to sue the plaintiff for money damages arising out of the same incident that forms the basis for the plaintiff's suit. A Claim of Defendant must be filed with the Small Claims Court clerk and served on the plaintiff. Time limits vary from state to state, as do the technical requirements for service. In California, a Claim of Defendant should be filed and served at least five days prior to the date that the court has set for the hearing on the plaintiff's claim. In New York, the time limit is seven days. Check your local rules. Often service can be accomplished by mail. But even if personal service is required and you can't find the plaintiff to serve the papers, all is not lost. Explain your problem to the court clerk. In most states, the clerk will either arrange to have the hearing date delayed or will tell you to show up for the first hearing with your papers. You can serve them on the plaintiff in the hallway (not the courtroom). Then explain to the judge why it was impossible to locate the plaintiff earlier. The judge will either put the whole case over (delay the case) for a few days, or allow you to proceed with your claim that day. Either way, she will accept your Claim of Defendant as validly served.

J. Serving Someone in the Military— Declaration of Nonmilitary Service

It is proper to serve someone who is on active duty in the armed forces. If she shows up, fine. If she doesn't, you have a problem. We learned in Chapter 10 that, as a general rule, if a properly served defendant doesn't show up, you can get a "default judgment" against her. This is not true if the person you are suing is in the military (the reserves don't count).

Default judgments cannot normally be taken against people on active duty in the armed forces because Congress has given our military personnel special protections. To get a default judgment, a statement normally must be filed under penalty of perjury that he or she is not in the military. This declaration is available from the clerk. Clerks almost always accept a Declaration of Nonmilitary Service signed by the plaintiff, as long as the plaintiff reasonably believes that the defendant is not on active duty. This constitutes a lenient interpretation of the law by clerks, but no one seems to be complaining. ■

The Defendant's Options

This chapter is devoted to a review of the concerns of the defendant. Most of this material has already been discussed in the first eleven chapters, but since the plaintiff, as the initiator of a lawsuit, gets more than half the space, let's even things a little and use this chapter to look at a Small Claims case from the point of view of the person being sued.

How should a defendant approach a Small Claims case? Start by understanding that there is no one correct course of action—it all depends on the facts of the dispute and your personal desires. In the rest of this small chapter, I'll review your principal options.

A. Claim Improper Service or Another Technical Defense

You may conclude that you were not properly (legally) served with the plaintiff's court papers. (See Chapter 11.) Perhaps the Claim of Plaintiff was left with your neighbors, or maybe you didn't have the correct number of days in which to respond, or maybe you believe you have been sued in the wrong district of your state. Figuring that since you weren't served properly, the case can't be heard, you may even be tempted to not show up in court. This is not smart. The judge can easily be unaware of, or overlook, the technical problem and issue a default judgment against you. If this happens, you will have to go to the trouble of requesting that the default be set aside. (See Chapter 10.) You are better off to contact the clerk, explain the problem with the service or the court location, and ask that the case be continued to a date that is convenient for you or transferred to the correct court. If the clerk can't help promptly, write the judge and explain the problem, or show up on the day in question and make your request.

Out-of-state defendants. As discussed in Chapter 9, if you don't live—or do business—in a state where you are sued, the court normally doesn't have power ("jurisdiction," in legalese) to enter a valid judgment against you, unless court papers are served on you while you happen to be in that state. (Exceptions exist for people who live elsewhere but own land in the state where the Small Claims case was filed or got into a traffic accident in that state.) If you are an out-of-state resident and receive Small Claims papers via the mail, promptly write a letter to the court explaining that you do not believe you are subject to the court's jurisdiction. Stay in touch with the court until you are sure the case has been dismissed.

B. You Have a Partial Defense—Try to Compromise

If you feel that perhaps the plaintiff has some right on his side, but that you are being sued for too much, contact the plaintiff and try to work out a compromise settlement. (See Chapter 6, Section A, for more on how to negotiate.) One good approach is to call or write the plaintiff and make an offer. How much depends on the relative merits of your position as compared to that of the plaintiff's, and whether the plaintiff is asking for a dollar amount you think is more or less fair, or greatly inflated. Assuming the plaintiff has a pretty strong legal position (you probably are legally liable), and is asking the court for an amount that's, broadly speaking, reasonable, I recommend that you make an initial compromise offer to pay about half of the amount the plaintiff has requested. Even with a strong case, the plaintiff may be motivated to accept your lowball offer, if for no other reason than saving the time it takes to prepare for and appear in court. More likely, your offer is likely to set in motion a little dance of offer and counteroffer, with an eventual compromise of somewhere between 65% and 80% of the plaintiff's original request. Obviously, if the plaintiff is asking for way too much, or you are not sure that a judge would find that you are liable in the first place, you'll want to offer less.

Any settlement you make should be set down in writing along the lines outlined in Chapter 6, "How to Settle Your Dispute," Section D.

Don't rely on being judgment proof. Some defendants who have at least a partial defense to the plaintiff's claim are tempted not to show up and defend a case in Small Claims Court because they have no money and figure that, even if they lose, the plaintiff can't collect. If you have a decent defense, this is just plain dumb. Judgments are normally good for from five to 20 years, depending on the state (see chart in Chapter 24, Section E), and can usually be renewed for a longer period of time, if necessary. Hopefully, you'll get a job or otherwise put a few dollars together sometime in the future and you probably won't want them immediately taken away to satisfy a Small Claims judgment that you believe shouldn't have been entered in the first place. So wake up and defend yourself while you can. The exception to this advice is where you plan to declare Chapter 7 bankruptcy, wiping out all your debts, including those that have been turned into a judgment.

C. You Have Absolutely No Defense

Now let's assume that the service of the plaintiff's papers was proper and you have no valid defense on the merits of the case. Perhaps you borrowed money under the terms of a written contract and haven't paid it back. Since you know you'll lose, you conclude that it makes little sense to fight back in court. Your decision not to show up will almost surely result in a default judgment being entered against you. The judgment will most probably be for the dollar amount demanded by the plaintiff, plus the amount of his filing fee and any reasonable costs to serve the papers on you. We discuss default judgments and how you can try to set them aside if you take action immediately in Chapters 10 and 15.

In a number of states, if you do not dispute the plaintiff's claim, but cannot afford to pay it all at once, the law allows you to request the right to make payments in installments. After checking with the Small Claims Clerk to see that installment payments really are allowed in your state, your best bet is to show up in court and explain your situation to the judge. If you can't be present, write a letter to the court prior to the court hearing (be sure to properly identify the case, using the case number from the Claim of Plaintiff form) explaining why it would be difficult or impossible to pay any judgment all at once. For example, if you are on a fixed income, have recently been unemployed and have a lot of debts, or have a low or moderate income and a large family, explain this to the judge. Just state the facts; there is no need to tell a long sob story. Assuming your state's law allows it, when the judge enters a judgment against you, she will very likely order you to pay in reasonable monthly installments.

D. You Want to Avoid Conflict—Try to Mediate

In Chapter 6, Section B, I discuss mediation in some detail. Please reread this material and, as you do, consider that engaging in this process is almost always beneficial to the defendant, because the very process of mediation tends to encourage a compromise settlement for a lower amount than the plaintiff has demanded. In addition, mediation gives the defendant a chance to raise issues that are not officially part of the plaintiff's lawsuit. For example, in a dispute between neighbors, small business people or relatives, it's often important to discuss and settle emotional (human) concerns in addition to sorting out how much is owed.

Ask the Small Claims clerk for help with mediation. Mediation of all Small Claims cases is mandatory in some areas of the country. In others, it is easily accessible on a voluntary basis, either right in the courthouse or at a nearby community mediation project. Ask the Small Claims Court clerk where mediation is available in your area. Then contact the mediation project and enlist their help in bringing the plaintiff to the table.

E.   Have Your Case Transferred to a Formal Court

Depending on state law and the facts of your case, it is often possible for a defendant to have a case transferred out of Small Claims Court to a formal court. This may be called municipal, district, county, justice, circuit, city or civil court. But whatever the name used in your state, the point is that this court will allow lawyers and require formal rules of evidence and procedure, including far more paperwork than is required in Small Claims Court.

Transfer rules are an area where Small Claims rules vary greatly around the U.S. Some states allow any defendant to transfer any case, others allow it only if the defendant files her own claim (a counterclaim) over the Small Claims limit or as part of a defendant's request for a jury trial. Still other states allow a case to be transferred only with the discretionary approval of a judge. And some states don't allow transfers at all.

What this amounts to is that if you are interested in the possibility of transferring your case and you think this may be possible, after looking at the brief summary for your state in the Appendix, you absolutely need to consult your state's rules. But first it makes sense to ask why transfer a case out of Small Claims Court. My answer is that it is rarely a good idea. Since Small Claims Court is cheaper, more user friendly and far less time consuming than formal court, you'll usually want to defend your case right there unless, of course, you want to file a defendant's claim (counterclaim) for an amount significantly over the Small Claims limit. However, in the following additional situations transfer may make sense.

1. To get a jury trial (in states where transfer for this reason is allowed). In my view, nonlawyers are almost always better off trying a case before a judge under relaxed Small Claims rules as compared to the extra level of formality a jury trial adds to the already fussy rules of formal court. But I know people who disagree, believing that there is no justice without a jury.

2. Because you know how to navigate in formal court far better than the plaintiff—or are willing to hire a lawyer to represent you. Yes, this approach may be a tad cynical, but given the opportunistic nature of many plaintiffs, why not take full advantage of every possible edge you have.

F. Fight Back

Now we get to the situation where you feel that you don't owe the plaintiff a dime and you want to actively contest the case filed against you. This means you must show up in court on the date stated in the papers served on you, unless you get the case delayed to a later date. (See Chapter 10.) In the great majority of states, a defendant need not file any papers with the court clerk; showing up ready to defend yourself is enough. However, a written response must be filed in a few states, including Alabama, Alaska, Connecticut, Oregon, South Carolina (oral is also okay), Vermont (oral is also okay), Virginia and West Virginia. To defend most types of cases successfully you'll want to back up your oral presentation with as much evidence as possible.

Beyond reviewing these basics, a defendant will want to focus energy on several broad areas, as follows:

*   *Analyze your opponent's case.* To do this, you will normally want to focus on any facts that show you are not legally liable (carefully reread Chapter 2 to see what plaintiffs must prove). Next, if you conclude that the plaintiff may have a winning case, focus on whether he has asked for the right dollar amount. For example, if you can convince a judge that you only owe a couple of hundred, not several thousand dollars, you will have won a substantial victory (see Chapter 4).
    Example: Assume the plaintiff sues you for a breach of contract. Assuming the facts support your position, you might claim that no contract existed in the first place. Or that even if it did, the plaintiff violated its terms so thoroughly that you were justified in considering it to be void. And even if you have to admit that you broke a valid contract, you can claim the plaintiff is asking for far too much damages.

*   *Develop evidence.* As emphasized in Chapters 13 and 14, the key to winning a Small Claims Court case is to convince the judge of your version of the facts. To do this, you need to back up your oral presentation. The best way to accomplish

this is with eyewitnesses (if you are lucky enough to have any), and expert witnesses who can lend credence to your position (a mechanic who agrees the plaintiff ruined your engine). In addition, you will want to present any documentary evidence, such as contracts, canceled checks and photos that support your position. For example, if you are a computer repair person sued by someone who claims you ruined her PC, you may want to get a written opinion from another repair shop that the current problem with the computer has nothing to do with what you fixed. In addition, you might want to present advertisements and trade pricing data to show that the plaintiff is placing an inflated value on her used computer.

- *Practice your court presentation.* Remembering that the plaintiff gets to present her case first, and understanding that the judge may interrupt or even upstage your presentation by asking questions, you want to be able to make an incisive, logical presentation of why the plaintiff should receive little or nothing. Once you have your arguments thought out, practice them in front of a friend or family member until you are thoroughly comfortable. One trick here is not to repeat uncontested facts presented by the plaintiff, but to immediately focus on why the plaintiff's case is misguided.

Example: Tom, the landlord, listens patiently as Evie, the tenant, spends five minutes explaining the history of their landlord/tenant relations before claiming she should have gotten her security deposit back because she left the rental unit clean and undamaged. When it's Tom's turn, he ignores several small discrepancies in Evie's long rendition of her rental history. Instead, he focuses on the exact point of the dispute by saying, "Your Honor, the key to my defense is that the plaintiff left the rental at 127 Spring Street in a dirty and damaged condition. I have pictures to demonstrate this and a reliable witness to back it up. But first I would like to briefly list the worst problems."

You don't need a lawyer just because the plaintiff has one. In states where it's allowed, if the plaintiff has a lawyer, a question that often arises is, "Am I at a disadvantage if I go it alone?" Considering the high costs of hiring a lawyer—and assuming you are willing to carefully prepare your case—my answer is no. Start by understanding that since there are no technical legal procedures, rules of evidence or legal jargon in Small Claims Court, a lawyer has no inherent advantage. Then remember that no one knows the facts of your case as well as you do. Finally, consider that most Small Claims judges go out of their way to even the playing field if they see that a lawyer is trying to use professional tricks to gain an advantage.

G. You, Not the Plaintiff, Were Wronged— File a "Claim of Defendant"

Finally, there are those of you who not only want to dispute the plaintiff's claim, but also want to sue him. Perhaps you believe you, not the plaintiff, suffered harm and are outraged that the plaintiff sued first. To assert your own claim against the plaintiff, you should promptly file a Claim of Defendant (often called a counterclaim) in Small Claims Court for up to the Small Claims Court maximum, or, if you wish to sue for more, have the case transferred to the appropriate formal court. (For more on what to do if you wish to sue the plaintiff, see Chapter 10, Section C, and Chapter 11, Section I.)

Assuming your case stays in Small Claims Court, both your claim and the plaintiff's will be heard together. You should prepare and present your case just as you would if you had filed first—that is, understand the legal basics that underlie your case, make a practical and convincing oral presentation and back it up with as much hard evidence as you can find. ■

Getting Ready for Court

Once your papers have been filed with the Small Claims clerk and the defendant(s) have been properly served, the preliminaries are over and you are ready for the main event—your day in court. Movies, and especially TV (yes, even "Court TV"), have done much to create false impressions of court proceedings. Ask yourself what a trial might have been like *before* every lawyer fancied himself Raymond Burr, Charles Laughton or even Johnnie Cochran, and judges acted "fatherly," or "stern" or "indignantly outraged" in the fashion of Judge Wapner of "People's Court."

There are people whose lives revolve around courthouses, and who have been playing movie parts for so long that they have become caricatures of one screen star or another. Lawyers are particularly susceptible to this virus. All too often, they substitute posturing and theatrics for good, hard preparation. Thankfully though, most people who work in our courts quickly recover from movieitis and realize that the majestic courtroom is, in truth, a large, drafty hall with a raised platform at one end; "His Honor" is only a lawyer dressed in a tacky black dress, who knew the right politician; and they, themselves, are not bit players in "L.A. Law," or even the murder trial of O. J. Simpson.

I mention movieitis because it's a common ailment in Small Claims Court. Cases that should be won easily are sometimes lost because one party or the other goes marching around the courtroom antagonizing everyone with comic opera imitations of Marcia Clark. And don't assume you are immune. Movieitis is a subtle disease, with many people never realizing they have it. To find out if you are likely to be infected, ask yourself a few self-diagnostic questions:

- Have you watched courtroom scenes on TV or in the movies?
- Have you ever imagined that you were one of the lawyers?
- How many times have you been in a real courtroom in comparison to watching movie-set or court TV courtrooms?

I'm sure you get the idea. Chances are good that, like most of us, your idea of what court is like comes mostly from the media. The best advice I can give you is to put all of this aside and just be yourself. To succeed in Small Claims Court, you don't need fancy clothes, words or attitudes. If you feel a little anxious about a first court appearance, drop by the court a few days before your case is heard and watch for an hour or two. You may not learn a great deal that will be helpful in your case, but you will be a lot more relaxed and comfortable when your turn comes.

Movieitis aside, most people I have watched in Small Claims Court have done pretty well. Those who really stood out had prepared their evidence carefully and were ready to make a clear, concise verbal presentation. As I'll emphasize in the next few chapters, the best way to be sure you are in top form is to practice ahead of time. Do this by having a savvy friend or family member play at being the Small Claims judge while you present your case, just as you plan to do in the courtroom.

The rest of this chapter contains basic information about how Small Claims Court works. I'll discuss how to prepare and present different types of cases in the next chapters.

A. Interpreter Services

In some states, Small Claims Courts make an effort to have interpreter services available for those who need and ask for this help. Notify the court clerk well in advance if you or one of your witnesses will need an interpreter. However, in many courts, interpreters are not routinely made available by the court. Where this is true, it is normally permissible to bring your own. But check with the Small Claims clerk in advance to be sure you understand the rules. Many ethnic and cultural organizations offer interpreter services to low-income persons free of charge.

B. Legal Advisors

If you are confused about any aspect of Small Claims Court, be sure to ask the court clerk whether assistance is available. In most Small Claims Courts, helpful "how-to" written pamphlets, videos or easy-to-use computer tutorials are available free or at a low cost. Even better, many Small Claims Courts—especially those in California—have free legal advisor programs. While there is no set approach, most court-sponsored legal advisor programs make it possible for people involved in Small Claims Court actions, either as plaintiffs or defendants, to talk to a lawyer or a person with paralegal training, either in person or by phone, before going to court. The idea is that the legal advisor will help the person using Small Claims Court to understand and prepare her case properly.

C. Lawyers

As noted several times, a number of states have, quite sensibly, banned lawyers from appearing in Small Claims Court on behalf of either plaintiff or defendant. However, the majority of states do continue to allow representation by an attorney. (See Appendix.) In my view, this is a mistake—it is past time that the lawyers be banned from appearing in what really should be the people's court.

Suppose you live in a state that allows lawyers to appear in Small Claims Court, and that your opponent has retained one. Does it make sense for you to hire one too? Probably not. Given the high costs that are inevitably involved, you will almost always be better off to handle the case yourself. As you will have gathered from this book, Small Claims Court rules and procedures are quite simple—with a little study, you should be able to do a fine job of preparing and presenting your case. And you may actually have a psychological advantage—as a person without formal legal training going up against a lawyer, you can play David to the lawyer's Goliath. You may also be reassured to know that two studies sponsored by the National Center for State Courts have found that, broadly speaking, having an attorney represent a person in Small Claims Court does not significantly enhance that person's chances of winning (see specifically "Small Claims and Traffic Courts," John Goerdt (National Center for State Courts). Or, put another way, in most situations, people who spoke for themselves did just as well as those who hired a mouthpiece.

It can be cost-effective to hire a lawyer for advice only. If you are worried about some legal aspect of your case, it can be sensible to get legal advice on that particular point. This should not be expensive as long as you don't hire the attorney to handle the entire case. If no free legal advisor program is available through your Small Claims Court and you are not a low-income person eligible for free legal assistance through a federally sponsored "legal aid" (often called "legal services") program, one good approach is to hire a lawyer for a short consultation. For $100–$150 or so, you should be able to find an attorney who will review your entire case and advise you on any tricky points. Also, you may wish to spend a few hours doing some of your own research in your local law library. (See Chapter 1, Section D.)

D. Mediation and Arbitration

As discussed in more detail in Chapter 6, Section B, many courts utilize mediation techniques to provide an opportunity for the parties to settle their cases without actually going to court.

Mediation: In mediation, the parties sit down with a third person whose job it is to help them arrive at their own solution. In most areas, the mediator is either a volunteer, or a retired person who is paid a modest amount—often about $30–$50 per mediation. Most mediators have received a week or two of training in the art of helping disputing parties arrive at their own negotiated settlement. In some states, however, the mediator may be a local volunteer attorney. A mediator has no power to make a "decision." Rather, her job is to help the parties settle their dispute consensually. If this proves impossible, the case is referred to Small Claims Court. If a mediation program is available in your area, I recommend that you give it a try, especially if the other party is a relative, neighbor, local business person or anyone else with whom it's important to preserve or restore a decent personal relationship.

Arbitration: In a few states, including New York, arbitration is offered as an option. This usually consists of a volunteer lawyer listening to both sides and actually making a decision just as a judge would. Although it's often possible to have a case heard sooner if you elect arbitration, I don't recommend it. Over the years, I have received more complaints from readers dissatisfied with the decisions of lawyer arbitrators and volunteer lawyer judges (often called "pro tem" judges) than for any other aspect of Small Claims Court. I'm convinced this is because most lawyers specialize in fairly narrow areas of the law, and are simply not up to speed in many others; as a result, they are prone to make mistakes.

⚠ **Be sure you know what you are agreeing to before you accept a non-court alternative.** The terms "mediation," "arbitration" and "conciliation" are often used so loosely you can't always be sure what they mean. For example, in a few courts, a hybrid process—nonbinding arbitration—is used, which allows an arbitrator to suggest a solution, but does not require the parties to accept it. So if anyone suggests you participate in any of these programs (sometimes called Alternative Dispute Resolution or ADR), be sure you understand exactly what's involved before agreeing.

E. Getting to the Courthouse

Before you locate the right courtroom, you obviously have to get to the right building. Sometimes, doing this can be tricky, because Small Claims Courts are often not in the main courthouse. Like a half-forgotten stepsister, many are housed wherever the city or county has an empty room. In short, don't assume you know where your Small Claims Court is unless you've been there before. Plaintiffs have already had to find the clerk's office to file their papers, so they probably know where the courtroom is, but defendants should check this out in advance. Be sure too, that your witnesses know exactly where and when to show up. And do plan to be a few minutes early—people who rush in flustered and late start with a strike against them.

F. Court Times

Small Claims Courts can schedule cases any time they wish on business days. The most user-friendly set five starting times (for example, 8:30 a.m., 10:30 a.m., 1:00 p.m., 3:00 p.m. and 7:00 p.m.), so no one has to wait long. Most commonly, however, court is scheduled at 9:00 a.m. or 1:00 p.m., with a considerable number of cases to be heard in turn. In larger judicial districts, Saturday or evening sessions may also be held. If it is not convenient for you to go to court during business hours, request that your case be scheduled at one of these other sessions, if available.

Also, be aware that courts in many areas of the country use a "hurry-up-and-wait" technique that would make the Army blush. For example, you might be told to show up for court at 8:15 a.m. At this time, the judges are still home having coffee, since court doesn't really start until 9:00, with delays to 9:15 or 9:30 being common. To avoid cooling my heels, I always ask the Small Claims clerk what time the judge really begins court.

A few minutes before the judge arrives, it's common for the clerk to ask everyone to swear (or affirm, if you wish) to tell the truth, although in some areas, this is done later, just before each case is presented.

G. Understanding the Courtroom and Basic Procedure

Most Small Claims proceedings are conducted in standard courtrooms that are also used for regular trials. Indeed, sometimes you will have to sit through a few minutes of some other type of court proceeding before Small Claims Court actually begins.

Most judges still sit on little elevated wooden throne boxes and wear depressing black dresses, both of which trace their history back over a thousand years to England, to a time when courts were largely controlled by kings, nobility and clergy. In addition to the judge, a clerk and a bailiff will normally be present. They usually sit at tables immediately in front of the judge. The clerk's job is to keep the judge supplied with necessary files and papers, and to make sure that proceedings flow smoothly. The bailiff is there to keep order in the courtroom if tempers get out of hand.

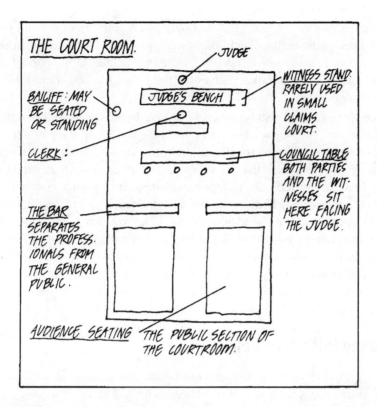

No written record of court proceedings is kept. A Small Claims clerk is not the same as a court reporter, who keeps a word-by-word record of proceedings. In most states, no such record is kept in Small Claims Court, and no court reporter is present, although in a few areas, tape recordings or video tapes are made and used if a case is appealed.

Courtrooms are divided about two-thirds of the way toward the front by a little fence (known to initiates as the "bar"). The public must stay on the opposite side of the bar from the judge, clerk, bailiff and attorneys, unless invited to cross. This invitation occurs when your case is called by name (*Smith vs. Jones Ford* or *Abercrombie vs. Lee*) by the clerk. At this point you, and any witnesses, will normally be asked to come forward and sit at a table (known as the "counsel table"). You will be facing the judge, with your back to the spectator section of the courtroom. However, in a few courtrooms, judges try to hurry things along by asking everyone to stand in front of the judge's bench. The idea seems to be that if people can't sit down, they will present their cases faster. This might be okay if the judge would stand, too, but since they never do, I feel it's insulting.

In the great majority of Small Claims Courts, you, your opponent and your witnesses will present the entire case from the counsel table. This means that neither you nor your witnesses sit in the witness box next to the judge. Many people (and judges) feel that it is polite to stand when addressing the judge, but you should do what feels most comfortable to you.

Normally, the plaintiff will be asked to present her case first and introduce any witnesses, who will also get a chance to have their say. When the plaintiff is done, it will be the defendant's turn to speak and present witnesses. Both sides should have any papers or other evidence that backs up their story carefully organized to present to the judge. This can include bills, receipts, estimates, photographs, contracts, letters to or from your opponent and other types of documentation or physical evidence. At the appropriate place in your presentation, tell the judge you have materials you want her to see, and then hand them to the clerk, who in turn will give them to the judge. As I have said before, documentation is a great aid to your case, but don't go overboard. Judges are a little like donkeys—load them too heavily and they are likely to lie down and go to sleep.

H. Dealing With Your Opponent

Before you get to the courtroom, you should do a little thinking about your opponent. Perhaps you can guess what sort of presentation he will make. If so, ask yourself how you can best deal with these arguments. This is a good way to take the negative energy you may feel (frustration, annoyance, anger) and turn it into creative planning and preparation. Always be polite when presenting your case. If you are hostile or sarcastic, you will gain nothing, and may lose the respect of the judge. Never interrupt your opponent when she is speaking—you will get your chance. When you do, lay out the key facts that support your position to the judge; don't conduct an argument with the other side.

Cope with lying by presenting convincing evidence. I am often asked what to do if your opponent tells huge fibs. Although not an everyday occurrence, big lies definitely are told in Small Claims Court and can be a big problem if you aren't prepared to poke holes in them. The best response to an opponent who tells whoppers is to wait calmly for your turn to speak and say something like this, "Your honor, almost everything defendant (or plaintiff) has said is simply not true. Please let me prove this to you with facts." Then present your evidence—or if you have already presented it, remind the judge of why it proves that your opponent's story is false. For example, if your opponent who has failed to return your cleaning deposit swears you left an apartment filthy, you should win if you show the judge photos of how clean you really left it. Fortunately, if you can demonstrate that your opponent has told one big lie, the judge will distrust and hopefully disbelieve the rest of what he says.

I. Dealing With the Judge

The person who hears your case may be a regular judge who also presides over other types of cases. But, increasingly, cities and counties are hiring full-time commissioners or referees to hear Small Claims cases. These are administrative categories designed to allow lawyers to be hired for lower salaries and benefits than are paid to judges (a bit like colleges hiring nontenured instructors instead of full professors). By and large, commissioners and referees—who usually hear Small Claims cases on a daily basis— do a very competent job, sometimes better than judges, who occasionally act as if they are too important to hear such small disputes.

In many states, volunteer lawyers are also routinely appointed as temporary judges when a judge, referee or commissioner is ill or on vacation. The legal slang for a temporary judge is often "Judge, pro tem," or "Arbitrator." Especially if your case comes up on a day when only a pro tem judge or arbitrator is present, you normally will be given a choice as to whether you want to accept that judge or ask that your case be heard by a regular judge. If your case is contested and you feel it involves fairly complicated legal issues, I recommend you ask that it be heard before a full-time judge or commissioner. Pro tem judges and arbitrators are not paid, rarely trained and often do not have much practical experience in the legal areas that are commonly heard in Small Claims Court. While many are excellent, enough are seriously substandard and, as a general rule, are best avoided.

Sometimes an attempt is made to hide your right to reject a temporary judge. In some courtrooms, clerks simply ask you to sign or otherwise indicate your approval of a judge, without explaining his temporary status and your right to say no. Don't fall for this. Whenever you are asked to approve a judge, you can be sure it's a substitute for the real judge, and you can say no.

You can't appeal from an arbitrator's decision in New York. To save time, residents of the Empire State are often encouraged to have their cases heard by a volunteer lawyer arbitrator instead of a Small Claims Court judge. But beware of this alternative. In addition to getting a less experienced decision-maker, there is no right of appeal from an arbitrator's decision, as there is from the decision of a regular Small Claims judge.

What if your case will be heard by a regular judge, commissioner or referee whom you don't like, either because you know the person or because you have been put off by the way she has handled other cases? Laws exist in nearly all states that allow you to "disqualify" a judge simply on your honest belief that he is "prejudiced" against you. (No one will ask you to prove it.) To disqualify a judge, in some states you can simply wait for your case name to be called and then stand up and say something like this: "Your Honor, I believe you are prejudiced against my interest, and I request a trial before another judge." Unfortunately, in other states, you need to put your disqualification request in writing and file it in advance. If you think you may want to take advantage of a disqualification procedure, check with the Small Claims clerk before your court date to be sure you understand the rules.

When thinking about presenting your case to a judge, referee or commissioner, there is one constructive thing you can do: Imagine yourself in the decision-maker's shoes. What would you value most from the people appearing before you? Before I ever sat as a judge, my answer to this question was "politeness, good organization of the material to be presented and reasonable brevity." After experiencing Small Claims Court from the judge's chair, I would add one word—"evidence." By this, I mean a presentation that consists of more than just your oral statement as to what happened. Witnesses, written statements, police accident reports and photographs all give the judge the opportunity to make a decision based on something more than who tells the better story. And one final thing—remember that the person who is deciding your case has heard thousands of stories very much like yours, and will either cease paying attention or get annoyed if you are needlessly repetitive.

J. Organizing Your Testimony and Evidence

As mentioned frequently in this text, it's essential that you carefully organize what you have to say and the physical evidence that backs up each point. Do this by dividing your testimony into a list of the several main points you want to make. Under each heading, note any items of physical or documentary evidence you wish to show the judge. If your evidence consists of a number of items, make sure that you put them in order so you can find each item quickly.

Example (from the plaintiff's point of view): Let's assume your case is based on a hotel's failure to return your deposit when you canceled a wedding reception three months before the event was to be held. Your list of key points—and the evidence to back them up—might look like this:

- Valley View Hotel refused to return my $500 deposit when I canceled my wedding reception.

- This was true even though I canceled 83 days before the event.

- The contract I signed with the hotel allowed a full refund if cancellation occurred more than 60 days before the event. (Show contract to the judge.)

- When I canceled, Valley View told me (and claims they sent me a letter) stating that their cancellation policy had been changed the previous month to require 90 days notice in order to get a refund.

- I never received a letter and had no idea of the policy change until I canceled and asked for my money back.

- Even if Valley View did send me a letter, the change should not affect my contract, which was signed prior to the policy change. The key point here is, since I never signed a new contract, the existing contract was still valid.

- In any event, the hotel has a duty to try and rerent the banquet room to minimize (mitigate) any damages they suffered. And they have plenty of time (83 days) to do so. (See Chapter 4, Section C1, for a discussion of the mitigation of damages point.)

- 90 days is an unreasonably long cancellation policy.

- Here is a list of short cancellation policies of five other hotels in the area, all of which allow a full refund on much shorter notice than 83 days. (Give list to the judge.)

Example (from the defendant's point of view): Since Valley View goes second, their representative can't know in advance what the plaintiff will say and what evidence it will present. It follows that Valley View will need to adopt a little more flexible approach. Still, since chances are that Valley View reps have talked to the plaintiff or exchanged letters, they probably have a pretty good idea of what to expect. Accordingly, Valley View's list might look something like this.

- True, we didn't refund the $500. The reason was we turned down two other receptions for that same day before plaintiff canceled. Since we ended up with no other function, we lost at least $500.

- Although it is true that the written contract allowed cancellation prior to 60 days before the event, plaintiff was notified that this policy had been changed to 90 days before the contract was signed in two ways:

  √ A sign on the reservations desk where the plaintiff sat to sign the contract. (Show sign to judge.)

  √ Testimony of Angie Ells, who booked the reservation. Angie will testify that she included written notice of the change with the contract package. (Show judge a copy of the notice.)

  √ A copy of the written notice changing the contract.

 Chapters 14–22 contain an extensive discussion about how to prepare for court and what to do once you get there. ■

Witnesses

It is often extremely helpful to have someone in court with you who has firsthand knowledge of the facts of your case and who can support your point of view. In many types of cases, such as car accidents or disputes concerning whether or not a tenant left an apartment clean, witnesses are particularly valuable. However, in other fact situations, they aren't as necessary. For example, if a friend borrowed $500 and didn't pay it back, you don't need a witness to prove that your friend's signature on the promissory note is genuine, unless you expect him to base his defense on the theory that his signature was forged.

A good witness should have firsthand knowledge of the facts in the dispute. This means that either she saw something that helps establish your case (for example, the car accident, dog bite or dirty apartment, etc.) or be an expert you have consulted about an important aspect of your case (for example, a car mechanic who testifies your engine wasn't fixed properly). The judge will not be interested in the testimony of a person who is repeating secondhand or generalized information such as "I know

Joe is a good, safe driver and would never have done anything reckless," or "I didn't see Joe's apartment before he moved out, but both Joe and his mother, who couldn't be here today, told me that they worked for two days cleaning it up."

A good witness is believable. This isn't always an easy quality to define. For example, a police officer may be a symbol of honesty to some people, while others will automatically react to him with hostility and fear. But remember, it's the judge you are trying to convince, and judges tend to be fairly establishment folk. They make comfortable salaries, own their own homes and generally tend to like the existing order of things. Most judges I know would tend to believe a police officer.

In many types of cases, such as a car accident, you won't have much choice as to witnesses. You will be lucky to have one person who saw what happened. Unfortunately, in some types of disputes, close friends and family are often your only eyewitnesses. There is no rule that says you can't have these people testify for you. Indeed, I have often seen a person's spouse, or the friend that she lives with, give very convincing testimony. But, given a choice, it is usually better to have a witness who is neither friend nor kin. A judge may discount testimony of people to whom you are close on the theory that they would naturally be biased in your favor. One little trick to dispel this judicial cynicism is to have a closely related witness bend over backwards to treat the other side as fairly as possible. Thus, if your brother is your only witness to the fact that ABC Painting splashed paint on your boat, he might point out to the judge not only that he saw them do it, but that it was a very windy day and ABC was having a hard time painting the breakwater.

In some types of disputes, such as whether your house was properly painted or the work on your car engine competently completed, you have an opportunity to plan ahead to locate witnesses. That's because the type of witness you need is usually not an eyewitness who saw the work in progress, but instead an expert in the field who can convincingly explain what went wrong. Obviously this type of witness is only valuable if she really does have good credentials in the field so that a judge is likely to believe what she says. Thus, in a dispute over whether car repairs were properly done, it's preferable to bring a working car mechanic with 20 years' experience who has completed a load of training courses rather than your neighbor "who knows a lot about cars."

I will talk more about witnesses as I go through the various case examples (Chapters 16–21), but let's outline a few basic rules here:

- Prepare your witness thoroughly as to what your position is, what your opponent is likely to say and what you want the witness to say. In court, the witness will be on her own, and you want to be sure that the story comes out right. It is completely legal and ethical to thoroughly discuss the case with your witness beforehand.

- Never bring a witness to court who is hostile to you or hostile to the idea of testifying.

- Do not ask a witness to testify unless you know exactly what he will say. This sounds basic, but I have seen people lose cases because their witnesses got mixed up, and in one instance, where the witness actually supported the other side.

- It's proper to pay an expert witness—say a car mechanic who has examined your engine—a reasonable fee in most Small Claims Courts (check with yours). However, it may be unnecessary to bring the person to court, since in most states the judge will accept written evidence. (See Chapter 17 for an example of an expert witness's written statement.)

- When a person must take off work—or if you are unsure if they will keep a promise to show up voluntarily—it makes sense to subpoena them. But never use a subpoena form to require a witness to be present unless you have made sure it is okay with the witness (more in Section A, below).

How to work with your witnesses in court: In the courtroom, your witness will normally sit next to you at the table facing the judge and talk to the judge from there (in some courtrooms, the judge may ask all parties and witnesses to approach the judge's bench and stand there in a little group). It is fairly rare for a witness to take the witness stand in Small Claims Court, but it happens in a few courts. Assuming your witness is seated at the counsel table, it is best for her to stand when it's her turn to speak and simply explain what happened. There is no need for you to pretend to be a lawyer and ask your witness a lot of leading questions. The judge is likely to ask the witness questions and may even interrupt her presentation and cause her to lose her train of thought. When the witness is done, if you feel he has left something out, ask a question designed to produce the information you want.

A. Subpoenaing Witnesses

In most states, you can require that a witness with firsthand knowledge of what happened be present if that person resides within a certain distance from the court-house. (The distance varies from state to state. It is often about 150 miles, but in some states subpoenas reach only within county boundaries.) To do this, go to the clerk's office and get a "subpoena" form. Fill it out and have it served on the person you wish to have present. But remember, you never want to subpoena a person unless you have talked to her first and gotten an okay. The very act of dragging someone into court who doesn't want to come may set her against you. A subpoenaed witness is normally entitled to a modest fee upon demand. The person serving the subpoena must have this money ready to pay if it is requested. If you win your case, you will probably be able to recover your witness fees from the other side. The judge has discretion as to whether to grant you your witness fees. Some judges are strict about this, making the loser pay the winner's witness fees only if he finds that the subpoenaed witness was essential to the presentation of the case. This means that if your case is so strong that you don't need a witness but you subpoena one anyway, you may well have to pay the witness even though you win.

Expert witnesses whom you locate after an event occurs to express an opinion cannot be subpoenaed. For this reason they often submit their opinions in writing, a practice that is allowed in most courts.

Below is the standard California subpoena form. You will need to prepare an original and two copies. Once prepared, take the subpoena form to the clerk, who will issue it. Service must be made personally, and the Proof of Service, which is probably on the back of the subpoena, returned to the clerk's office. Rules for service are discussed in Chapter 11.

B. Subpoenaing Police Officers

You have probably already noticed that on the California subpoena form there is a special box to use if you wish to subpoena a police officer. The box is easy to fill out, but expensive to pay for in most states. The deposit to subpoena a police officer is at least $125. This money must be paid to the clerk at the time the subpoena is issued. Depending on the amount of the officer's time that is used, you may eventually get a refund of some of your $125. Be sure to check your local rules.

CIVIL SUBPOENA

ATTORNEY OR PARTY WITHOUT ATTORNEY *(Name and Address)* :	TELEPHONE NO.:	FOR COURT USE ONLY
John O'Gara 15 Scenic St. Albany, CA		

ATTORNEY FOR *(Name)*: In Pro Per

NAME OF COURT:	Municipal Court, County of Alameda
STREET ADDRESS:	2000 Center St.
MAILING ADDRESS:	
CITY AND ZIP CODE:	Berkeley, CA 94704
BRANCH NAME:	Berkeley-Albany Judicial District

PLAINTIFF/PETITIONER: Public Library

DEFENDANT/RESPONDENT: John O'Gara

CIVIL SUBPENA

☐ **Duces Tecum**

CASE NUMBER:

THE PEOPLE OF THE STATE OF CALIFORNIA, TO (NAME):

Jane Doe

1. **YOU ARE ORDERED TO APPEAR AS A WITNESS in this action at the date, time, and place shown in the box below UNLESS you make a special agreement with the person named in item 3:**

   a. Date: Time: ☐ Dept.:   ☐ Div.:   ☐ Room:
   b. Address:

2. **AND YOU ARE**
   a. ☒ ordered to appear in person.
   b. ☐ not required to appear in person if you produce the records described in the accompanying affidavit and a completed declaration of custodian of records in compliance with Evidence Code sections 1560, 1561, 1562, and 1271. (1) Place a copy of the records in an envelope (or other wrapper). Enclose your original declaration with the records. Seal them. (2) Attach a copy of this subpena to the envelope or write on the envelope the case name and number, your name and date, time, and place from item 1 (the box above). (3) Place this first envelope in an outer envelope, seal it, and mail it to the clerk of the court at the address in item 1. (4) Mail a copy of your declaration to the attorney or party shown at the top of this form.
   c. ☐ ordered to appear in person and to produce the records described in the accompanying affidavit. The personal attendance of the custodian or other qualified witness and the production of the original records is required by this subpena. The procedure authorized by subdivision (b) of section 1560, and sections 1561 and 1562, of the Evidence Code will not be deemed sufficient compliance with this subpena.

3. **IF YOU HAVE ANY QUESTIONS ABOUT THE TIME OR DATE FOR YOU TO APPEAR, OR IF YOU WANT TO BE CERTAIN THAT YOUR PRESENCE IS REQUIRED, CONTACT THE FOLLOWING PERSON BEFORE THE DATE ON WHICH YOU ARE TO APPEAR:**
   a. Name: **b.** Telephone number: (510) 555-1212

4. **Witness Fees:** You are entitled to witness fees and mileage actually traveled both ways, as provided by law, if you request them at the time of service. You may request them before your scheduled appearance from the person named in item 3.

> DISOBEDIENCE OF THIS SUBPENA MAY BE PUNISHED AS CONTEMPT BY THIS COURT. YOU WILL ALSO BE LIABLE FOR THE SUM OF FIVE HUNDRED DOLLARS AND ALL DAMAGES RESULTING FROM YOUR FAILURE TO OBEY.

Date issued:

▶

....
(TYPE OR PRINT NAME)   (SIGNATURE OF PERSON ISSUING SUBPENA)

                                                            (TITLE)

(See reverse for proof of service)

Form Adopted by Rule 982
Judicial Council of California
982(a)(15) [Rev. January 1, 1991]

CIVIL SUBPENA

Code of Civil Procedure, §§ 1985, 1986, 1987

C. Subpoenaing Documents

In addition to witnesses, you can also subpoena documents. This is rarely done in Small Claims Court, but it may occasionally be helpful. Someone (such as a police department, phone company, hospital or corporation) may have certain books, ledgers, papers or other documents that can help your case. To get them, in many states, you must prepare a form entitled "Subpoena Duces Tecum." This is very similar to the standard subpoena form, except that there is a space to describe the papers or other documents you want brought to court. To get a "Subpoena Duces Tecum" issued, you must normally follow a procedure along the following lines: Attach an affidavit stating why you need the written material. Prepare three copies of all papers and, after you get the clerk to issue the subpoena, serve it on the witness, using personal service, as described in Chapter 11. As with a regular subpoena, the witness is entitled to ask for a fee. The Proof of Service is on the back of the subpoena form and must be filled out and returned to the clerk.

Rules for subpoenas vary from state to state: Technical rules on filing and serving papers, as well as paying witness fees, vary considerably from one state to the next. Make sure you know what will be required in plenty of time. Also, before subpoenaing documents, be sure to ask if the other side will simply give you photocopies in advance.

A Subpoena Duces Tecum must be directed to the person who is in charge of the documents, books or records you want. It may take a few phone calls to find out who this is. Be sure you get this information accurately. If you list someone on the Subpoena Duces Tecum who has nothing to do with the documents, you won't get them. When dealing with a large corporation, public utility, municipal government, etc., it is wise to list the person who is in overall charge of the department where the records are kept. Thus, if you want records having to do with library fines from a public library, or having to do with business license fees from the city tax and license department, you should not list the city manager or the mayor, but should list the head librarian or the director of the tax and license office.

Example: Let's take a hypothetical case. You are being sued by the city on behalf of the public library for $300 for eight rare books which they state you failed to return. You know that you did return the books, but can't seem to get that across to the library, which insists on treating you like a thief. You learn that each April the library takes a yearly inventory of all books on their shelves. You believe that if you can get access to that inventory, you may be able to figure out where the library misplaced the books, or at least show that a significant percentage of the library's other books are not accounted for, raising the implication that they, not you, lost the books.

Your first step is to ask the library officials to voluntarily open the inventory to you. If they refuse, you may well want to subpoena it. Here's how:

1. Check the "Duces Tecum" box on the Subpoena form.

2. Prepare an affidavit using a form available from the court. It should be brief. Describe the documents you need and why they are necessary to prove issues involved in the case. If you want the custodian of the records to show up in person, give a reason. Don't argue the merits of your case on this form.

3. Have the subpoena issued by the Small Claims clerk. Then have the subpoena served, being sure that the Proof of Service (see Chapter 11) is properly filled out and returned to the clerk.

DECLARATION FOR SUBPOENA DUCES TECUM

Name and Address of Court: Municipal Court, County of Alameda
Berkeley-Albany Judicial District
2000 Center Street
Berkeley, CA 94704

SMALL CLAIMS CASE NO. (fill in number)

PLAINTIFF/DEMANDANTE *(Name, address, and telephone number of each)*:

Public Library
100 Allston Way
Berkeley, CA 94704

Telephone No.:

Telephone No.:

DEFENDANT/DEMANDADO *(Name, address, and telephone number of each)*:

John O'Gara
100 Scenic Drive
Berkeley, CA 94702

Telephone No.:

Telephone No.:

[ ] See attached sheet for additional plaintiffs and defendants.

DECLARATION FOR SUBPENA DUCES TECUM

1. I, the undersigned, declare I am the [ ] plaintiff [X] defendant [ ] judgment creditor [ ] other *(specify)*:
in the above entitled action.
2. This action has been set for hearing on *(date)*:(fill in date) at *(time)*: (fill in time) in the above named court.
3. *(Name)*: Robert Riwyle   has in his or her possession or under his or her control
the following documents relating to *(name of party)*   :

a. [ ] Payroll receipts, stubs, and other records concerning employment of the party. Receipts, invoices, documents, and other papers
or records concerning any and all accounts receivable of the party.
b. [ ] Bank account statements, cancelled checks, and check registers from any and all bank accounts in which the party has an interest.
c. [ ] Savings account passbooks and statements, savings and loan account passbooks and statements, and credit union share account
passbooks and statements of the party.
d. [ ] Stock certificates, bonds, money market certificates, and any other records, documents, or papers concerning all investments
of the party.
e. [ ] California registration certificates and ownership certificates for all vehicles registered to the party.
f. [ ] Deeds to any and all real property owned or being purchased by the party.
g. [X] Other *(specify)*:

Book inventory information collected by the main branch of the
public library during the calendar year 19__.

These documents are material to the issues involved in this case for the following reasons *(specify)*:

My contention is that I returned the books for which the library
is suing me. The inventory should back me up on this.

I declare under penalty of perjury under the laws of the State of California that the foregoing is true and correct.

Date: (fill in)

...........John O'Gara..........................   ▶ John O'Gara
(TYPE OR PRINT NAME)   (SIGNATURE OF JUDGMENT CREDITOR)

Form Approved by the
Judicial Council of California
SC-107 [New January 1, 1992]

DECLARATION FOR SUBPENA DUCES TECUM
(Small Claims)

Code of Civil Procedure, §§ 1985–1987.5

Note: On the day of the hearing, the person you have subpoenaed will show up with the documents in question. The documents will be presented to the court—not to you. If you need an opportunity to examine the documents, request it from the judge. He may well let you do your examining right there in the courtroom while other cases go ahead, or, if necessary, he may continue the case for a few days and arrange to have you make your examination at the place of business of the owner of the records.

D. Written Evidence

In most Small Claims Courts, there are no formal rules of evidence requiring that a witness testify in person (but be sure to check your local rules). While it is best to have a witness appear in court, this isn't always possible, and a judge will accept written statements from both eyewitnesses ("I was there and saw the filthy apartment") and expert witnesses ("I examined the transmission and found that a rebuilt part was installed improperly"). If you do present the written statement of a witness, make sure the witness covers the following points:

For an eyewitness:
- Who the witness is.
- The date of the event.
- What she saw, heard, smelled, felt or tasted, and where and how she did so.

For an expert witness:
- Who the witness is.
- The witness's work and education credentials, which demonstrate her expertise in the field she is commenting on. (If credentials are lengthy, it's a good idea to include the person's resume or vitae.)
- What he did to be able to render his opinion. ("I examined the paint on Mr. Jones's 35-foot Cabin Cruiser and subjected it to the following test....")

- When he did it.
- His conclusion (the paint used was not suitable for salt water immersion).
- If possible, an estimate of the cost to redo the work properly.
- Any other facts that have a bearing on the dispute.

It's a good idea to attach a separate list of the expert's credentials. If your expert has a resume or vitae listing educational and experiential credentials, attach it to the letter in which she states her findings. The more distinguished your expert, the more likely the judge is to respect her opinion.

Here are examples of letters an eyewitness and an expert witness might write (see Chapter 17 for another written statement by an expert witness):

---

37 Ogden Court
Kansas City, Kansas
September 30, 19__

Presiding Judge
Small Claims Court
Kansas City, Kansas

Re: John Swift vs. Peter Petrakos
Small Claims Case No. 11478

Your Honor:

My name is Victor Van Cleve, I work at Racafrax Engineering in Kansas City, Kansas, as a mechanical engineer, and I am 43 years old.

On September 15, 19__, I witnessed an auto accident a little after 7:30 a.m., involving John Swift and Peter Petrakos. I was about 50 feet away from the accident and could see what happened clearly.

I saw Mr. Petrakos' Toyota, which was heading north on South Dora, go through a red light and hit Mr. Swift's blue van, which was proceeding east on West 7th, well inside the 25 MPH speed limit. I assume the light was green facing Mr. Swift, but since I was waiting for the red light on South Dora, I couldn't actually see it. I also noticed that the traffic light facing Mr. Petrakos did not turn to green for ten seconds or so after the accident, so this was not a case of Mr. Petrakos just being a little early going through an intersection at a light change.

Sincerely,

Victor Van Cleve

Gail McClosky
47 Penrod Street
Helena, Montana

Sept. 30, 19__

Judge
Small Claims Division
Helena, Montana

Re: John Swift vs. Peter Petrakos
Small Claims Case No. 11478

Dear Judge:

I am a fully licensed contractor with 20 years' experience here in Helena
(Contractor's License (4021B)). For the last ten years I've run my own five-person
contracting company specializing in building enclosures and buildings to be used to
house horse and other large animals. I enclose a resume outlining my specialized training
and experience in this field.

On April 23, 19__, I was asked by James Dills to inspect several new stalls he had
built in the main barn of his Lazy T Ranch by R&B Construction.

In my opinion these stalls are markedly below normal industry standards for three
reasons.

1) They are too small for the animals intended to be kept in them. [Continue with
details.]

2) Walls and doors are built of plywood too thin to safely contain an agitated
animal. [Continue with details.]

3) Construction is so rough in several regards as to pose a danger of injury to an
animal intended to be kept there. [Continue with details.]

In conclusion, I believe the stalls are so poorly constructed they can't reasonably be
upgraded to provide safe habitable housing for horses. Were they mine, I would rip them
out and start over.

Sincerely,

Gail McClosky

E. Judges as Witnesses

Using a judge as a witness is a valuable technique in many situations. This is done routinely in many types of disputes, such as clothing cases in which you bring the damaged garment into court for the judge's examination. Always bring into the court any physical evidence that meets these two criteria:

• Showing it to the judge will help your case;

• It will fit through the door.

But what if your evidence is impossible to bring into the courtroom (a car with a poor paint job or a supposedly pedigreed puppy that grew up looking as if Lassie were the mother and Rin Tin Tin the father)? Why not ask the judge to accompany you outside the building to examine the car, or the dog, or whatever else is important to your case? Many (but not all) judges are willing to do so if they feel it is necessary to better understand the dispute and won't take too long. But never ask a judge to take time to leave her court to view evidence if you can prove your case just as well by other means, such as witnesses and pictures. A good approach is to do as much as you can in court, and to ask the judge to view evidence outside of court only if it is essential. Sometimes it clearly is. For example, one excellent judge I know was disturbed one morning when two eyewitnesses gave seriously contradictory testimony about a traffic accident. He questioned both in detail and then took the case under submission. That evening, he drove over to the relevant corner. Once there, it was clear that one of the witnesses couldn't possibly have seen the accident from the spot on which she claimed to be standing (in front of a particular restaurant). The judge decided the case in favor of the other.

F. Testimony by Telephone

A surprising number of Small Claims Court judges will take testimony over the phone if a witness cannot be present because he or she is ill, disabled, out-of-state or can't take time off from work. While procedures vary, some courts will set up conference calls so that the opposing party has the opportunity to hear what is being said and to respond.

Don't just assume that your local court will allow telephone testimony. Ask the clerk. If you get a negative response, don't give up—ask the judge when you get into the courtroom. It is also an extremely good idea to have a letter from the witness whom you want to reach by phone, explaining what he or she will testify to (for example, your opponent's car ran a red light and broadsided you) and why it is impossible for him to be in court. Such a letter might look like the one above, except the witness should add:

"Mr. Swift has asked me to testify on his behalf, and normally I would be happy to do so—however, I will be in New York City on business during the months of October, November and December 19__ and cannot be present.

"I have asked Mr. Swift to let me know the day and approximate time of the court hearing and have told him that I will give him a phone number where I can be reached. If you think it desirable, I will be pleased to give my testimony by phone."

■

CHAPTER

15

Presenting Your Case to the Judge

A. Uncontested Cases—Getting a Judgment by Default

Surprisingly often, presenting your case in court will be easy—your opponent simply will not show up on the date of your hearing. If this occurs, in most states you will be asked to briefly state the basic facts of your case and possibly to provide some documentary evidence, such as a copy of the written contract you claim the defendant broke. Once this is done you will be eligible to have a default judgment entered on your behalf. In the few states that require a defendant to file a written answer (see Appendix), you should be able to find out before the court date whether the other side will appear when you do ask what, if anything, you must do to get your default judgment.

Assuming you will be required to make an in-court presentation, you should be prepared to accomplish it in a few sentences.

Example: "Your Honor, I own the Racafrax Auto Repair Shop. On January 11, 199x, I repaired defendant's 1994 Eagle Talon. He paid me $500 and agreed to pay another $500 on March 1. He has not made the second payment. I have copies of the contract defendant signed and of several unpaid bills I sent him. I am asking for a judgment of $500 plus $55 for my court filing fee and the cost of having the papers served."

No need for a longwinded presentation at a default hearing: If the other side doesn't show up, a judge only wants to hear facts necessary to support a judgment on your behalf. Since your opponent is not present to contest these facts, they should be taken as true by the court, meaning there is no need to present an extended argument.

After you state your case, the judge may check to see that your opponent was properly served and may ask you a question or two to make sure that there is no obvious flaw in your case, such as the statute of limitations having run out two years ago. Assuming she is satisfied that all is in order, she will enter a judgment for the amount of your request. A defendant who doesn't show up to argue his or her case usually can't appeal to a formal court (see Chapter 23) unless the default is first set aside. (See Chapter 10, Section F.)

In some Small Claims Courts, such as those in Washington, D.C., you won't even have to enter the courtroom if your case is for an unpaid debt and you have good documentation, such as a contract and copies of unpaid bills. A court clerk, not the judge, will enter the default judgment.

Occasionally, a person who has defaulted will show up in court a few days later with a good excuse. If the defaulting party makes a motion to set aside the default within a relatively short time (almost always under a month), the judge in most states may—but does not have to—set it aside. The party who missed the first hearing always has the job of convincing the judge that the reason she didn't show up or phone earlier is good enough to justify setting aside the default. (See Chapter 10 for more on setting aside a default.)

B. Contested Cases

Assuming now that both sides show up and step forward when the case is called by the clerk, what happens next? First, the judge will establish everyone's identity. These will often be the principal people involved in the dispute, but in some states, might be a collection agency or an attorney. Also, in many states, businesses can be represented by employees. Thus a dentist or store owner could send a bookkeeper to establish that a bill wasn't paid.

Next, the judge will ask the plaintiff or his representative to briefly state his case. But before we focus on the plaintiff's and defendant's presentations, here are a few tips that both should find helpful.

- Stand when you make your initial presentation. Standing gives most people a sense of presence and confidence at a time when they may be a little nervous. It's fine to sit while your opponent is talking. If the judge interrupts her presentation to ask you a quick question, there is no need to jump to your feet to answer it.

- Be as brief as you can and still explain and document your case thoroughly.
- Don't read your statement. Reading in court is almost always a bore. But you may find it helpful to make a few notes on a card to serve as a reminder in case you get nervous or forget something. If you decide to do this, list the headings of the various points you want to make in an outline form. Be sure your list is easy to read at a glance and that the topics are in the correct order. (I give a sample list in Chapter 13.)
- Never interrupt your opponent or any of the witnesses, no matter how outrageous their "lies." You will get your chance to respond.
- Try to present any portion of your case that is difficult to explain verbally in another way. This often means bringing your used car parts, damaged clothing or other exhibits, such as photographs or canceled checks, with you, and having them organized for easy presentation.
- There will be a blackboard in court. If drawings will be helpful, as is almost always true in cases involving car accidents, be sure to ask the judge for permission to use it. You will want to draw clearly and legibly the first time, so it's wise to have practiced in advance.
- If you are the defendant, don't repeat uncontested facts that the plaintiff already presented (for example, that the two of you had a fender bender at a certain corner in a certain city at a certain time during certain weather conditions). Instead, focus on the point of your principal disagreement (whether the light facing you was green or red, for example) and introduce evidence to prove that point.

Be sure to practice your presentation. A key to preparing your case well is to practice making your oral presentation ahead of time. Have a tough-minded friend or family member play the part of judge and be ready to ask questions and try to poke holes in your best points. Run through your presentation several times until you get it right.

1. From the Plaintiff's Side

The plaintiff should clearly tell the judge what the dispute is about before she starts describing the details of what happened. I call this starting with the end, not the beginning, of your story.

If your case involves a car accident, you might start by saying, "This case involves a car accident at Cedar and Rose Streets in which my car suffered $872 worth of damage when the defendant ran a red light and hit my front fender," not "It all started when I was driving down Rose Street after having two eggs and a danish for breakfast."

Only occasionally have I seen a case where the plaintiff's initial presentation should take longer than five minutes. As part of his statement, the plaintiff should present and explain any relevant papers, photos or other documentary evidence. These should be handed to the clerk, who will pass them on to the judge. The plaintiff should also be sure to indicate the presence of any witnesses to the judge, and be sure they get a chance to have their say. If either the plaintiff or defendant has done legal research and believes that a statute or court decision supports his position, he should call it to the attention of the judge. The best way to do this is to write the statute number or case name, along with its official citation, on a piece of paper and hand it to the judge. (See Chapter 1, Section D, for an explanation of how statutes and cases are cited.)

If the plaintiff has witnesses, it's important to tell the judge at the beginning of his presentation. And if a witness has key information (as would be the case if she saw a traffic accident or inspected an apartment immediately after a departing tenant cleaned up), she should be well prepared to state it clearly. Too often, when a witness is asked to testify, she either leaves out important points or is so disorganized that the force of her testimony is lost.

The best way to be sure your witness really will be able to succinctly and concisely explain to the judge the key facts that support your case is to have her practice her testimony in advance. As long as she sticks to the truth, rehearsing the exact words she will say in court is both proper and legal. One good way to rehearse is to meet with your witness and a friend you have asked to act as a mock judge. First you present your case to the pretend judge exactly as you plan to do it in court. Then ask your witness to stand and explain, firsthand, her version of what happened.

If at first your witness is a little disorganized or unsure, work with her to develop a short convincing presentation that covers all key points. When you have something that sounds good, ask her to write it down and practice it several times before your court date.

When the plaintiff is finished—or often even before the plaintiff has made all of her points—the judge may begin to ask questions. Each judge will control the flow of evidence differently. It's best to go with the judge's energy, and directly answer any questions. Just be sure that you and your witnesses eventually get a chance to make all of your points. If you feel rushed, say so. The judge will normally slow things down a little. Especially if you appear before a volunteer lawyer (called an arbitrator, in New York), you can expect the case to be heard even less formally, with the arbitrator taking an active role in questioning the parties and witnesses.

2. From the Defendant's Side

Sooner or later it will be your turn. Defendants often get so angry at something the plaintiff has said that when they finally get to speak, they attack angrily. This is usually counterproductive. Far better to calmly and clearly present your side of the dispute to the judge. Start with the key event of the dispute and then fill in the details of the story. If the plaintiff has made false or misleading statements, these should be answered, but normally towards the end of your presentation, not at the beginning.

> **Example:** "Your Honor, it's true that the bumper of my truck hit defendant's fender and pushed it in slightly, but it happened because defendant entered the intersection before it was clear and was therefore at fault. I was driving south on Cedar and entered the intersection just as the light first turned yellow. I slowed briefly near the center line behind a car that was turning left and then continued across, at which point defendant's car darted in front of me...."

Like the plaintiff, the defendant should be prepared to present documentary evidence and, if possible, witnesses that will back up her story. And if any statutes or court decisions are relevant, she should call them to the judge's attention by preparing a brief memo, as described in Section B1, just above.

3. A Sample Case

Now let's look at how a contested case might be presented from both the plaintiff's and defendant's perspectives.

Clerk: "The next case is *John Andrews v. Robertson Realty.* Will everyone please come forward?" (Four people come forward and sit at the table facing the judge.)

Judge: "Good morning. Which one of you is Mr. Andrews? Okay, will you begin, Mr. Andrews?"

John Andrews: (stands) "This is a case about my failure to get a $700 cleaning deposit returned, your Honor. I rented a house from Robertson Realty at 1611 Spruce Street in Rockford in March of 199x on a month-to-month tenancy. On January 10, 199x, I sent Mr. Robertson a written notice that I was planning to move on March 10. In fact, I moved out on March 8 and left the place extremely clean. I know it was clean because I spent eight hours, a lot of them on my hands and knees, cleaning it. In addition, all of my rent was properly paid. A few days after I moved out, I asked Mr. Robertson to return my $700 deposit. He wrote me a letter stating that the place was dirty and he was keeping my deposit.

"I have with me a copy of a letter I wrote to Mr. Robertson on March 15 setting out my position in more detail. I also have some photographs that my friend, Carol Spann, who is here as a witness, took on the day I moved out. I believe the pictures show pretty clearly that I did a thorough clean-up. (John Andrews hands the letter and pictures to the clerk, who hands them to the judge.)

"Your Honor, I am asking not only for the $700 deposit, but also for $500 in extra damages, plus 2% monthly interest, which the law of this state allows a tenant when a landlord improperly refuses to return a deposit."

Judge: "Mr. Andrews, will you introduce your witness."

Andrews: "Yes. This is Carol Spann. She helped me clean up and move on March 7 and 8."

Judge: (looking at the pictures) "Ms. Spann, were you in the apartment the day John Andrews moved out?"

Carol Spann: (standing) "Yes, your Honor, I was—and the day before, too. I helped clean up, and I can vouch that we did a good job. Not only did we do the normal washing and scrubbing, but we waxed the kitchen floor, cleaned the bathroom tile and shampooed the rugs."

Judge: (turning to Mr. Robertson) "Okay, now it's your turn to tell me why the deposit wasn't returned."

Harry Robertson: (standing) "I don't know how they could have cleaned the place up, your Honor, because it was filthy when I inspected it on March 9. Let me give you a few specifics. There was mildew and mold around the bathtub, the windows were filthy, the refrigerator hadn't been defrosted and there was dog—how shall I say it—dog manure in the basement. Your Honor, I have brought along Clem Houndstooth as a witness. Mr. Houndstooth is the tenant who moved in three days after Mr. Andrews moved out. Incidentally, your Honor, the place was so dirty that I only charged Mr. Houndstooth a $200 cleaning deposit, because he agreed to clean it up himself."

Judge: (looking at Clem Houndstooth) "Do you wish to say something?"

Clem Houndstooth: (standing) "Yes, I do. Mr. Robertson asked me to come down and back him up and I am glad to do it, because I put in two full days cleaning that place up. I like a clean house, your Honor, not a halfway clean, halfway dirty house. I just don't think that a house is clean if the oven is full of gunk, there is mold in the bathroom, and the insides of the cupboards are grimy. All these conditions existed at 1611 Spruce St. when I moved in. I just don't believe that anyone could think that place was clean."

Judge: "Mr. Andrews, do you have anything to add?"

John Andrews: (standing up) "Yes, I sure do. First, as to the mildew problem. The house is 40 years old and there is some dampness in the wall of the bathroom. Maybe there is a leaky pipe someplace behind the tile. I cleaned it a number of times, but it always came back. I talked to Mr. Fisk in Mr. Robertson's office about the problem about a month after I moved in and he told me that I would have to do the best I could because they couldn't afford to tear the wall apart. As to the cupboards and stove, they are both old. The cabinets haven't been painted in 10 years, so, of course, they aren't perfect. And that old stove was a lot dirtier when I moved in than it is now, since I can tell you I personally worked on it with oven cleaner for over an hour."

Judge: "What about the refrigerator, Mr. Andrews? Was that defrosted?"

John Andrews: "No, your Honor, it wasn't, but it had been defrosted about three weeks before I moved out and I thought that it was good enough the way it was."

Judge: "Okay, if no one else has anything to add, I want to return your pictures and letters. You will receive my decision by mail in a few days."

Now, I have a little surprise for you. The case I just presented was a real case. As they used to say on *Dragnet,* "Only the names have been changed to protect the innocent." And I have another surprise for you. I spoke to the judge after the court session and I know how the case came out. The judge explained his reasoning to me as follows.

"This is a typical case in which both sides have some right on their side. What is clean to one person may be dirty to another. Based on what I heard, I would have to guess that the old tenant made a fairly conscientious effort to clean up and probably left the place about as clean as it was when he moved in, but that the new tenant, Houndstooth, had much higher standards, and convinced the landlord that it was filthy. The landlord may not have needed too much convincing, since he probably would just as well keep the deposit. But I did hear enough to convince me that Andrews, the old tenant, didn't do a perfect job cleaning up. My decision will be that Andrews gets a judgment for the return of $450 of the $700 deposit, with no extra damages. I believe that $250 is more than enough to compensate the landlord for any damages he suffered as a result of the apartment 'being a little dirty.'"

I then asked the judge if he felt the case was well presented. He replied substantially as follows:

"Better than average. I think I got a pretty good idea of what the problems were. The witnesses were helpful and the pictures suggested that the place wasn't a total mess. Both sides could have done better, however. Andrews could have had a witness talk about the condition when he moved in if it was truly dirtier than when he left. Another witness to testify to the apartment's cleanliness when he moved out would have been good, too. His friend, Carol Spann, seemed to be a very close friend and I wasn't sure that she was objective when it came to judging whether the place was clean. The landlord, Robertson, could also have done better. He could have presented a more disinterested witness, although I must say that Houndstooth's testimony was pretty convincing. Also, he could have had pictures documenting the dirty conditions and an estimate from a cleaning company for how much they would have charged to clean the place up. Without going to too much trouble, I think both sides could have probably done somewhat better with more thorough preparation."

C. Don't Forget to Ask for Your Costs

Both plaintiff and defendant are entitled to ask that a judgment in their favor include any recoverable costs, such as for filing and serving court papers or subpoenaing essential witnesses. Sometimes defendants have no costs, unless a necessary witness is subpoenaed. In most states, you can recover for:

- *Your court filing fee* (usually charged to the plaintiff, but not the defendant).

- *Service of process costs.* A plaintiff must pay this fee unless a friend serves the papers, as is allowed in some states. Fees vary from a few dollars in states where certified mail is allowed, to considerably more if a professional process service is required. A defendant will normally only pay to serve papers if she files a countersuit. (In some states, both parties must try and fail to serve papers by mail as a condition of the court awarding higher fees for a process server—see Chapter 11.)

- *Subpoenaed witness fees.* Both the plaintiff and defendant can incur this cost if a witness must be subpoenaed and claims a fee. (In some courts, witness fees must be approved by the judge ahead of time.) Generally, fees for subpoenaing witnesses and documents are only recoverable if the judge believes the person or documentary evidence was really necessary.

- *The cost of obtaining necessary documents,* such as verification of car ownership by the D.M.V. (Both plaintiffs and defendants can have these.)

As I discussed in Chapter 10, you can't recover for such personal expenses as taking time off from work to prepare for or attend court, paying a babysitter or photocopy charges. For information on recovering collection costs incurred after judgment when your opponent won't voluntarily pay, see Chapter 24. ■

Motor Vehicle Repair Cases

Most Small Claims Court cases fall into a dozen or so broad categories, with perhaps another dozen subcategories. In the next six chapters, we look at the most common types of cases and discuss strategies to handle each. Even if your fact situation doesn't fit neatly into one of these categories, it makes sense to read them. By picking up a few hints here and a little information there, you should be able to piece together a good plan of action. For example, many of the suggestions I make to handle motor vehicle repair disputes can be applied to cases involving major appliances, such as televisions, washers and expensive stereos.

Let's start by imagining that you go to the auto repair shop to pick up your trusty, but slightly graying, steed after a complete engine overhaul. The bill, as agreed to by you in advance, is $1,225. This always seemed a little steep, but the mechanic had talked you into it based on his claim that he would do a great job and that, when the work is done, the engine should last another 50,000 miles. At any rate, you write out a check and drive out of the garage in something approaching a cheerful mood. One of life's more disagreeable hassles has been taken care of, at least temporarily. Unfortunately, as most of us have learned through hard experience, "temporarily" can sometimes be a very short time. In this case, it lasts only until you head up the first hill. What's that funny noise, you think? Why don't I have more power? "Oh shit," you say (you never swear, but there are some extreme provocations where nothing else will do). You turn around and drive back to the garage. Not only are you out $1,225, but your car runs worse than it did when you brought it in.

Funny, no one seems as pleasant as they did before. And no one appears to have time to listen to you. Finally, after a bit of foot stomping, you get someone to say they will look the car over. You take a bus home, trying not to be paranoid. The next day you call the garage. Nothing has been done. You yell at the garage owner and then call your bank to stop payment on the check. You are told it has already been cashed. The next day the garage owner tells you the problem is in a part of the engine they didn't work on. You only paid for a "short block job," they tell you. "Give us another $500 and we can surely solve this new problem," they add.

In disgust, you go down and pick up your handicapped friend and drive it home—slowly. You are furious, and you decide to pursue every legal remedy, no matter what the trouble. How do you start?

First, park your car, take a shower and have a glass of wine. Nothing gets decided well when you're mad. Now, going back to the reasoning we used at the beginning of this book, ask yourself some basic questions:

A. Have I Suffered a Loss?

That's easy. Your car doesn't work properly, you paid out a lot of money and the garage wants more to fix it. Clearly, you have suffered a loss.

B. Did the Negligence of the Garage Cause My Loss?

Ah ha, now we get to the nitty gritty. In this type of case, you can almost always expect the garage to claim they did their work properly and the car simply needs more work. Maybe the garage is right—it's your job to prove that their work was not up to a reasonable standard of competence. Doing so will make your case; failing to do so will break it. You better get to work.

Step 1. Collect Available Evidence

First, get all evidence together where time is of the essence. In this situation, this means getting your used parts (it's a good idea to do this anytime you have major work done—something the law of some states requires.) If the garage will not give them to you, make your request by letter, keeping a copy for your file. If you get the parts, fine—if you don't, you have evidence that the garage is badly run or has something to hide.

Step 2. Have the Car Checked

Before you drive many miles, have your car checked by an established local mechanic
or mechanics. Sometimes it is possible to get a free estimate from a repair shop if the
shop thinks it will get the job of fixing your car. In this situation, however, you may be
better off paying for someone to look at the engine thoroughly, as you want to be sure
that at least one of the people who looks the car over is willing to come with you to
Small Claims Court if the need arises, or at the very least, will write a convincing letter
stating what's wrong with the engine. One way to try to accomplish this is to take your
car to a garage that someone you know already has a good personal relationship with.
A few states require that you present three written estimates in Small Claims Court.
Whether this is required or not, it's a good idea to have them.

Step 3. Try to Settle Your Case

By now, you should have a pretty good idea as to what the first garage did wrong.
Call them and ask that either the job be redone, or that they give you a refund of part
or all of your money. Often the repair shop will agree to do some, or all, of the work
over to avoid a further hassle. If they agree to take the car back, insist on a written
agreement detailing what they will do and how long it will take. Also, talk to the
mechanic who will actually work on the car to be sure he understands what needs to
be done. Naturally, you may be a little paranoid about giving your car back to the
garage that screwed it up, but unless they have been outrageously incompetent, this is
probably your best approach at this stage. If you sue and the garage owner shows up
in court and says he offered to work on the car again but you refused, it may weaken
your case.

Step 4.   Write a Demand Letter

If the garage isn't cooperative, it's time to write them a formal demand letter. Remember our discussion in Chapter 6. Your letter should be short, polite and written with an eye to a judge reading it. In this situation, you could write something like the one below.

Jorge Sotomayor
15 Orange St.
Hamden, CT

Happy Days Motors
100 Speedway
New Haven, CT

Dear People:

On August 13, 19_, I brought my 1988 Dodge to your garage. You agreed to do a complete engine rebuild job for $1,225. You told me, "Your car will be running like a watch when we're through with it." The car worked well when I brought it in, but was a little short on power. Two days later, when I picked up my car, it barely moved at all. The engine made such a clanging noise that I have been afraid to drive it.

I have repeatedly asked you to fix the car or to refund my money. You have refused. Shortly after the work was done, I asked for my used parts to be returned. You refused to give them to me, even though it is a violation of state law.

I have had several mechanics look my car over since you worked on it. They all agree that you did your job improperly and even installed some used parts instead of new ones. The work you did on the engine rings was particularly badly done.

After receiving no response from you, I had the work redone at a cost of $900. (Most Small Claims Courts do not require that you actually have the work redone before going to court, but a few, such as New York City, require a repair bill marked "Paid.") My car now works well. Please refund my $1,225. Should you fail to do so, I will exhaust all my legal remedies, including complaining to interested state and local agencies and taking this dispute to Small Claims Court. I hope to hear from you promptly.

Jorge Sotomayor

cc: Connecticut Dept. of Consumer Affairs
      Bureau of Automotive Repair
      Hartford, CT

Note: Most small independent garages don't make any written warranty or guaranty of their work. However, if you were given any promises in writing, mention them here in your letter. Also, if you were told things orally about the quality of the work the garage planned to do and you relied on these statements as part of your decision to have the work done, you should call attention to this express verbal warranty. (See Chapter 2.)

Step 5. File Your Court Papers

If you still get no satisfactory response from the garage, file your papers at the Small Claims clerk's office of your local Small Claims Court. Reread Chapters 7–10.

Step 6. Prepare for Court

If you want the judge to understand your case, you must understand it yourself. Sounds simple, doesn't it? It did to me too until I got involved with a case involving a botched car repair. All I really knew was that after I had paid to have the engine fixed, the darn thing was not supposed to belch black smoke and make a disgusting noise. I really wasn't interested in the details.

But fortunately, I realized that for me to argue my case in Small Claims with this level of knowledge would likely end in a bad loss. Clearly, to convince a judge that the mechanic had ripped me off, I needed to do some homework. After all, I could expect the people from the garage to show up in court with a terrific-sounding story about the wonderful job they did. I clearly needed to be prepared to cope with their talk about pistons, bearings and turning the cam shaft so as to convince the judge that they botched the job.

It turned out that fifteen minutes' conversation with a knowledgeable mechanic was all I really needed to understand what the mechanic did wrong. (Also, my local library had several car manuals, complete with diagrams, which were a big help.) In court, armed with my new knowledge, I had no trouble explaining to the judge that the mechanic had done a substandard job and getting a judgment for the full amount I had paid.

Remember the Judge: In Chapter 13, I mentioned that it's important to pay attention to the person to whom you are presenting your case. Most Small Claims judges don't understand the insides of cars any better than you do. People often become lawyers because they don't like to get their hands dirty. So be prepared to deal with a person who nods his head but doesn't really understand the difference between the drive shaft and the axle. Car cases are sometimes easier to present to a woman judge. Cultural changes in the last few years notwithstanding, women still don't usually have the same ego involvement with being mechanical car experts that men do. They are often more willing to say "I don't know," and to listen.

Step 7. Appearing in Court

When you appear in court, be sure you are well organized. Bring all the letters you have written, or received, about your car problem, as well as written warranties (if any), photographs if they are helpful and your used parts if they aid in making your case. If you have a witness to any oral statements (warranties) made by the garage, be sure to bring that person with you to court. Also, be sure to present any written letters by independent garage people who have examined your car. A well-written letter from an expert saying that for the amount of money you paid, the engine should have been fixed, is likely to be particularly effective.

If you are well prepared, you should win the sort of case outlined here without difficulty. Judges drive cars and have to get them fixed, so they tend to be sympathetic with this type of consumer complaint. Simply present your story (see Chapter 15), your documentation and your witnesses. If you feel your opponent is snowing the judge with a lot of technical lingo, get His Honor back on track by asking that the technical terms be explained in ordinary English. This will be a relief to everyone in the courtroom except your opponent. You will likely find that, once his case is shorn of all the magic words, it will shrink from a tiger to a pussycat.

Step 8: Ask for a Continuance in the Middle of Your Presentation If It Is Essential

The best-laid plans can occasionally go haywire. Perhaps a key witness doesn't show up, or maybe, despite careful preparation, you overlook some aspect of the case that the judge feels is crucial. If this occurs, you may want to ask the judge to reschedule the case on another day so that you can prepare better. It is proper to make this sort of request. Whether or not it will be granted is up to the judge. If he or she feels that more evidence isn't likely to change the result, or that you are making the request to stall, it will not be granted. If there is a good reason for a delay, however, it will usually be allowed. But if you want a delay, you have to ask for it—the judge isn't going to be able to read your mind. ■

Motor Vehicle Purchase Cases

All too often someone buys a motor vehicle, drives it a short way, only to have it fall apart. And all too often the seller won't stand behind the product sold or work out some sort of fair adjustment. There are major differences in approach between buying a new vehicle from a dealer, buying a used vehicle from a dealer and buying a used vehicle from a private party. Let's look at each situation individually.

A. New Vehicles

The most common problem with new vehicles is the lemon with major manufacturing defects. Here is an example:

Example: You trade in your rusty '84 bomb that served you well for longer than you want to remember and fork over a ridiculously large pile of money on a shiny new car. Your new carriage runs fine for a few months, but then it begins to vibrate uncontrollably whenever you drive over 50 mph. You take it back to the dealer, who tries to fix it, but it still shakes. You take it back again, but it's still not right. By now you're tired of countless repairs. You paid for a new car that's supposed to work and you feel you should either get a full refund or a replacement. How can you do this?

A large majority of states have enacted some sort of "lemon law" to protect consumers in your situation. Although the laws vary a little from state to state, most follow the same basic structure: If your new car has a substantial defect that cannot be repaired after repeated attempts or 30 days of service, you have a right to a refund or replacement vehicle from the manufacturer if you notify them of the problem and submit to arbitration. The arbitration is free and you don't need a lawyer.

 The Lemon Book, by Ralph Nader and Clarence Ditlow (Center for Auto Safety), contains an excellent state-by-state rundown of rights and remedies under state lemon laws.

Enforcing Your Lemon Rights

To qualify for a refund or replacement under most lemon laws you (or, rather, your car) must meet the following conditions:

1. *Substantial Defect.* Your new car must have a defect within the first year. The defect must substantially impair the car's use, value or safety (or some combination of the three). Unfortunately, many lemons have lots of little problems rather than one big one, and most lemon laws don't recognize this. Massachusetts and Rhode Island, however, do allow a bunch of "little" defects to be lumped together and treated as one "substantial" one.

2. *Opportunity to Repair.* The dealer or manufacturer gets three or four (depending on the state) chances to fix the defect within the first year, but can't keep the car in the shop for more than a total of 30 days. If the defect can't be fixed, the car is legally a lemon. (Note that the 30 total days during the year need not be consecutive days; also, some states only count "business" days.) Most states treat each defect separately, and thus allow four repair attempts or 30 days for each one. A few states, however, allow the dealer only four repairs or 30 days to cure all the defects.

3. *Notice to Manufacturer.* You must notify the manufacturer about the repairs as they are being done. In most states, this requirement is satisfied by simply taking the car to the dealer, since the dealer contacts the manufacturer for reimbursement for all repairs done under warranty. A few states, however, including California and Washington, additionally require that you notify the manufacturer *in writing*. Merely taking it into the dealer is not enough.

Once you've given the manufacturer three or four attempts or 30 days to fix your car, you have to notify the manufacturer again, in writing, that you want a refund or replacement vehicle.

4. *Arbitration.* After you've made your demand, you must submit to arbitration. In most states (except Texas and Vermont), you must use the manufacturer's arbitrator, if it has one (most major companies do). These arbitrators or arbitration boards must meet federal and/or state standards of impartiality. Arbitration must be free and designed to be conducted without a lawyer. You explain the problem to the arbitrator, either in person or in writing, and the arbitrator rules within 60 days whether your car is a lemon and whether you're entitled to a refund, replacement or something less. The arbitrator, however, will not award consequential damages, such as the cost of a car you had to rent while your car was in the shop. For that you have to go to court.

In all likelihood, the manufacturer will try to settle before you ever get to arbitration. Manufacturers hate to buy back cars or give replacements because they get stuck with a defective car that they have to resell as a used car, at a substantial loss. (One study showed that GM settled 90% of its cases before they reached arbitration. Of the 10% who did arbitrate, 60% got more than GM's final offer.)

If the arbitrator decides you don't qualify for a refund or a replacement, you can take your case to court. If you go to Small Claims Court, you'll be limited by the maximum amount your state allows in recovery. If you go to a formal court and hire an attorney, the attorney's fees may exceed the cost of fixing the car, and your case may not be heard for several years.

Unfortunately, many disputes involving new vehicles don't fall under the lemon law. This would be the situation if the same defect didn't recur four times, or if problems develop just after the warranty expires.

Sometimes it seems as though there is a little destruct switch set to flip 15 minutes after you hit the end of the warranty period. Often, too, a problem starts to surface while the car is still under warranty and a dealer makes inadequate repairs that last scarcely longer than the remainder of the warranty term. When the same problem develops again after the warranty has run out, the dealer refuses to fix it.

Not long ago I saw a case involving this sort of problem. A man—let's call him Bruno—with a new, expensive European car was suing the local dealer and the parent car company's West Coast representative. Bruno claimed that he had repeatedly brought the car into the dealer's repair shop with transmission problems while it was still under written warranty. Each time adjustments were made that seemed to eliminate the problem. But each time, after a month or so, the same problem would reappear. A few months after the written warranty ran out, the transmission died. Even though the car was only a little over a year old, and had gone less than 20,000 miles, both the dealer and the parent car company refused to repair it. Their refusals continued even though the owner repeatedly wrote them, demanding action.

How did Bruno go about dealing with his problem? First, because he needed his car, he went ahead and had the repairs made. Then, although the repairs cost slightly in excess of the Small Claims limit, he decided that because it was too expensive to hire a lawyer and sue in a formal court, he would scale down his claim and sue for the Small Claims maximum. Because the dealer was located in the same city as Bruno was, he sued locally. In this situation, it would have been adequate to sue only the local dealer and not the car company, but it didn't hurt to sue both, following the general rule, "When in doubt, sue all possible defendants."

In court, Bruno was well prepared and had a reasonably easy time. Both he and his wife testified as to their trials and tribulations with the car. They gave the judge copies of the several letters they had written the dealer, one of which was a list of the dates they had taken the car to the dealer's shop. They also produced a letter from the owner of the independent garage that finally fixed the transmission, stating that, when he took the transmission apart, he discovered a defect in its original assembly. The new car dealer simply testified that his mechanics had done their best to fix the car under the written warranty. He then contended that, once the written warranty had run out, he was no longer responsible. The dealer made no effort to challenge the car owner's story, nor did he bring his own mechanics to testify as to what they had done while the car was still under warranty. Bruno won. He presented a convincing case to the point that the defect had never been fixed when it should have been under the written warranty. The dealer did nothing to rebut it. As the judge noted to me after the hearing, an $18,000 car should come with a transmission that lasts a lot longer than this one did. Bruno would have had an even stronger case if he had brought the independent garage man to court, but the letters, along with his own testimony and that of his wife, were adequate in a situation where the dealer didn't put up much of a defense.

Document all attempts to have your vehicle repaired. In this sort of case, it can be very convincing to present to the court a list of all the trips you have made to the dealer's repair shop. You may be able to find copies of work orders you signed, or your canceled checks. If you don't have this sort of record, sit down with a calendar and do your best to make an accurate list. Give the list to the judge in court. He will accept it as true unless the car dealer disputes it.

Even if your car is no longer covered by a written warranty when trouble develops, you may have a case. When a relatively new car falls apart for no good reason, many Small Claims Court judges bend over backwards to give you protection over and above the actual written warranty period that comes with the vehicle. One reason for this is that many states have warranty laws that require that a product be reasonably fit for normal use. These laws have been interpreted to give the consumer more rights than the limited warranty that comes with the car. Thus, if the engine on your properly maintained car burns out after 25,000 miles, you will stand a good chance of recovering some money even if the written warranty has expired.

If your car develops problems. Particular models of cars are prone to particular problems. After a car has been in production for awhile, a pattern develops. Manufacturers are extremely sensitive to complaints in "high problem" areas and may even have issued an internal memo telling dealers to fix certain types of problems upon request. One reason for this is that they want to avoid federal government-required recalls. How can knowing this benefit you? By giving you the opportunity to pressure the company where it is most vulnerable. If your car that is no longer covered by a written warranty develops a serious problem before it should, talk to people at independent garages that specialize in repairing this model. If they tell you the problem is widespread and the company has fixed it for some persistent customers, write a demand letter to the car dealer and manufacturer. (See Chapter 6.) Mention that if your problem is not taken care of, you will sue in Small Claims Court and will subpoena all records having to do with this defect. (See Chapter 14.) This may well motivate the company to settle with you. If not, follow through on both counts.

B. Used Vehicle Dealers

Recovering from used vehicle dealers can be tricky for several reasons, unless you live in Connecticut, Massachusetts, New York or Rhode Island, where at least some used cars are covered by the lemon law. Otherwise, recovering for a defective used car can be tough unless you deal with a reputable dealer who provides an adequate written warranty.

Traditionally, unlike new vehicle dealers, who are at least somewhat dependent upon their reputation in the community for honesty, many used vehicle dealers commonly have had no positive reputation to start with and have survived by becoming experts at self-protection. Also (and don't underestimate this one), judges almost never buy used vehicles and therefore aren't normally as sympathetic to the problems used vehicle owners encounter. Chances are a judge has had a problem getting her new car fixed under a warranty, but has never bought a 10-year-old Plymouth in "tip-top shape," only to have it die two blocks after leaving Honest Al's.

The principal self-protection device employed by used vehicle dealers is the "as is" designation in the written sales contract. The salesperson may promise the moon, but when you read the fine print of the contract, you will see it clearly stated that the seller takes absolutely no responsibility for the condition of the vehicle and that it is sold "as is."

Time and again I have sat in court and heard hard luck stories like this:

"I bought the car for $1,200 two months ago. The man at Lucky Larry's told me that it had a completely reconditioned engine and transmission. I drove the car less than 400 miles and it died. I mean really died—it didn't roll over and dig itself a hole, but it may as well have. I had it towed to an independent garage and they told me that, as far as they could see, no engine or transmission work had ever been done. They estimated that to put the car right would cost $800. I got one more estimate which was even higher, so I borrowed the $800 and had the work done. I feel I really got taken by Lucky Larry. I have with me the canceled check for the $800 in repairs, plus the mechanic who did the work, who will testify as to the condition of the car when he saw it."

Unfortunately, this plaintiff will probably lose. Why? Because going back to the sort of issues we discussed in Chapter 2, Section A, he has proven only half of his case. He has shown his loss (he bought a $1,200 car that wasn't worth $1,200), but he has not dealt with the issue of the defendant's responsibility to make the loss good ("liability"). Almost surely, the used car dealer will testify that he "had no way of knowing how long a 10-year-old Plymouth would last and that, for this very reason, sold the car 'as is.'" He will then show the judge a written contract that not only has the "as is" designation, but that will say someplace in the fine print that "this written contract is the entire agreement between the parties and that no oral statements or representations made by the dealer or any salesperson are part of the contract."

How can you fight this sort of cynical semi-fraud? It's difficult to do after the fact. The time for self-protection is before you buy a vehicle, when you still have time to have it checked by an expert and can insist that any promises made by the salesperson as to the condition of the car or the availability of repairs be put in writing. Of course, good advice given after the damage has been done "isn't worth more than a passel of warm spit," as former Vice President John Nance Garner so graphically put it. If you have just been cheated on a used car deal, you want to know what, if anything, you can do now. Here are some suggestions:

- If you reside in Connecticut, Massachusetts, New York or Rhode Island, your state's lemon law applies to used as well as new cars. Check to see if your situation is covered.

- If the car broke down almost immediately after you took it out of the used car lot, you can file in Small Claims Court and argue that you were defrauded. Your theory is that, no matter what the written contract said, there was a clear implication that you purchased a car, not a junk heap. When the dealer produces the "as is" contract you signed, argue that it is no defense to fraud. I discuss fraud in more detail in Chapter 2.

- If the dealer made any promises, either in writing or orally, about the good condition of the vehicle, he may be required to live up to them. Why? Because, as noted in Chapter 2, statements about a product that you rely on as part of deciding whether to purchase may constitute an express warranty. This is true even if the seller had you sign an "as is" statement that disclaims all warranties. The key to winning this sort of case is to produce a witness to the dealer's laudatory statements about the vehicle, copies of ads that state the car is in good shape, plus anything else that will back up your story. Although not every state will let you make this argument (under the theory that the written agreement is the sum total of what applies), try making it anyway. I have seen it succeed.

- You may also want to claim an implied warranty. One type—the implied warranty of fitness—means that the vehicle is warranteed to work for a particular purpose (say consistency). The more common implied warranty is for merchantability. Here, if the car doesn't run at all, your basic claim is that because you haven't gotten a car worth anything at all, it isn't merchantable.

- You may want to consider having the car towed back to the lot and refusing to make future payments. This is a radical remedy and should only be considered in an extreme situation. It does have the beauty of shifting the burden of taking legal action to the other side, at which point you can defend on the basis of fraud. If you take this approach, be sure you have excellent documentation that the car was truly wretched. And be sure to set forth in writing the circumstances surrounding the difficulties, sending copies to the dealer and the bank or finance company to whom you pay your loan. Of course, you will probably have made some down payment, so even in this situation, you may wish to initiate action in Small Claims Court.

- Have your car checked over by someone who knows cars and will be willing to testify, if need be. If this person can find affirmative evidence you were cheated, you will greatly improve your Small Claims case. They might, for example, find that the odometer had been tampered with in violation of federal or state law, or that a heavy grade of truck oil had been put in the crankcase so the car wouldn't belch smoke. Also, this is the sort of case where a Subpoena Duces Tecum (subpoena for documents) might be of help. (See Chapter 14.) You might wish to subpoena records the car dealer has pertaining to his purchase price of the car, or its condition when purchased. It might also be helpful to learn the name of the car's former owner, with the idea of contacting him. With a little digging, you may be able to uncover information that will enable you to convince a judge that you have been defrauded.

- Consider other remedies besides Small Claims Court. These can include checking with your state Department of Consumer Affairs, or the local Department of Motor Vehicles, to see if used car lots are regulated. In many states, the Department of Motor Vehicles licenses used car dealers and can be very helpful in getting disputes resolved, particularly where your complaint is one of many against the same dealer for similar practices. Also, contact your district attorney's office. Most now have a consumer fraud division, which can be of great help. If you can convince them that what happened to you smells rotten, or your complaint happens to be against someone they have already identified as a borderline criminal, they will likely call the used car dealer in for a chat. In theory, the D.A.'s only job is to bring a criminal action, which will be of no direct aid in getting your money back, but in practice, negotiations often go on that can result in restitution. In plain words, this means that the car dealer may be told, "Look, buddy, you're right on the edge of the law here (or maybe over the edge). If you clean up your act, which means taking care of all complaints against you and seeing that there are no more, we will close your file. If you don't, I suggest you hire a good lawyer, because you are going to need one."

C. Used Vehicles From Private Parties

Normally, it is easier to win a case against a private party than a used vehicle dealer. This runs counter to both common sense and fairness, as a private party is likely to be more honest than a dealer. But fair or not, the fact is that a nondealer is usually less sophisticated in legal self-protection than is a pro. Indeed, in most private party sales, the seller does no more than sign over the title slip in exchange for the agreed-upon price. No formal contract is signed that says the buyer takes the car "as is."

If trouble develops soon after you purchase the vehicle and you are out money for unexpected repairs, you may be able to recover. Again, the problem is usually not proving your loss, but convincing the judge that the seller of the vehicle is responsible ("liable") to make your loss good. To do this, you normally must prove that the seller represented the vehicle to be in better shape than, in fact, it was, and that you relied on these promises when you made the deal.

Recently, I watched Barbara, a 20-year-old college student, succeed in proving just such a case. She sued John for $1,150, claiming that the BMW motorcycle she purchased from him was in far worse shape than he had advertised. In court, she ably and convincingly outlined her conversations with John around the purchase of the motorcycle, testifying that he repeatedly told her that the cycle was "hardly used." She hadn't gotten any of his promises in writing, but she did a creative job of developing and presenting what evidence she had. This included:

- A copy of her letter to John, which clearly outlined her position, such as the following letter.

14 Harrison St.
Moline, IL
January 27, 19___

John Malinosky
321 Adams St.
Moline, IL

Dear Mr. Malinosky:

This letter is a follow-up to our recent phone conversation in which you refused to discuss the fact that the BMW motorcycle I purchased from you on January 15 is not in the "excellent condition" that you claimed.

To review: on January 12, I saw your ad for a motorcycle that was "almost new—hardly used—excellent condition" in the local flea market newspaper. I called you and you told me that the cycle was a terrific bargain and you would never sell it except that you needed money for school. I told you I didn't know much about machinery.

The next day, you took me for a ride on the cycle. You told me specifically that:

1. The cycle had just been tuned up.

2. The cycle had been driven less than 30,000 miles.

3. The cycle had never been raced or used roughly.

4. That if anything went wrong with the cycle in the next month or two, you would see that it was fixed.

I didn't have the cycle more than a week when the brakes went out. When I had them checked, the mechanic told me that the carburetor also needed work (I confirmed this with another mechanic—see attached estimate). The mechanic also told me that the cycle had been driven at least 75,000 miles (perhaps a lot more) and that it needed a tune-up. In addition, he showed me caked mud and scratches under the cycle frame, which indicated to him that it had been driven extensively off the road in rough terrain and had probably been raced on dirt tracks.

The low mechanic's estimate to do the repairs was $1,150. Before having the work done, I called you to explain the situation and to give you a chance to arrange for the repairs to be made, or to make them yourself. You laughed at me and said, "Sister, do what you need to do—you're not getting dime one from me."

Again, I respectfully request that you make good on the promises (express warranty) you made to me on January 15. I relied on the truth of your statements (express warranty) when I decided to buy the bike. I enclose a copy of the mechanic's bill for $1,150, along with several higher estimates that I received from other repair shops.

Sincerely,

Barbara Parker

- Copies of repair bills (and three estimates) dated within two weeks of her purchase of the cycle, the lowest of which came to $1,150.
- A copy of John's newspaper ad that she answered. It read: "BMW 500, almost new—hardly used—excellent condition—$3,500."
- Finally, Barbara presented the judge with this note from the mechanic who fixed the cycle.

To Whom It May Concern:

   It's hard for me to get off work, but if you need me, please ask the judge to delay the case a few days. All I have to say is this: the BMW that Barbara Parker brought to me was in *fair* shape. It's impossible to be exact, but I guess that it had been driven at least 75,000 miles, and I can say for sure that it was driven a lot of miles on dirt.

                                            Respectfully submitted,

                                            Al "Honker" Green

                                            February 3, 19__

   Barbara quickly outlined the whole story for the judge and emphasized that she had saved for six months to get the money to make the purchase. True, testimony about financial hardship isn't relevant, but it never hurts. As an old appeals court judge who had seen at least 75 summers told me when I graduated from law school and was proud of my technical mastery of the law, "Son, don't worry about the law—just convince the judge that truth and virtue are on your side and he will find some legal technicality to support you." No one ever gave me better advice.

   Next, John had his turn. He helped Barbara make her case by acting like a weasel. His testimony consisted mostly of a lot of vague philosophy about machinery. He kept asking, "How could I know just when it would break?" When the judge asked him specific questions about the age, condition and previous history of the cycle, he clammed up as if he was a mafioso called to testify by a Senate anti-racketeering committee. When the judge asked him if he had, in fact, made specific guarantees about the condition of the bike, John began a long explanation about how, when you sell things, you "puff them up a little," and that "women shouldn't be allowed to drive motorcycles anyway." Finally, the judge asked him to please sit down.

Bring witnesses or witness statements when possible. In this type of case, absent a written warranty such as an ad that states the vehicle is in great shape, it's often one person's word against another's. Any shred of tangible evidence that the seller has made an express verbal warranty as to the condition of the goods can be enough to shift the balance to that side. Of course, if you have a friend who witnessed or heard any part of the transaction, his or her testimony will be extremely valuable. Getting a mechanic to check over a vehicle and then testify for you is also a good strategy. Sometimes you can get some help from publications such as Blue Books that list wholesale and retail prices for used cars. Several times I have seen people bring Blue Books (car dealers have them) into court and show the judge that they paid above the Blue Book price for a used car "because the car was represented to be in extra good shape." This doesn't constitute much in the way of real proof that you were ripped off, but it is helpful to at least show the judge that you paid a premium price for unsound goods. ■

Bad Debts: Initiating and Defending Cases in Which Money Is Owed

A. Is Small Claims Court a Good Place to Sue on Bad Debts?

Well over 60% of Small Claims cases involve a claim that the defendant has improperly failed to pay the plaintiff a sum of money. Usually this means a bill for goods or services hasn't been paid, but it also can involve failure to pay a promissory note (for example, a loan from a friend or relative), or even a civil fine for something as simple as the failure to return a library book. In over 90% of these cases, the plaintiff wins (often because the defendant defaults), making Small Claims Court potentially a very effective part of any business's bill collection strategy. But paradoxically, Small Claims Court can also work well for a defendant who believes that no money is owed or that the plaintiff is asking for too much and, as a result, puts up a spirited defense. Unlike formal court, in Small Claims, a defendant has to jump through few, if any, procedural hoops to show up and present her side of the story.

Some business people, and especially professionals such as doctors, dentists and lawyers, don't use Small Claims Court to collect unpaid bills because they think it takes too much time, or is "undignified." You will have to worry about your "dignity" yourself, but realize that Small Claims Court actions can be handled with very little time and expense once you get the hang of it. And in many states, the job of actually appearing in court can be delegated. By contrast, business people who don't use Small Claims Court as part of a self-help debt collection strategy must normally either write off the loss or turn the bill over to a collection agency.

Probably no aspect of Small Claims Court practice varies more from state to state than who can sue to collect unpaid bills. As listed in the state-by-state Appendix, some states:

* allow bill collectors to use Small Claims Court
* ban bill collectors but let lawyers carry out much the same task, by representing multiple creditors
* ban both bill collectors and lawyers, allowing only businesses, themselves, to sue.

And even among the states where businesses can't hire third parties but must represent themselves to sue on bad debt claims, there are important differences. For example, a few states entirely prohibit corporations from suing in Small Claims Court while others make it difficult for unincorporated businesses to send anyone but an owner or partner to court. By contrast, most states allow corporations to sue and make it reasonably easy for both incorporated and unincorporated businesses to designate a bookkeeper or other employee to handle court appearances. (See Chapter 7 for more on who can sue in Small Claims Court.)

After first checking the summary of rules in the Appendix, if you are still interested in using Small Claims Court to collect unpaid bills, contact your Small Claims Court clerk and find out exactly what rules govern bill collection activities in your state. Then talk to other small business people (or business associations, such as the Chamber of Commerce) to learn practical strategies to cope with any rules that hinder using Small Claims as part of a cost-efficient bill collection strategy. Also, if you are in a state where bill collectors or lawyers do Small Claims collection work, you will want to find out how much they charge and how efficient they are, and then compare this to the time and energy it would take for you to do it yourself. Chances are you'll find that, since bill collectors and lawyers typically charge from 30% to 50% of any money they collect, there is plenty of opportunity to do this work cheaper yourself.

A bookkeeper or other representative is often, but not always, a good choice to appear in Small Claims Court. In many states a business owner does not have to appear in court herself, but can send an employee. Where money is owed, a bookkeeper or financial manager is normally a good choice, since she can testify that a valid contract existed and the defendant has not paid the promised amount. However, if the defendant shows up and defends on the basis that the goods or services were defective, delivered late or were otherwise not acceptable, the bookkeeper is likely to be at a serious disadvantage, since she probably has no firsthand knowledge of anything except that the check was not in the mail. For example, if you own a graphics business and are suing on an unpaid bill in a situation where you expect the defendant may show up in court and falsely claim you did lousy work, you will obviously need to have someone in court who knows the details of the particular job. Typically, this should be the employee(s) who dealt with the customer and did the work.

B. Bad Debt Cases From the Plaintiff's Point of View

The job of the plaintiff in a case where he or she is suing for nonpayment of a debt is usually easy, since in the majority of cases, the debtor doesn't show up (defaults, in legalese). In the absence of a defendant, the plaintiff need only prove that a valid debt exists and it has not been paid. With no opposition, in a few Small Claims Courts this is done by showing your documentation to the court clerk who enters the default order. But in most courts the plaintiff must make a very brief court presentation, showing the judge proof of the debt in the form of a contract, work order, promissory note or purchase order signed by the defendant. At this point, the court will issue a judgment—which, of course, is necessary if you wish to collect from a debtor who refuses to pay voluntarily. Here are a few suggestions.

1. Don't Bother Suing on Some Types of Debts

Although using Small Claims Court as part of your debt collection process often makes sense, there are exceptions. Here are the principal ones:

* **When there isn't enough money at stake.** For disputes involving a few hundred dollars or less, your costs of filing, preparing and presenting a Small Claims case are likely to be unacceptably high relative to what you are likely to receive. This is doubly true if you doubt whether a court judgment will be collectible.

* **When the defendant is a deadbeat.** As discussed in more detail in Chapter 3, most court judgments are fairly easy to collect, because the defendant has a job, bank account, investments or real property. However, it's also true that some people are judgment proof and are likely to stay that way. Although probably making up only between 10%–20% of the U.S. population, people who have so little money or property that they can effectively thumb their noses at creditors undoubtedly run up a disproportionate share of bad debts. One thing is sure—as a sensible business person, you don't want to spend your time and energy chasing people who are never likely to have enough money to pay you. If the person who owes you

money has no job or property—and no prospects of getting either soon—your best bet is to write off the debt and tighten up your credit-granting procedures. (See Chapter 3, "Can You Recover If You Win?")

- **When you want to get along with the person in the future.** Any court action, even a Small Claims case, tends to polarize disputes and risks deepening enmities. This isn't a problem when dealing with people or businesses you don't plan to have future contact with. But in other circumstances, such as a situation where a former friend or local business owes you money, it's possible that your ongoing relationship with a debtor may be more important than collecting all that you are owed. In these situations, you may sensibly try to minimize conflict by trying to work out your dispute through mediation. (See Chapter 6, Section B.)

Extra damages for bad checks: Every business is stuck with a rubber check now and then. Until recently, it usually didn't pay to take a bad check writer to court, especially for smaller checks. Today, many states permit a person holding a bad check to obtain a judgment for a specified amount of money in damages in addition to the amount of the check. I discuss how to take advantage of these laws in Chapter 4, Section C1(b), "Extra Damages for Bad Checks."

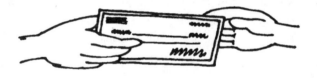

2. Ask for Your Money Before You Sue

In Chapter 6, I discuss techniques to settle your case without going to court, including writing an effective letter demanding your payment. Because this will result in payment in a significant number of cases, you should always do this before filing in Small Claims Court. Unfortunately, many businesses rely on fill-in-the-blanks past due notices and dun letters purchased from commercial sources. While these may be better than nothing, it's much better to write your own, more personal, demand letter (see the sample in Chapter 6) and modify it slightly to fit the circumstances. But realize that whenever you are demanding payment of a bill, a number of laws protect debtors from overzealous creditors. For do's and don'ts in collecting bills, see *The Legal Guide for Starting and Running a Small Business,* by Fred Steingold (Nolo Press).

Plan in advance to counter any claim that your bill wasn't paid for a good reason. If you provide goods or services, it's wise to include a statement on all your bills and collection letters requesting that the debtor notify you if the goods are defective or services substandard. Bring copies of these notices to court. Then, if the debtor shows up and, for the first time, claims he didn't pay you because of some problem or defect, you can show the judge that you consistently asked to be informed about any problems with your product or service. The fact that, in most instances, no complaints were previously made will normally go far toward convincing the judge that the defendant is fabricating, or at least exaggerating, his current complaint in an effort to avoid paying you.

3. It Pays to Bring Debt Collection Cases Promptly

For maximum success in collecting on bad debts, file suit as soon as you conclude that informal collection methods are unlikely to work. For starters, you'll be pleasantly surprised that a small but significant number of debtors will quickly pay up—or call you to work out a payment plan—to avoid having a court judgment appear in their credit records. But fast action is also advisable for other reasons, the most important being that people who owe you money are likely to have other debts as well, and may be considering bankruptcy. The quicker you act, the faster you'll get a judgment and be eligible to start collection activities, such as a wage garnishment or property attachment.

In addition, if you file promptly, you will avoid having to worry about whether you are within the legal filing deadline, called the "statute of limitations." Depending on the state and the type of debt, this can be anywhere from one to four years. (You will find a discussion of the statutes of limitations applicable to different sorts of debts in Chapter 5.) Even when there is no danger that your period in which to file will run out, it makes sense to get to court as soon as reasonably possible. One good reason for this advice is that judges tend to be skeptical of old claims. For example, several times when I served as a pro tem (temporary) judge, I wondered why someone waited three years to sue for $500. Was it because she wasn't honestly convinced that her suit was valid? Was it because she and the defendant got into a spat about something else and she was trying to get even? In one case, my curiosity caused me to ask the plaintiff several questions about a four-year-old debt for car repairs. When the plaintiff's answers weren't satisfactory, I dismissed the case, even though the defendant hadn't bothered to show up.

4. Special Rules Apply to Installment Debts

If you lend money or sell an item with payments to be made in installments, and a payment is missed, you normally are only entitled to sue for the amount of the missed payment, not the whole debt. Before you can sue for the entire amount, you must wait until all payments are missed. But there is a major exception to this rule: You can immediately sue for 100% of the debt—plus any interest—if your contract contains an "acceleration clause." This is legal jargon stating that if one payment is missed, the whole debt is due. Read any written installment contract carefully.

5. Written Contracts—Bring Documentation to Court

Most debts are based on a written contract. This may be a purchase order, credit agreement, lease or formal contract. It normally makes no difference what your document is called, as long as you have something in writing with the defendant's signature.

A few courts require that a copy of a purchase contract, signed work order or any other written evidence of indebtedness be submitted at the same time your action is filed. (Check your local rules.) In most states, however, there is no need to file anything in advance. Simply bring your written documentation to court on the day your case is heard, both as proof of the debt and so that, in some states, the court can mark it canceled when a judgment in your favor is entered. Also, bring any ledger sheets, computer printouts or other business records documenting any payments that have been missed.

Take your responsibility to be organized seriously. Often I have seen otherwise sensible-looking business people show up with botched records and become flustered when closely questioned by the judge. The courtroom is not the place to straighten out a poor accounting system.

6. How to Prove Debts Covered by Oral Contracts

Generally, a debt based on an oral contract is legal as long as the contract was (or could have been) carried out in one year, is not for the sale of real estate or for goods (personal property) worth more than $500. (See Chapter 22 for more on written documentation rules for the sale of goods.) Of course, you may face a problem proving that the debt exists if the defendant denies that he borrowed the money or bought the goods or services. Your best bet is to attempt to come up with some written documentation that your version of what occurred is true. For example, even if there is no written agreement, the defendant may have written you a down payment check or a letter asking for more time to pay. Either would be a huge help in convincing the judge that a debt exists. If you can't come up with anything in writing, try to think of a person who has firsthand knowledge of the debt and who is willing to testify. For example, if you asked the defendant to pay you and he said in the presence of a friend, "I know I owe you $1,000. I'll pay you next month," or even, "Too bad you will never get your money back," or anything similar to indicate that a loan existed, bring your friend as a witness.

Unfortunately, in many situations, there is no direct written or verbal evidence sufficient to prove the existence of a contract. If so, you will have to try to establish the existence of the contract by reference to the conduct of the parties. In law school, this is referred to as establishing the existence of an "implied contract." It is easiest to do this when one person provides services in a commercial context and the other accepts them.

Example: Jane is a commercial illustrator who works as a freelancer for a variety of ad agencies, publishers and other clients. One day she got a call from Harold, a dress designer, asking her to do a series of drawings of his new line of evening wear. Jane did the drawings and submitted her bill for $2,000. Harold refused to pay, alternately claiming that payment was conditional on the drawings being published in a fashion magazine (they weren't) and that Jane was charging too much. Jane filed in Small Claims Court. The judge had no trouble finding the existence of an oral contract based on Harold's admission that he asked Jane to do the work. However, the judge only awarded Jane $1,400, because she could not document her claim that she was to be paid $100 an hour, and Harold made a convincing presentation that illustrators usually charge no more than $70 per hour. (Also see Chapter 2, Section C, for more on oral and implied contracts.)

C. Bad Debt Cases From the Debtor's Point of View

While there are an increasing number of ordinary folks using Small Claims Court, the majority of plaintiffs are business people or employees of government entities trying to collect debts. Over 20 years ago, when I first observed debt collection cases, I did so with scant attention. I assumed that individuals being pursued by businesses were likely to lose, especially since I guessed they mostly did owe the money. I even wondered why a lot of folks bothered to show up—knowing in advance they had no realistic defense.

But then a curious thing happened. As I sat in on more Small Claims Court sessions, I saw that many debtors refused to play the stereotyped deadbeat role I had assigned them. Instead of shuffling in with heads down, saying "I'm short of money right now," they often presented well-thought-out, convincing defenses, with the result that the judge reduced or sometimes even eliminated the debt. I had learned something very valuable—people who owe money can fairly often have the amount reduced, and sometimes win an outright victory. This conclusion has been corroborated by a prominent study of Small Claims Court cases, which concludes that when a defendant shows up to contest a case, the plaintiff's chance of winning 100% of the amount asked for declines substantially ("Small Claims and Traffic Courts," by John Goerdt (National Center for State Courts)). In fact, defendants win outright in 26% of debt cases and pay half or less of what the plaintiff asked for in an additional 20%.

Here are some examples of cases in which defendants succeeded in whole or part:

- A local hospital sued an unemployed man for failure to pay an emergency room bill for $478. It seemed an open-and-shut case—the person from the hospital had all the proper records, and the defendant hadn't paid. Then the defendant told his side of it. He was taken to the emergency room suffering from a superficial but painful gunshot wound. Because it was a busy night and he was not about to die, he was kept waiting four hours for treatment. When treatment was given, it was minimal, and he suffered later complications that might have been avoided if he had been treated more promptly and thoroughly. He said he didn't mind paying a fair amount, but that he didn't feel he got $478 worth of care in the 20 minutes the doctor spent with him. The judge agreed and awarded judgment to the hospital for $150, plus court and service of process costs. After the defendant explained that he had only his unemployment check, the judge took advantage of a state law that allowed time payments and ordered that he pay the judgment at the rate of $10 per month.

- A large local tire retailer sued a woman for not paying the balance on a tire bill. She had purchased eight light truck tires manufactured by a major tire company and still owed $512. The tire company presented the judge with the original copy of a written contract, along with the woman's deficient payment record, and then waited for judgment. It is still waiting. The woman, who ran a small neighborhood gardening and landscaping business, produced several advertising flyers from the tire company that strongly implied that the tires would last at least 40,000 miles. She then testified and presented a witness to the fact that the tires had gone less than 25,000 miles before wearing out. The defendant also had copies of four letters written over the past year to the headquarters of the tire company in the

Midwest complaining about the tires. Both in the letters, and in court, she repeatedly stated that the salesperson at the tire company told her several times that the tires were guaranteed for 40,000 miles. Putting this all together, the judge declared the total price of the tires should be pro-rated on the basis of 25,000 miles and, after figuring what the defendant had already paid, gave the tire company a judgment for only $150. The woman wrote out a check on the spot and departed feeling vindicated.

- A rug company sued a customer for $686 and produced all the necessary documentation showing that the carpet had been installed and that no payment had been received. The defendant testified that the rug had been poorly installed, with a seam running down the center of the room. He brought photographs that left little doubt that the rug installer was either drunk, blind or both. The defendant also presented drawings that illustrated that there were obviously several better ways to cut the carpet to fit the room. The rug company received nothing.

The point of these examples is not the facts of the individual situations—yours will surely differ—but to say that if you feel goods or services you received were worth less than the amount for which you are being sued, there are several possible defenses, and it often makes good sense to fight back.

1. Kinds of Common Defenses

As discussed in more detail in Chapter 2, defenses can include:

- *Breach of contract:* The other party failed to live up to (perform) the terms of the agreed-upon act within the correct period of time. For example, you contracted to have your kitchen counter remodeled using white ceramic tile, and ended up with beige plastic tile. Or, you hired a florist to provide fresh flower arrangements for a party and the flowers arrived half dead, and six hours late.

> ⚠️ **Trivial defects won't void a contract.** To succeed with a breach of contract defense, you must show that the breach was material—that it prevented you from receiving all or a substantial amount of the product (or benefit) you entered into the contract to obtain. For example, if you order light yellow flowers for a wedding, and cream-colored flowers are delivered, you can be pretty sure the judge will decide in favor of the plaintiff if you are sued for failure to pay your bill. By contrast, if you had ordered yellow flowers and received dark red ones, which clashed with your color scheme, your chances of winning would be much better.

- *Fraud:* The other party intentionally lied to you about a key fact in a transaction. For example, you buy a used car from a car lot with 25,000 miles on the odometer. Later, you meet the first owner who says it went 100,000 miles and that the odometer had reflected that when he sold it to the lot.

- *Breach of warranty:* An express written or implied warranty (assurance) made by the seller of goods turned out to be bogus. For example, a roofer claims in writing that your new roof will last five years. In fact, it leaks in the first big storm.

- *Violation of statute:* Many federal and state laws require the seller of a particular type of goods or service to comply with certain rules. For example, the Federal Trade Commission provides that a seller of door-to-door goods and services for more than $25 must give you notice of your right to cancel within three days, along with a cancellation form. If he fails to do so, your right to cancel continues forever.

2. Evidence to Defend Your Case

To successfully defend a suit claiming you owe money, you'll normally need to document a very good reason why you were dissatisfied with the goods or services you received. Sorry, but this means you'll normally need to do more than tell the judge a sad story. If shoddy goods are involved, show them to the judge, or bring a picture or written report from an expert. (See Chapter 14, Section D.) If you received truly bad service, bring a witness (see Chapter 14) or other supporting evidence to court. For example, suppose the new paint on your recently refinished boat immediately began to chip and peel and, as a result, you notified the boat yard that you would not pay for the job. In case you are later sued, you will want to take pictures clearly showing the problem, and get a written opinion from another boat refinisher stating the work was substandard, as well as an estimate to fix or redo the job.

3. Appearing in Court

There is often a tactical advantage for the debtor in the fact that the person who appears in court on behalf of the creditor is not the same person with whom he had dealings. If, for example, you state that a salesperson told you X, Y and Z, that person probably won't be present to state otherwise. This may tilt a closely balanced case to you. It is perfectly appropriate for you to point out to the judge that your opponent has only books and ledgers, not firsthand knowledge of the situation. The judge may sometimes delay (continue) the case until another day to allow the creditor to have whatever employee(s) you dealt with present, but often this is impossible because the employee in question will have left the job, or will be otherwise unavailable.

You can ask the judge for a little more time to pay. In California, the District of Columbia, New York, Rhode Island, Washington and in many other areas, the judge has considerable discretion to order that a judgment be paid in installments. Thus, if you lose your case in whole or part, the judge can allow you to pay it off in small monthly installments, instead of all at once. Time payments can be particularly helpful if you really can't come up with all the money at once, thereby preventing the creditor from initiating a wage attachment or other intrusive collection activity. Don't be afraid to ask the judge for time payments—he or she won't know that you want them if you don't ask for them. ■

Vehicle Accident Cases

It is a rare Small Claims Court session that does not include at least one fender bender. Often these cases are badly prepared and presented. The judge commonly makes a decision at least partially by guess. I know from personal experience when I sat as a "pro tem" judge that it sometimes wouldn't take much additional evidence for me to completely reverse a decision.

The average vehicle accident case that ends up in Small Claims Court doesn't involve personal injury, but is concerned with damage to one, or both, parties' car, cycle, RV, moped or whatever. Because of some quirk of character that seems to be deeply embedded in our overgrown monkey brains, it is almost impossible for most of us to admit that we are bad drivers, or were at fault in a car accident. We will cheerfully acknowledge that we aren't terrific looking or geniuses, but we all believe that we drive like angels. Out of fantasies such as these are lawsuits made.

In Chapter 2, I discuss the concept of negligence. Please reread this material. Except in states that follow no-fault rules (see below), to recover in a vehicle accident case you have to either prove that the other person was negligent and you were driving safely or, if both of you were negligent, that you were less so. Normally, dealing with concepts of negligence in a vehicle accident is a matter of common sense; you probably have a fairly good idea of the rules of the road and whether you or the other driver screwed up. One key is often whether either you or the other party was cited for breaking a law having to do with highway safety (see Section D, below). When a safety-related law is broken, negligence is usually presumed.

File personal injury cases in formal court. Cases involving all but very minor personal injuries don't belong in Small Claims Court, as they will involve claims for far more money than the Small Claims maximum. And in states that have no-fault insurance, personal injury cases may not be allowed in court at all unless you've first complied with the requirements of your state's no-fault insurance law.

Check rules in no-fault states. States with no-fault insurance laws generally require that auto accident disputes—especially those involving less serious injuries—be submitted to the no-fault administrative system, not to court. Check your state's rules.

A. Who Can Sue Whom?

The owner of a vehicle is the person who should file a claim for damage done to the vehicle, even if he wasn't driving when the damage occurred. Your lawsuit should be brought against the negligent driver, and if the driver is not also the registered owner, you should also sue the owner. To find out who owns a car, contact the Department of Motor Vehicles. As long as you can tell them the license number, they can tell you the registered owner. (Some states require that you provide a good reason in order to get this information—telling them you are filing a lawsuit based on a vehicle accident should do it.)

B. Was There a Witness to the Accident?

Because the judge has no way of knowing what happened unless one or more people tell her, a good witness can make or break your case. It is better to have a disinterested witness than a close friend or family member, but any witness is better than no witness. If the other guy is likely to have a witness who supports his point of view (even though it's wrong) and you have none, you will have to work extra hard to develop other evidence to overcome this disadvantage. Reread Chapter 14 for more information on witnesses. If you do have an eyewitness but can't get that person to show up in court voluntarily, bring a written statement.

C. Police Accident Reports

When you have an accident and believe the other person was more at fault than you were, it is almost always wise to call the police so that a police report can be prepared. A police report is admissible as evidence in Small Claims Court in most states. The theory is that an officer investigating the circumstances of the accident at the scene is in a better position to establish the truth of what happened than is any other third party. So, if there was an accident report, buy a copy for a few dollars from the police station. If it supports you, bring it to court. If it doesn't, be prepared to refute what it says. This can best be done with the testimony of an eyewitness. If both an eyewitness and a police report are against you, try prayer.

Of course, many of you will be reading this book some considerable period of time after your accident. Obviously, my advice to call the police and have an accident report prepared will be of no use. Unfortunately, if the police are not called at the time of the accident, it's too late.

D. Determining Fault

In Chapter 2, I discussed the general concept of negligence. While that discussion is fully applicable to motor vehicle cases (go back and read it if you haven't already), negligence can also be determined in these types of cases by a showing that the other driver caused the accident (in whole or in part) as a result of a Vehicle Code violation or other similar statutory violation. For instance, if Tommy runs a red light (prohibited by state law) and hits a car crossing the intersection, Tommy is negligent (unless he can offer a sufficient excuse for his action). On the other hand, if Tommy is driving without his seatbelt on (also prohibited by most states) and has an accident, the violation cannot be said to have caused the accident and therefore can't be used to determine negligence.

If there is a police report, the reporting officer may have noted any vehicle code violations that occurred relative to the accident. The report may even conclude that a code violation caused the accident. If there is no police report, or the report does not specify any violations, you may wish to do a little research on your own. Your state's vehicle code is available in most large public libraries, all law libraries and sometimes at the Department of Motor Vehicles. You can use its index to very quickly review dozens of driving rules that may have been violated by the other driver. If you discover any violations that can fairly be said to have contributed to the accident, call them to the attention of the judge. Congratulations, you have gone far towards establishing your negligence claim.

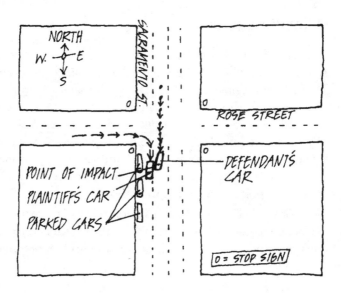

E. Diagrams

With the exception of witnesses and police accident reports, the most effective evidence is a good diagram. I have seen a good case lost because the judge never properly visualized what happened. All courtrooms have blackboards, and it is an excellent idea to draw a diagram of what happened as part of your presentation. If you are nervous about your ability to do this, you may want to prepare your diagram in advance and bring it to court. Use crayons or magic markers and draw on a large piece of paper about three feet square. Do a good job, with attention to detail. Here is a sample drawing that you might prepare to aid your testimony if you were going eastbound on Rose St. and making a right-hand turn on Sacramento St. when you were hit by a car that ran a stop sign on Sacramento. Of course, the diagram doesn't tell the whole story—you have to do that.

F. Photos

Photographs can sometimes be of aid in fender bender cases. They can serve to back up your story about how an accident occurred. For example, if you claimed that you were sideswiped while you were parked, a photo showing a long series of scratches down the side of your car would be helpful. It is also a good idea to have pictures of the defendant's car if you can manage to get them, as well as photos of the scene of the accident.

G. Estimates

In a few courts, including those in New York City, you must normally have the repairs completed and paid for before you are eligible for a Small Claims Court judgment (bring your canceled check or a receipt marked paid). But in most states you can prove your property loss by bringing estimates from repair shops to court.

It is important that you obtain several estimates for the cost of repairing your vehicle. Three is usually a good number. Be sure to get your estimates from reputable shops. If, for some reason, you get an estimate from someone you later think isn't competent, simply ignore it and get another. You have no responsibility to get your car fixed by anyone suggested to you by the person who caused the damage. Common sense normally dictates that you don't. Unfortunately, you can't recover money from the other party to cover the time you put in to get estimates, take your car to the repair shop or to appear in court.

In addition to damage to your car, you can also recover for the fair market value of anything in your car that was destroyed. You must be prepared not only to establish the fact of the damage, but the dollar amount of the loss. You can also recover for alternate transportation while your car is disabled. However, you can only recover for the minimum reasonable time it should take to get your car fixed. Thus, if you could arrange to get a fender fixed in two days, you are only entitled to rent a car for two days, even if an overworked mechanic takes four.

If you think the plaintiff's repair bill is too high. Sometimes plaintiffs dishonestly try to get already existing damage to their car fixed as part of getting the legitimate accident work done. If you think the repair bill is high, try developing your own evidence that this is so. If you have a picture of the plaintiff's car showing the damage, this can be a big help. Also, remember that the plaintiff is only entitled to get repairs made up to the total value of the car before the accident. If the car was worth only $500 and the repairs would cost $750, the plaintiff is only entitled to $500. (See Chapter 4.)

H. Your Demand Letter

Here again, as in almost every other type of Small Claims Court case, you should write a letter to your opponent with an eye to the judge reading it. See the example letters in Chapter 6. Here is another:

---

18 Channing Way
Eugene, OR
August 27, 19__

R. Rigsby Rugg
27 Miramar Crescent
Eugene, OR

Dear Mr. Rugg:

On August 15, 19__ I was driving eastbound on Rose Street in Eugene, Oregon, at about 3:30 p.m. on a sunny afternoon. I stopped at the stop sign at the corner of Rose and Sacramento and then proceeded to turn right (south) on Sacramento. As I was making my turn, I saw your car going southbound on Sacramento. You were about 20 feet north of the corner of Rose. Instead of stopping at the stop sign, you proceeded across the intersection and struck my car on the front left fender. By the time I realized that you were coming through the stop sign, there was nothing I could do to get out of your way.

As you remember, after the accident the Eugene police were called and cited you for failure to stop at a stop sign. I have gotten hold of a copy of the police report, which confirms the facts as I have stated them here.

I have obtained three estimates for the work needed on my car. The lowest is $612. I am proceeding to get this work done, as I routinely need my car in the course of my employment.

I will appreciate receiving a check from you as soon as possible. If you wish to talk about any aspect of this situation, please don't hesitate to call me, evenings, at 486–1482.

Sincerely,

Sandy McClatchy

In court, Sandy would present her case like this:

Clerk: "Next case, *McClatchy v. Rugg.* Please come forward."

Judge: "Please tell me what happened, Ms. McClatchy."

Sandy McClatchy: "Good morning. This dispute involves an auto accident that occurred at Rose and Sacramento Streets on the afternoon of August 15, 19_. I was coming uphill on Rose (that's east) and stopped at the corner. There is a four-way stop sign at the corner. I turned right, or south, on Sacramento Street, and as I was doing so, Mr. Rugg ran the stop sign on Sacramento and crashed into my front fender. Your Honor, may I use the blackboard to make a quick diagram?"

Judge: "Please do. I was about to ask you if you would."

Sandy McClatchy: (makes drawing like the one on page 19/4, points out the movement of the cars in detail and answers several questions from the judge) "Your Honor, before I sit down, I would like to give you several items of evidence. First, I have a copy of the police accident report from the Eugene police, which states that Mr. Rugg got a citation for failing to stop at the stop sign. Second, I have some photos that show the damage to the front fender of my car. Third, I have my letter to Mr. Rugg, trying to settle this case and finally I have several estimates as to the cost of repairing the damage to my car. As you can see from my canceled check, I took the lowest one."

Judge: "Thank you, Ms. McClatchy. Now, Mr. Rugg, it's your turn."

R. Rigsby Rugg: "Your Honor, my case rests on one basic fact. Ms. McClatchy was negligent because she made a wide turn into Sacramento Street. Instead of going from the right-hand lane of Rose to the right-hand, or inside lane, on Sacramento Street, she turned into the center lane on Sacramento Street. (Mr. Rugg moves to the blackboard and points out what he says happened.) Now it might be true that I made a rolling stop at the corner. You know, I really stopped, but maybe not quite all the way—but I never would have hit anybody if she had kept to her own side of the road. Also, your Honor, I would like to say this—she darted out; she has one of those little foreign cars, and instead of easing out slow, like I do with my Lincoln, she jumped out like a rabbit being chased by a red fox."

Judge: "Do you have anything else to say, Ms. McClatchy?"

Sandy McClatchy: "I am not going to even try to argue about whether Mr. Rugg can be rolling and stopped at the same time. I think the policeman who cited him answered that question. I want to answer his point about my turning into the center lane on Sacramento St., instead of the inside lane. It is true that, after stopping, I had to make a slightly wider turn than usual. If you will look again at the diagram I drew, you will see that a car was parked almost to the corner of Sacramento and Rose on Sacramento. To get around this car, I had to drive a little farther into Sacramento before starting my turn than would have been necessary otherwise. I didn't turn into the center lane, but as I made the turn, my outside fender crossed into the center lane slightly. This is when Mr. Rugg hit me. I feel that since I had the right of way and I had to do what I did to make the turn, I wasn't negligent."

Judge: "Thank you both—you will get my decision in the mail."

(The judge decided in favor of Sandy McClatchy and awarded her $612 plus service of process and filing costs.)

Don't assume you will lose if you were partially at fault. You can win, or partially win, a case involving negligence in most states, even if you were not completely in the right. If the other person was more at fault than you were, you have a case. This concept of "comparative" negligence is a new one in many states. It used to be that if you were even a little at fault, you couldn't recover because of a legal doctrine known as "contributory negligence."

Professional drivers have added incentive to lie. Be particularly wary when you are opposing a bus or truck driver. Many of these people suffer problems on their jobs if they are found to be at fault in too many accidents. As a result, they deny fault almost automatically. Judges usually know this and are often unsympathetic when a bus driver says that there has never been a time when he "didn't look both ways twice, count to 10 and say the Lord's Prayer" before pulling out from a bus stop. Still, it never hurts to question the driver in court as to whether his employer has any demerit system or other penalty for being at fault in an accident. ■

CHAPTER

20

Landlord-Tenant Cases

In most states, Small Claims Court can be used by a tenant to sue for money damages for such things as the failure of a landlord to return a cleaning or damage deposit, invasion of the tenant's privacy by the landlord, the landlord's violation of his duty to provide habitable premises and rent control violations, to name but a few. Similarly, a landlord can use Small Claims Court to sue a tenant or former tenant for damage done to the rental property and for failure to pay rent. In some states, it is also possible for a landlord to use Small Claims Court to evict a tenant. (See Appendix for state-by-state information.) This is an exception to the general rule that only money damage cases can be handed down by Small Claims Court.

Practically, it makes great sense to use Small Claims Court for money damage cases, and sometimes less sense, in many states, to use it for evictions. Why? Because, Small Claims Court rules, even in those states where evictions are allowed, tend to limit a landlord's rights when it comes to getting the tenant out in the minimum time and getting a judgment for the maximum amount of rent and other damages. In a few states, a Small Claims defendant even has an automatic right to appeal the eviction judgment and to remain living in the rental unit while the appeal is pending, even though no rent is paid.

So before you bring an eviction action in Small Claims Court, check out the answers to the following questions in your state rules:

- If you win an eviction order, can you get the sheriff or marshal to enforce it immediately?
- If the defendant appeals, can he or she stay in the dwelling while the appeal is pending?
- Can you sue for enough damages to fully or at least mostly cover your legitimate claim for back rent and damages to the premises?
- If the defendant can stay in the dwelling during an appeal, is there a requirement that he or she must post some money in the form of a bond that will go to you to cover lost rent if the appeal fails?

A. Deposit Cases

The most common landlord-tenant disputes concern the failure of a landlord to return a tenant's cleaning and damage deposits after the tenant moves out. These days, deposits can add up to many hundreds of dollars, and tenants understandably want them returned.

Going to court if a landlord refuses to return a deposit can be easy or difficult, depending upon both the facts of the situation and on how much homework a tenant has done in advance of filing suit. Many landlords are experienced with Small Claims proceedings and come to court prepared with a long list of damaged and dirty conditions they claim the tenant left behind. All too often, the landlord's presentation leaves the tenant sputtering with righteous indignation. Unfortunately, evidence, not indignation, wins cases. Think about it—if the tenant testifies the apartment was clean, and the landlord that it was dirty, the judge (unless he is psychic) is stuck making a decision that is little more than a guess. Faced with this sort of situation, most judges will split the difference.

How should a tenant prepare a case involving failure to return deposits? Ideally, preparation should start when he moves in. Any damage or dirty conditions should be noted as part of the lease or rental agreement. The tenant should also take photographs of substandard conditions and have neighbors or friends look the place over. When the tenant moves out and cleans up, he should do much the same thing—take photos, have friends check the place over, keep receipts for cleaning materials, try to get the landlord to agree that it's in satisfactory condition.

In most states, it is up to the landlord to prove that dirty or damaged conditions exist that justify the landlord keeping all or part of a deposit. Often state law also provides that if a deposit is not returned within a short time after the tenant moves out (usually somewhere between 14 and 30 days, depending on the state), and if the landlord acted in bad faith in retaining the deposit, the tenant may be entitled to extra ("punitive") damages over and above the actual amount of the withheld deposit. Whether or not the tenant actually gets these extra damages is a matter of judicial discretion, but after checking your state's rule, it never hurts to bring your Small Claims suit for an amount large enough to allow you to recover any extra damages.

Now let's assume you are a tenant and have not gotten $600 in cleaning and damage deposits returned even though you moved out of an apartment three weeks ago, having paid all your rent and having given proper notice. Start by writing the landlord a letter like this:

750 Lampost Lane
Costa Mesa, CA
October 15, 19___

Anderson Realty Co.
10 Rose St.
Costa Mesa, California

Dear People:

As you know, until September 30, 19_, I resided in apartment #4 at 300 Oak Street in Costa Mesa and regularly paid my rent to your office. When I moved out, I left the unit cleaner than it was when I moved in.

As of today, I have received neither my $300 cleaning deposit nor my $300 damage deposit. Indeed, I have never received any accounting from you for any of my money. Please be aware that I know my rights under California Civil Code 1950.5 and that, if I do not receive my money within the next week, I will regard the retention of these deposits as showing "bad faith" on your part and shall sue you, not only for the $600 deposit, but also for the $200 punitive damages allowed by Section 1950.5 of the California Civil Code.

Hoping to hear from you soon.

Sincerely,

Farah Shields

If you get no satisfactory response, file your case. Sometimes it is hard to know whom to sue, since rent is often paid to a manager or other agent instead of the owner. In most states, multiple occupancy buildings with two or more units must have ownership information posted on the premises, or list the name of the owner (or his agent for purposes of suit) on the rental agreement. If you are in doubt as to who owns your unit, you are probably safe if you sue both the person to whom you pay your rent, and the person who signed the rental agreement, unless you have received notice that the building has been transferred to a new owner, in which case you would sue that person.

On court day, a well-prepared tenant would show up in court with as many of the following pieces of evidence as possible:

- Photos of the apartment on moving in, which show any dirt or damage that already existed.
- Photos of the apartment on moving out, which show clean conditions.
- Receipts for cleaning supplies used in the final clean-up.
- A copy of your written lease or rental agreement, if any.
- A copy of a demand letter to the landlord, such as the one set out above.
- One, or preferably two, witnesses who were familiar with the property and saw it after you cleaned up, and who will testify that it was immaculate. People who helped in the clean-up are always particularly effective witnesses. If you also have a witness who saw the place when you moved in and who will say that it wasn't so clean (or damage already existed), so much the better.
- A copy of an inventory of conditions when moving in and moving out, signed by the landlord and tenant, if one was prepared.

Proceedings in court should go something like this:

Clerk: "*Shields v. Anderson Realty.* Please step forward."

Judge: "Good morning. Please tell me your version of the facts, Ms. Shields."

Farah Shields: "I moved into the apartment at 300 Oak St. in Costa Mesa, in the spring of 19__. I paid Mr. Anderson, here, my first and last months' rent, which totaled $400. I also paid him a $300 damage security deposit and a $300 cleaning deposit.

"When I moved into #4 at 300 Oak, it was a mess. It's a nice little apartment, but the people who lived there before me were sloppy. The stove was filthy, as was the bathroom, the refrigerator, the floors and just about everything else. In addition, the walls hadn't been painted in years. But I needed a place and this was the best available, so I moved in despite the mess. I painted the whole place—everything. Mr. Anderson's office gave me the paint, but I did all of the work. And I cleaned the place thoroughly, too. It took me three days. I like to live in a clean place.

"Here are some pictures of what the place looked like when I moved in *(hands photos to clerk, who gives them to the judge)*. Here is a second set of photos that were taken after I moved out and cleaned up *(again hands pictures to clerk)*. Your Honor, I think these pictures tell the story—the place was clean when I moved out. I also have receipts *(hands to clerk)* for cleaning supplies and a rug shampooer that I used during the clean-up. They total $18.25. I have also brought with me two people who saw the place the day I left and can tell you what it looked like."

Judge: *(looking at one of the witnesses)* "Do you have some personal knowledge of what this apartment looked like?"

John DeBono: "Yes, I helped Farah move in and move out. I simply don't understand what the landlord is fussing about. The place was a smelly mess when she moved in, and it was spotless when Farah moved out."

Judge: (*addressing the second witness*) "Do you have something to add?"

Puna Polaski: "I never saw 300 Oak when Farah moved in because I didn't know her then. But I did help her pack and clean up when she moved out. I can tell you that the windows were washed, the floor waxed and the oven cleaned, because I did it. And I can tell you that the rest of the apartment was clean too, because I saw it."

Judge: "Mr. Anderson, do you want to present your case."

Adam Anderson: "Your Honor, I am not here to argue about whether the place was clean or not. Maybe it was cleaner when Miss Shields moved out than when she moved in. The reason I withheld the deposits is that the walls were all painted odd, bright colors, and I have had to paint them all over. Here are some color pictures of the walls taken just after Miss Shields moved out. They show pink and purple walls, two of which are adorned with rainbows. And in one of the bedrooms, there were even animals painted on the walls. I ask you, your Honor, how was I going to rent that place with a purple bulldog painted on the wall? It cost me more than $300 to have the place painted over white."

Judge: (*looks at the pictures and gives up trying to keep a straight face, which is okay, as everyone in the courtroom is laughing—except Mr. Anderson*) "Let me ask a few questions. Was it true that the place needed a new coat of paint when you moved in, Ms. Shields?"

Farah Shields: "Yes."

Judge: "Do you agree, Mr. Anderson?"

Adam Anderson: "Yes, that's why my office paid her paint bills, although we never would have if we had known about that bulldog, not to mention the rainbows."

Judge: "How much did the paint cost?"

Adam Anderson: "$125."

Judge: "I normally send decisions by mail, but today I am going to explain what I have decided. First, the apartment needed repainting anyway, Mr. Anderson, so I am not going to give you any credit for paying to have the work redone. However, Ms. Shields, even though the place looked quite—shall I say, cheerful—when you moved out, Mr. Anderson does have a point, in that you went beyond what is reasonable. Therefore, I feel it's unfair to make Anderson Realty pay for paint twice. My judgment is this: The $125 for the paint that was given to Ms. Shields is subtracted from the $600 deposits. This means that Anderson Realty owes Farah Shields $475 plus $9.00 for costs."

Note: We have focused here on deposit cases from the tenant's point of view. This is because tenants are the ones who initiate this sort of case. Landlords, who commonly must defend deposit cases, should carefully read the list of evidence that is helpful in court. Often the best witness for a landlord is the new tenant who has just moved in. This person is likely to feel that the place isn't as clean as did the person who moved out.

B. Money Damage Cases—Unpaid Rent

In most states, landlords can initiate Small Claims actions to sue for unpaid rent. Often the tenant has already moved out and doesn't bother to show up in court. If this happens, the landlord wins by default. Sometimes the tenant does show up but presents no real defense and is only there to request the judge to allow him to make payments over time.

The landlord (or bookkeeper-manager, if you're in a state that allows bookkeepers to appear on behalf of business owners—see Chapter 7) should bring the lease or rental agreement to court and simply state the time periods for which rent is due but unpaid. Nothing else is required unless the tenant presents a defense, as discussed below. Sometimes a landlord will sue for three times the amount of rent owed (triple damages) under a lease or rental agreement that states he is entitled to them if the tenant fails to pay rent but stays in the rental unit. Doing this will almost guarantee that the tenant will put up a fight. In my experience, landlords are rarely awarded more than their actual out-of-pocket loss, and it makes little sense to request more.

There are several valid defenses to a suit based on a tenant's failure to pay rent. The principal one is where the tenant claims that rent was withheld because the condition of the premises was so bad that it was "uninhabitable." This amounts to the tenant saying to the landlord: "I won't pay my rent until you make essential repairs." Assuming the rental unit really does have major problems, it is legal to withhold rent for this reason in most states. In addition, in some states a tenant may pay withheld rent to a contractor and have essential repairs made directly.

The important thing for a tenant to understand, however, is that rent withholding is not legal where the landlord refuses to fix some minor defect. For rent to be legally withheld (whether or not the tenant actually hires someone to make the repairs), the problem must be sufficiently serious so as to make the home "uninhabitable," "unhealthy" or "unsafe." In addition, the landlord must have been given reasonable notice to correct the problem. Thus, a broken furnace that a landlord refuses to fix in February would qualify as a condition making a unit uninhabitable, but lack of heat in the summer probably wouldn't.

If you are involved in a rent withholding case as a tenant, your job is to prove (using pictures, witnesses, etc.) that the condition that caused you to withhold rent is indeed serious. Thus, you might call the building inspector or an electrician to testify that the wiring was in a dangerous state of decay. The landlord, of course, will probably testify that the rental unit is in fundamentally sound shape, even though there may be some minor problems. A landlord has the right to inspect the property, as long as she gives the tenant reasonable notice. In many states, 24 hours' notice is presumed by the law to be reasonable in the absence of an emergency.

Laws allowing a tenant to withhold rent when a rental unit is uninhabitable and those allowing a tenant to authorize repairs to be made using rent money not paid to the landlord are slightly different in every state. To find out more, take a look at the excellent and extensive material on these subjects in

- *Every Landlord's Legal Guide,* by Marcia Stewart & Attorneys Ralph Warner & Janet Portman (Nolo Press).
- *Every Tenant's Legal Guide,* by Attorney Janet Portman and Marcia Stewart (Nolo Press).

C. Obnoxious Behavior

Occasionally, a particular landlord or tenant can get pretty obnoxious. This is also true of plumbers, physics teachers and hair stylists, but since this chapter is about landlord-tenant disputes, we will concentrate on these folks.

From the start, there is a major difference between how landlords and tenants handle problems. This is because landlords have two advantages tenants don't have. First, they can charge deposits, and if a tenant fails to pay rent, or damages the place, a landlord can often recover her loss by subtracting the amount in question from the deposit. In addition, the landlord usually has the right to ask a tenant to move out. (If the tenant has a lease or the unit is located in a city requiring just cause for eviction, this right is restricted.) Tenants, on the other hand, have neither of these rights and, as a result, are much more likely to sue for money damages in Small Claims Court when they are seriously aggrieved.

Typically, tenants have problems with landlords who cannot stop fidgeting and fussing over their property. Smaller landlords tend to develop this problem to a greater extent than do the larger, more commercial ones. Nosy landlords are always hanging around or coming by, trying to invite themselves in to look around and generally being pests. In addition, a tenant may also run into a manager who is on a power trip.

If a landlord or manager is difficult or unpleasant to deal with, she can make a tenant's life miserable. There is no law that protects a tenant from a landlord's disagreeable personality, and, if the tenant has no lease, she is especially unprotected from all but the most outrageous invasions of privacy or trespass. However, if the landlord's conduct is truly obnoxious, courts in some states recognize that tenants have a right to sue for the intentional infliction of emotional distress. In the case of *Newby v. Alto Riviera Apts.*, 60 Cal.App.3d 288 (1976), a California court found it was necessary to prove four things in this sort of lawsuit:

1. Outrageous conduct on the part of the landlord;

2. Intention to cause, or reckless disregard of the probability of causing, emotional distress;

3. Severe emotional suffering;

4. Actual suffering or emotional distress.

D. The Landlord's Right of Entry and the Tenant's Right of Privacy

One area where tenants are easily and understandably upset is when they feel their privacy is invaded. Landlords, on the other hand, have a legal right to enter their rental units in certain situations. Sometimes a tenant's needs to be left alone and a landlord's need to enter conflict. If they do, it is extremely important that both parties understand their rights.

In California, Section 1954 of the Civil Code establishes the circumstances under which a landlord can enter his tenant's home, and Section 1953 (a)(1) provides that these circumstances cannot be expanded, or the tenant's privacy rights waived or modified, by any lease or rental agreement provision. The first thing to realize is that there are only four broad situations in which a landlord may legally enter while a tenant is still in residence. They are:

1. To deal with an emergency;

2. To make needed repairs (or assess the need for them);

3. To show the property to prospective new tenants or purchasers; and

4. When you invite the landlord in.

In most instances (emergencies and tenant invitations excepted), a landlord can enter only during "normal business hours" (9:00 a.m. to 5:00 p.m.) and then only after "reasonable notice," presumed to be 24 hours.

If a landlord does not follow these rules, a tenant's first step is to politely ask him to do so. If violations persist, a letter is in order. If this doesn't help, it is possible to sue in Small Claims Court for invasion of privacy if the landlord's conduct is persistently outrageous.

E. Evictions

In some states, it is legal to do some types of evictions (known technically as "unlawful detainer," "summary dispossess" and "forcible entry and detainer," depending on the state) in Small Claims Court. A few, including Illinois, New York and Massachusetts, even have, in their larger cities, separate "landlord-tenant" courts that amount to Small Claims Courts for this one specific purpose. Without question, landlords should have a simple and cheap way to free themselves of tenants who don't pay their rent. As noted at the beginning of this chapter, in many states, if a landlord wants to be sure to get a tenant out without ridiculous delays, an "unlawful detainer" action must be filed in formal court. Traditionally this has required the expense of a lawyer, but more and more landlords are learning to handle their own eviction actions.

In states where eviction actions are allowed in Small Claims Court, a landlord should check the rules carefully before using the court, especially those governing the tenant's right to appeal. This can be a trap for the unwary. In some states, the defendant has an automatic right to appeal, and there is no requirement that an adequate bond be posted. In this situation, a tenant's appeal can mean a long and costly delay for the landlord who is trying to get the tenant out.

When a landlord gets to Small Claims Court, he must prove that the rent was not paid and that a correct notice was properly served. Bring a copy of the notice to court and Proof of Service form filled out by the person doing the service. The fact that a tenant is suffering from some hardship, such as illness, poverty, birth of a child, etc., is not a defense to failure to pay rent. Possible tenant defenses are discussed briefly above under "Money Damage Cases—Unpaid Rent" in Section B of this chapter. In most states, these include withholding rent because one or more serious problems cause the rental property to be uninhabitable. But remember, a tenant cannot legally raise the existence of a defect for the first time on the day of the court hearing. The landlord must be given reasonable notice that a defect exists before rent is withheld or repairs are made by the tenant. ■

Miscellaneous Cases

By now you should have a clear idea of how a Small Claims case can be sensibly presented. The facts of each situation will vary, but the general approach will not. Here I will discuss a few of the common types of cases not covered in the previous few chapters. If I don't cover your situation in detail, simply make your own outline of steps to be taken, adapting to your own case the general approaches I have suggested.

A. Clothing (Alteration and Cleaning)

Several years ago, before I started attending Small Claims Court regularly, I stopped by one morning when I had a few free moments to kill before a criminal hearing. The case being argued involved an elderly German-American gentleman with a strong accent suing an equally aged Armenian-born tailor, who was also seriously uncomfortable with the English language. The dispute centered around whether a suitcoat that the tailor had made for the plaintiff should have had two or three buttons. After ten minutes of almost incomprehensible testimony, I understood little more than that the plaintiff had never owned a suit with two buttons and the tailor had never made one with three. The two men ended by standing and facing one another—each pulling a sleeve of the suitcoat and each yelling as loud as he could in his own language, apparently about how many buttons a suit ought to have. Much to their credit, the judge and bailiff just sat and smiled. What happened? I don't know. I was still actively practicing law then and had to bustle off to argue before another judge that my client thought the two pounds of marijuana he was carrying in a money belt was really oregano. You can probably guess how that argument ended.

While I have never seen another clothing case quite as colorful as that of the two-button suit, I have been consistently surprised at how often I have encountered people in Small Claims Court clutching an injured garment. We must indeed come to view our clothing as an extension of ourselves, because so many of us react with an indignation out of proportion to our monetary loss when some favorite item is damaged. I will never forget the morning I saw a particularly sour-looking fellow with neither word nor smile for anyone, including his obviously long-suffering wife, draw himself up to full height and wax poetic for five minutes about a four-year-old leather vest that a cleaner had mutilated.

Winning a significant victory in a case involving clothing is often difficult. Why? Because while the liability is often easy to prove (that is, the seamstress cut off the collar instead of the cuff), a reasonable amount of compensation for damages is difficult or impossible to establish, for the obvious reason that used clothing has little actual market value, even though it may have cost a lot to start with or may have enormous sentimental value to its owner. In theory, a court can award a plaintiff only the fair market value of the damaged clothing, not its replacement cost. But because this rule of law commonly works a severe injustice in clothing cases (a $400 suit bought last week may be worth only $100 this week), many judges tend to bend it a little in favor of the person who has suffered the loss.

They do this by allowing an amount pretty close to the original purchase price when the clothing involved was almost new, even though its fair market value for resale would be much less. Thus, the owner of a $300 dress that had been ruined by a seamstress after only one wearing might recover $250. Judges are not required to take this approach, but many do. With older clothing, I have also seen some judges take a flexible approach. They do this by making a rough estimate of the percentage of total use that remains in a garment and then awarding the plaintiff this percentage of the original purchase price. Thus, if a cleaner ruined a $300 suit that had been worn about 50 percent of its useful life, the plaintiff might recover $150.

Here are some hints:

- Bring the damaged clothing to court. It's hard for a tailor to say much in his own defense when confronted with a coat that is two sizes too big or has three sleeves.

- Be ready to prove the original purchase price with a canceled check, newspaper ad, credit card statement, etc.

- Be sure that the person you are suing (tailor, cleaner, seamstress, etc.) caused the problem. As noted in the example of the suede coat in Chapter 2, some problems that develop during cleaning or alterations may be the responsibility of the manufacturer.

Don't let the cleaner take you to the laundry! Dry cleaning shops are particularly apt to offer "proof" from "independent testing laboratories" that damage caused to your garment during cleaning wasn't their fault. You will want to ask: "How much did the cleaner pay the testing lab for the report?" "How many times had the same cleaner used the same testing lab before?" "How did the cleaner know about the testing lab?"

B. Dog-Bite Cases

Many states have dog-bite statutes that make dog owners completely liable for injuries their dogs cause—no ifs, ands or buts. Some statutes cover only injuries occurring off the owner's property. Also, some statutes cover only bites, while others apply to any injury (for example, the dog jumps on you, scratches you and knocks you over) or property damage (for example, the dog digs up your rose garden) the dog causes. See Chapter 1, Section D, "Legal Research," to find out if your state has a dog-bite statute. If it does, your task in court could be a lot easier.

If your state doesn't have a dog-bite statute, the old "common law" rule probably applies. This means you'll have to prove that the owner was aware of, or should have been aware of, the fact that the dog was vicious. So, if you're bitten by a dog and can show that the dog had snarled, snapped and lunged at people before and the owner knew about it but let her dog run free anyway, she's probably liable (unless you provoked the dog or offered the dog your hand).

Be ready to prove the extent of the injury, the location where it occurred, time off from work without compensation, doctor's bills, etc. If the dog is mean-looking, a picture will be a great help.

 Dog Law, by Attorney Mary Randolph (Nolo Press), answers common legal questions about biting, barking, leash laws, problems with veterinarians and other common dog-related problems.

C. Damage to Real Property (Land, Buildings, etc.)

There is no typical case involving damage to real property, as facts vary greatly. So instead of trying to set down general rules, let's look at a situation that happened recently to a friend of mine (let's call her Babette).

Babette owns a cinder-block building that houses two stores. One morning, when she came to work, she noticed water pouring in through the back of her building. Because the building was set into a hill, it abutted about eight feet of her uphill neighbor's land (let's call her neighbor Boris). After three days of investigation involving the use of green dye in Boris's plumbing system, it was discovered that the water came from an underground leak in Boris's sewer pipe. At this point, Babette had spent considerable effort and some money to pay helpers to get the water mopped up before it damaged anything in the stores.

Instead of fixing the leak promptly, Boris delayed for four days. All of this time, Babette and her helpers were mopping frantically. Finally, when Boris did get to work, he insisted on digging the pipe out himself, which took another four days. (A plumber with the right equipment could have done it in one.) In the middle of Boris's digging, when his yard looked as though it was being attacked by a herd of giant gophers, it rained. The water filled the holes and trenches instead of running off, as it normally would have. Much of it ran though the ground into Babette's building, bringing a pile of mud with it.

When the flood was finally over, Babette figured out her costs as follows:

First three days (before the source of the water was discovered)	$148 (for help with mopping and cleaning)
Next four days (while Boris refused to cooperate)	$188 (for help with mopping and cleaning)
Final four days (including day it rained)	$262 (for help with mopping and cleaning)
One secondhand water vacuum purchased during rain storm	$200
Her own time, valued at $8.00 per hour.	$600

Assuming that Boris is unwilling to pay Babette's costs, for what amount should she sue and how much is she likely to recover? Remembering the lessons taught in Chapter 2, before Babette can recover for her very real loss, she must show that Boris was negligent or caused her loss intentionally. Probably, she can't do this for the first three days when no one knew where the water was coming from, and it's probably impossible to show that Boris was negligent for failing to replace a pipe that, up until then, had worked fine. However, once the problem was discovered and Boris didn't take immediate steps to fix it, he was clearly negligent, and Babette can recover at least her out-of-pocket loss ($450 for her labor and $200 for the water vacuum). Can Babette also recover for the value of her own time? The answer to this question is "maybe." It would depend on the state and the judge. If Babette could show she had to close her store or take time off from a job to stem the flood, she probably could recover. If I were she, I would sue for about $1,250 ($450 for labor she paid for, $200 for the vacuum and $600 for the value of her own labor) and count on getting most of it.

D. Police Brutality—False Arrest Cases

Now and then actions against the police end up in Small Claims Court. Usually, the plaintiff is an irate citizen who has tried and failed to get an attorney to represent him in a larger suit and, as a last resort, has filed for the maximum amount his Small Claims Court will allow. Put simply, most of the people I have seen bringing this sort of case have been run out of court in a hurry. Why? Because the police and jailers have excellent legal advice and aren't afraid to lie to back each other up. The unwritten rule in any law enforcement agency is to protect your own derriere first and to protect your buddies' derrieres right after that. Police officers are not going to sit politely still and collect black marks on their service records without fighting back. Most law enforcement people have testified many times, and know how to handle themselves in court.

The reason many plaintiffs must use Small Claims Court to sue law enforcement personnel pretty much tells the story. Lawyers normally won't invest their time and money in this sort of case because they find them almost impossible to win. Does this mean I believe that people bringing false arrest, police brutality and similar types of cases are wasting their time? Balancing the trouble involved against the unlikely chance of success, I would have to say "yes." That said, let me also say I believe that lots of things that make little sense at a practical level are worthwhile at many other levels. I can't help but admire people who will fight for principle even though they have small chance of winning.

If you do sue a police officer, jailer or anyone else with a badge, be sure that you have several witnesses who will back you up and won't be intimidated into keeping their mouths shut. Never, never rely on one officer to testify against another. They simply won't do it. It may be cynical, but it is also realistic to assume that all law enforcement personnel will tell whatever lies are necessary to protect themselves and each other. This isn't always true, but it happens often enough so that you may as well be prepared for the worst. You would also be wise to spend a few dollars and talk to a lawyer who specializes in criminal cases. For a $75–$100 fee, you can probably pick up some valuable pointers on how to convince the judge that you were treated in an illegal and unreasonable way.

Sue the city or county as well as the officer. In most cases alleging police misconduct, you will want to sue the city, county or state government that employs the officer, as well as the individual involved. But remember, in most states, before you can sue a government entity, you must file an administrative claim. (See Chapter 8.)

E. Defamation (Including Libel and Slander)

In California, libel and slander cases may be brought in Small Claims Court. However, many states, among them Colorado, Connecticut, Massachusetts, Michigan, Ohio and Oklahoma, bar libel, slander and other defamation cases from Small Claims Court.

⚠ Think twice before bringing a libel or slander case. Even in states that allow defamation cases to be brought in Small Claims Court, these lawsuits are hard to win. A big reason is that it's usually tough to show that your reputation was really damaged by a false statement or article. (For example, if your brain-dead neighbor refers to you as an idiot in a flyer she circulates around the neighborhood, your reputation may not be damaged one bit.) If you wish to learn more about the many intricacies of defamation law, a good place to start is with a law student course outline on torts (a negligent or intentional "wrong" that results in damage). These are carried by all law bookstores (usually located near law schools) or from Nolo's self-help law stores (510-704-2262).

F.   Suits Against Airlines or Hotels

Because of overbooking, it is not uncommon for an airline or a hotel to refuse to honor your reservation. In some situations, this can cause considerable financial loss, especially if, as in the case of an airline bumping, you miss work or an important meeting. Airlines are not required to provide any amount of compensation; however, public goodwill and trust may move them to. Try contacting the airline's consumer complaint office. If that doesn't work, you can use Small Claims Court to try to recover. To prepare your case for Small Claims Court, do as much of the following as possible:

*   At the airline gate when you are being bumped, tell the airline you will suffer financial loss if you don't get to your destination promptly, and ask that they request other passengers to take a later flight.
*   Find out the name of the local airline manager and put him on notice that you will sue if you are bumped.
*   Note down all out-of-pocket expenses the delay causes you.
*   Compute any loss of wages, commissions or paid vacation time the delay causes.
*   Write to the airline requesting payment of your loss, and inform them you will file in Small Claims Court if they don't pay up.
*   File your case in Small Claims Court for the amount of your out-of-pocket expenses and lost business. If your claim appears reasonable, the airline may pay voluntarily or allow you to win on a default judgment. ■

CHAPTER

Disputes Between Small Businesses

More and more, people who own or manage small businesses are turning to Small Claims Court to settle business disputes with other businesses when they have been otherwise unable to negotiate or mediate an acceptable compromise. They have learned that Small Claims Court is a relatively fast and cost-efficient way to resolve intractable problems. In several states, business-friendly changes in the law are making it easier for businesses to use the court efficiently. For example, New York state has established a separate commercial Small Claims Court in Manhattan and other areas.

This chapter focuses on how to handle substantive disputes between businesses in Small Claims Court. Typically, these center on a claim that work one party contracted for was done poorly, late or not at all by the other. (Cases involving the simple failure to pay a bill are covered in Chapter 18.)

Typical small business disputes involve situations such as these:

- A dentist is furious at a dental equipment wholesaler who passed off slightly used equipment as being new.
- An architect wasn't paid for drawing preliminary plans for a small retail complex when the development failed to get financing.

- A phototypesetter refused to pay its former accountant in a dispute involving the value of the latter's services.
- A landscape designer tries to enforce a verbal agreement, which he claims allowed him to increase his fee when a client asked for changes in final plans.
- An author claims that her publisher had taken too long to publish her book.
- A client cites his lawyer's incompetence as a prime reason he paid too much to settle a case.

A. Remember That You Didn't Always Hate Your Opponent

Although the disputes set out above seem very different from one another, they all have one thing in common—in each situation, the disputants had enjoyed friendly business, and possibly personal, relationships at some time in the past. And in each case, at least part of the reason the plaintiff brought the dispute to court was that he or she was personally upset with (mad at) the other.

In short, disappointment is a significant factor driving many small business disputes. Unfortunately, feeling let down by the other party doesn't help you evaluate whether you have a good case. Nor does it help you prepare for court or collect your money should you win. In fact, aside from its value as a goad to taking action in the first place, it often gets in the way of the clear thinking necessary to make good decisions. It follows that your first job is to try to cool off your emotions. If you are having trouble doing this, enlist another small business person as your mentor. After explaining both sides of the dispute as carefully as you can, ask your mentor for a frank evaluation both of the merits of the argument and whether the dispute is serious enough to take to court.

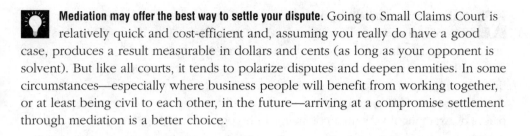 **Mediation may offer the best way to settle your dispute.** Going to Small Claims Court is relatively quick and cost-efficient and, assuming you really do have a good case, produces a result measurable in dollars and cents (as long as your opponent is solvent). But like all courts, it tends to polarize disputes and deepen enmities. In some circumstances—especially where business people will benefit from working together, or at least being civil to each other, in the future—arriving at a compromise settlement through mediation is a better choice.

B. Organizing Your Case

Small business people normally have two advantages over run-of-the-herd mortals when it comes to preparing for court. First, as a matter of course, they establish and maintain a record-keeping system. Depending on the type of business, this typically includes a good filing system to maintain bids, contracts and customer correspondence, as well as a bookkeeping system that tracks payables and receivables. Taken together, these resources normally contain considerable raw material helpful to successfully proving a Small Claims case. The second advantage is more subtle, but no less real. It involves the average small business person's organizational skill—that is, his or her ability to take a confused mess of facts and organize them into a coherent and convincing narrative. Of course, when one business person sues another, those advantages often cancel out, meaning that both sides are more likely to be well organized and prepared.

Throughout this book I talk about how to decide if you have a good case (Chapter 2) and, if so, how to prepare and present it in court (Chapters 13–15). I don't attempt to repeat this information here. Instead, I'll supplement it with material of particular interest in small business disputes.

1. Most Business Disputes Involve Contracts

The majority of business cases involve one business claiming that the other has broken a contract. (See Chapter 2, Section C, for more on contract law.) Start by taking a close look at any contract involved in your case. Specifically, ask yourself, what were your obligations and expected benefits from the deal? Similarly, what was the other person supposed to do, and how was she going to benefit?

Oral contracts are usually legal. Most oral contracts—except those that involve the sale of real estate, or involve the sale of goods (tangible property) worth $500 or more or which can't be carried out in one year—are legal and enforceable in all states if they can be proven. But when nothing has been written down, proof can be difficult, unless you can present strong indirect or circumstantial evidence that a contract existed. This is easiest to do when you did work for someone and weren't paid. For example, if you are a commercial photographer and spend a day taking pictures of a hat designer's new creations, a judge is likely to agree with your contention that, by implication, you wouldn't have done the work unless she had promised to pay you.

You should also remember that, as discussed in Chapter 2, a written contract need not be a formal negotiated document with both parties' signatures at the end. Under the Uniform Commercial Code (UCC)—which has been adopted in all states and applies to the sale of goods, but not services—to be a contract, a letter or other document doesn't even have to state the price or time of delivery, only that the parties agree on the sale of goods and the quantity of goods sold. If it meets this modest requirement, any letter, fax or other writing can constitute a contract.

Example: Hubert, a pest control operator, sends a fax to Josephine, the business manager of a company that manufactures rodent traps, saying: "I would like to order 1,000 gopher traps at $14 per trap." Josephine faxes back, saying: "Thank you for your order. The traps will be sent next week." There is a contract. In fact, even if Josephine didn't write back at all but simply sent the traps in a reasonable period of time, there would also be a contract implied from the circumstances of the transaction.

You should also be aware that the business usage and practices in a particular field are commonly viewed as being part of a contract and can be introduced as evidence in Small Claims Court to support or thwart your case. Thus, if Hubert ordered rodent traps in February and Josephine didn't send them until September, Hubert could present evidence in court that everyone in the rodent control business knows that traps are only salable in the spring and summer, when rodents attack crops, and that Josephine's failure to deliver the traps in the correct season constituted a breach of contract.

Finally, keep in mind that contracts can be, and often are, changed many times as negotiations go back and forth and circumstances change. The important agreement is the most recent one.

The Sale of Goods

The Uniform Commercial Code (UCC), adopted by all states, contains special rules affecting contracts for the sale of goods. While it requires that you produce something in writing if you want to enforce a contract for a sale of goods and the price is $500 or more, it provides that this writing can be very brief—briefer than a normal written contract. Under the UCC, the writing need only:

- indicate that the parties have agreed on the sale of the goods, and
- state the quantity of goods being sold.

If items such as price, time and place of delivery or quality of goods are missing, the UCC fills them in based on customs and practices in the particular industry. And where specially manufactured goods are ordered, the UCC doesn't require any writing at all once a party makes a significant effort towards carrying out the terms of the contract.

Example: A restaurant calls and orders 500 sets of dishes from a restaurant supply company. The dishes are to feature the restaurant's logo. If the supply company makes a substantial beginning on manufacturing the dishes and applying the logo, the restaurant can't avoid liability on the contract simply because it was oral.

2. Presenting Your Evidence in Court

In addition to the general techniques of presenting evidence efficiently in court, here are a few more suggestions of special interest to small business people. Start by understanding that in business disputes, the problem is often having *too much* evidence, rather than too little. If this is your situation, your job is to separate the material that is essential to proving your case from that which is less important. The best approach is to organize both your verbal presentation and the backup evidence around the central issue in dispute, rather than trying to fill in the background to work up to the point. In other words, the longer your story and the more evidence you have, the more important it is to start with a brief summary of the heart of the dispute.

Example: Ted, an interior decorator, was hired by Alice, the owner of Ames Country Inn, to freshen up the decor of the bed and breakfast accommodation. Ted had submitted an estimate, which Alice verbally accepted on the telephone. Later, Alice stopped by Ted's office and dropped off a set of detailed architectural drawings. Ted had worked for three days on the new decor plan when Alice, quite suddenly, called and canceled the deal because, on second thought, she didn't like the colors Ted was proposing. Ted's bills were not paid.

Ted filed in Small Claims Court, asking for three days' pay plus the money he was out of pocket for supplies. He should begin his presentation in Small Claims Court something like this. "Your Honor, the defendant hired me to prepare a detailed plan to redecorate the Ames Country Inn. I had worked on the job for three days and bought $200 worth of supplies when she canceled. Today, I'm asking for a judgment for my normal rate of pay of $80 per hour for the 24 hours I worked, plus the $200 for supplies. The total is $2,120."

Of course, there is a lot more to Ted's story and, after stating the crux of his claims, he will need to fill in the key points. Were I Ted, I would next make these points:

- He and Alice had worked together before and his work had always been acceptable.
- He really did the 24 hours of work he claimed, as documented by drawings and worksheets presented as evidence.
- He had a list of the supplies purchased for the job, plus canceled checks.

This should be enough to make Ted a winner. But it is always a good idea for any litigant to anticipate and deflect the other side's key points. For example, in this instance, if Ted was pretty sure Alice was going to claim she canceled because Ted was using a theme and colors she had specifically rejected, he would be wise to make it clear that no such restrictions were contained in their contract.

Many business people have employees, partners or business associates who have intimate knowledge of the dispute. By all means, bring them to court as witnesses. A witness who is knowledgeable about the transaction is almost always worth more than a stack of documentary evidence.

Example: Assume Ted's assistant, Doris, attended a preliminary meeting with Alice at which Ted asked for a list of Alice's suggestions. Great! Doris can testify that when the subject of color came up, Alice just waved her hand and said, "You know I don't like purple too much, but it's really up to you—you're the designer."

In some situations, having a witness testify as to the normal business practices in a particular field can also be helpful. Thus, if in your field goods are normally shipped within five to 15 days after an order is received (unless written notice of a delay is sent), but the person you are having a dispute with is claiming you must pay for goods that were shipped 90 days after your order was received, it would be a good idea to present an "expert" witness—or a letter from someone knowledgeable about relevant business practices—who could testify that unfilled orders are never good for more than 30 days.

C. The Drama of the Distraught Designer

Now let's review another typical small business case, with an eye to identifying good strategies. Don Dimaggio is a successful architect and industrial designer who heads his own small company, which specializes in designing small manufacturing buildings. He has offices in a converted factory building, and prides himself on doing highly innovative and creative work.

Recently Don did some preliminary design work for an outfit that wanted to build a small candle factory. When they didn't pay, he was out $6,500. In Don's view, the dispute developed like this:

"Ben McDonald, who makes custom candles, had a good year and wanted to expand. He called me and asked me to rough out a preliminary design. McDonald claims now that we never had a contract, but that's simply not true. What really happened is that McDonald authorized me to do some preliminary work before his company got their financing locked down. When interest rates went through the roof, the whole deal collapsed. I had already completed my work, but they got uptight and refused to pay. My next step was to get Stephanie Carlin, a lawyer who has done some work for me, to write McDonald a letter demanding payment. When that didn't do any good, I took Stephanie's advice and filed a Small Claims Court suit against McDonald. To do it, I had to scale my claim back to $5,000, the Small Claims maximum, since I couldn't afford to pay Stephanie $200 an hour to file in formal court."

Don's immediate problem was that he had never used Small Claims Court before. He wasn't sure how he needed to prepare, but knew, at the very least, he had to develop a coherent plan—if for no other reason than to overcome his anxiety. Here is how I coached him to do this:

RW: "Your first job is to establish why McDonald owed you money. Presumably it's because you claim he broke a contract with you that called for him to pay you for your work."

DD: "True, but unfortunately, nothing was written down."

RW: "Oral contracts to provide service are perfectly legal if they can be proven, and judges typically bend over backwards to see that freelancers get paid. But don't be so sure you have nothing in writing. Tell me, how did McDonald contact you?"

DD: "Mutual friends recommended me to him. He phoned me and we talked a couple of times. There was some back and forth about how much I would charge for the whole job and how much for parts of it. After a little garden-variety confusion, we decided that I would start with the preliminary drawings and be paid $6,500. If the whole job came through, and we felt good about one another, I would do the entire thing. On big jobs, I always insist on a written contract, but this one was tiny and I couldn't see wasting the time. They just stopped by the next day and we hashed out the whole thing in person."

RW: "Did you make notes?"

DD: "Sure. In fact, I made a few sketches, and then they gave me specifications and sketches they had made."

RW: "Do you still have those?"

DD: "Of course, in a file along with a couple of letters they sent later thanking me for my good ideas and making a few suggestions for changes. And of course, I have copies of the detailed drawings I made and sent them."

RW: "Well, that's it."

DD: "What do you mean, that's it?"

RW: "You've just told me that you can prove a contract exists. The combination of the sketches they provided and the letters McDonald's company wrote you pretty convincingly prove they asked you to do the work. Of course, it helps that legally there is a strong presumption in law that when a person is asked to do work in a situation where compensation is normally expected, he must be paid when the work is completed." (Lawyers call this legal doctrine "quantum meruit.")

DD: "That really is it, then? I just present my case and I win?"

RW: "Not so fast. First, let me ask a basic question—are you positive you can present your case coherently? Most people do a poor job unless they prepare an outline and practice. After you make your opening statement, you need to back it up with the key facts that show that McDonald hired you, you did the work and he broke the contract by failing to pay you. Pick someone who has a critical mind and appoint him your pre-trial judge. Then present your case as if you were in court. Encourage your friend to interrupt and ask questions, since that's what a judge will likely do. Finally, be sure you have organized all your evidence, especially the plans and letters, so you are ready to present them to the judge at the appropriate time."

DD: "What about McDonald? Is he likely to show up?"

RW: "Many cases involving money being owed result in defaults, meaning the person being sued ignores the whole proceeding. (See Chapter 15.) But since you know that McDonald claims he doesn't owe you the money, it's my guess he will probably show up and claim no contract existed. You should be prepared to counter the points he is likely to make."

DD: "You're right. Although it's a total crock, he will probably claim I agreed to do the work on speculation that he would get financing and hire me for the rest of the job."

RW: "And if your case is typical, McDonald will also probably try and claim your work was substandard in some way. That way, even if you prove that a contract existed, the judge may award you less than you asked for."

DD: "But they wrote me that my design was of excellent quality."

RW: "Great, but don't wait until they raise the issue. Since you are pretty sure this point will come up, emphasize how pleased McDonald was with your work in your opening statement. Now, what about McDonald's argument that there was no deal in the first place? Do you ever do preliminary work without expecting to be paid unless the deal goes through? And is that a common way to operate in your business?"

DD: "Me? Never! I don't have to. I suppose some designers do, or at least prepare fairly detailed bid proposals without pay, but I have so much work coming my way these days, I'm turning jobs down right and left, so when I do submit a bid, I make it clear to all potential clients that I charge for preliminary drawings. In this situation, as I said, we agreed on the price in advance."

RW: "What about witnesses to that conversation?"

DD: "Well, Jim, my partner, sat in on one of the early discussions. We hadn't agreed on the final price yet, but we weren't too far apart."

RW: "Was it clear to Jim that you intended to charge for your work and that McDonald knew you did?"

DD: "Yes, absolutely."

RW: "Great, bring Jim to court with you as a witness. Here is how I would proceed. Organize your statement as to what happened so it takes you no longer than five minutes to present it to the judge. Bring your sketches, and most important, the sketch that McDonald made, along with the letters they sent you, and show them to the judge. (See Chapter 15.) Then introduce your partner and have him state that he was present when money was discussed."

This little scenario is a simplified version of a real case. What happened? Don was given a judgment for the entire amount he requested and McDonald paid it.

D. Old Friends Fall Out

Finally, let's review another typical Small Claims dispute. Toni, a true artist when it comes to graphics, is an ignoramus when it comes to dollars and cents. Recognizing this, she never prepares her own tax returns. For the past several years, she has turned all of her tax affairs over to Phillip, a local C.P.A. Price was discussed the first year, but after that, Toni just paid Phillip's bill when the job was done.

One spring, things went wrong. As usual, Toni's records weren't in great shape, and she was late in getting them to Phillip. Phillip was busy and put Toni's tax return together quickly, without discussing it with her in detail. When Toni saw the return, she was shocked by the bottom line. She was sure she was being asked to pay way too much to Uncle Sam.

She called Phillip and reminded him of a number of deductions she felt had been overlooked. There was some discussion of whether Phillip should have known about these items or not. Things began to get a little edgy when Phillip complained about Toni's sloppy records and her delay in making them available, and Toni countered by accusing Phillip of doing a hurried and substandard job. But after some grumpy talk back and forth, Phillip agreed to make the necessary corrections. In a week this was done and the return was again sent to Toni.

While her tax liability was now less, Toni was still annoyed, feeling that not all of the oversights had been corrected. Toni called Phillip again, and this time they quickly got into a shouting match, which ended with Phillip very reluctantly agreeing to look at the return a third time but Toni saying "hell, no," she was taking her business to an accountant who could add.

Toni was true to her word and did hire another accountant, who made several modifications that resulted in a slightly lower tax liability. The second accountant claimed that because he needed to check all of Phillip's work to satisfy himself that it was correct, he ended up doing almost as much work as if he had started from scratch. As a result, he billed Toni for $2,300, saying that this was only $500 less than if he had not had the benefit of Phillip's work.

Phillip billed Toni for $3,000. Toni was furious and refused to pay. Phillip then sent Toni a demand letter stating that most of the problems were created by Toni's bad records, that he had made a number of changes when requested to do so and had offered to make relatively minor final changes at no additional charge. Phillip also suggested in his letter that he was willing to try and mediate the claim using a local mediator who specialized in small business disputes.

When Toni didn't answer the letter, Phillip filed suit. Were I Phillip, here is how I would prepare my case:

Phillip's Case

Step 1. Phillip has already written a clear, concise demand letter (see Chapter 6) and suggested mediation—a good idea, since both he and Toni work in the same area and Phillip has an obvious interest in not turning Toni into a vocal enemy. Unfortunately, Phillip's suggestion of mediation didn't work.

Step 2. Phillip knows that Toni's business makes money, so he is pretty sure he can collect if he wins, which of course should be a big consideration in deciding whether to file any Small Claims case. (See Chapter 3.)

Step 3. In court, Phillip's main job will be to prove that he did work that was worth $3,000 and to refute Toni's likely contention that his work was so bad it amounted to a breach of their contract. Bringing copies of Toni's tax returns as well as his own worksheets is the simplest way for Phillip to accomplish this. The returns should not be presented to the judge page by page, but as a package. The purpose is to indicate that a lot of work has been done, not go into details.

Step 4. Phillip should then testify as to his hourly rate and how many hours he worked. He should emphasize that extra hours were required because Toni did not have the raw data well organized. To illustrate his point, Phillip should present to the judge any raw data Toni gave him that he still has (for example, a shoebox full of messy receipts). If he no longer has Toni's material, he might create something that looks like it, carefully pointing out to the judge that this is a simulation of Toni's data, not the real thing.

Step 5. Phillip has now presented his basic breach of contract case, by testifying that he was hired to do a job, he did it and he wasn't paid. However, Phillip would be wise to go beyond this and anticipate at least some of Toni's defenses, which will almost surely involve the claim that Phillip broke the contract by doing poor quality work and doing it late. In addition, Phillip should anticipate Toni's backup claim that he charged too much and that the judge should award him less than $2,500. To accomplish this, were I Phillip, I would make a statement along these lines:

> *"Your Honor, when I finished my work, my client pointed out that several deductions had been overlooked. I believed then and believe now that this was because the data she provided me with was disorganized and inadequate, but I did rework the return and correct several items that were left out. When my client told me that she felt the revised draft needed additional changes, I again told her that I would work with her to make any necessary modifications. It was at this point that she refused to let me see the returns and hired another accountant. In my professional opinion, very little work remained to be done at this stage—certainly nothing that couldn't be accomplished in an hour or two.*
>
> *"Now, as to the amount charged—it took me ten hours to reconstruct what went on in the defendant's business from the mess of incomplete and incoherent records I was given. At $90 per hour, this means that $900 of my bill involved work that had to be done prior to actually preparing the return. Taking into consideration the difficult circumstances, I believe I charged fairly for the work I did, and that I did my work well."*

Toni's Case

Okay, so much for getting into the head of an indignant accountant. Now let's see how Toni, the upset graphic artist, might deal with the situation.

Step 1. For starters, I think Toni made a mistake by refusing to negotiate or mediate with Phillip. Especially since this is the sort of dispute over the quality of work where a judge is likely to enter a compromise judgment, it would have saved time and anxiety for Toni and Phillip to settle outside of court. (See Chapter 6).

Step 2. Once Toni decided not to try to settle the case, she should write a letter of her own, rebutting Phillip's demand letter point by point. (See Chapter 6.) She should bring a copy of this letter to court and give it to the judge as part of her presentation.

In some states, the judge doesn't have to accept it (it's not really evidence of anything but the fact that Phillip's request for payment was rejected), but more often than not, the judge will probably look at both Phillip's and Toni's letters.

Step 3. Next, Toni should testify that she refused to pay the bill because she felt that Phillip's work was so poorly done that she didn't trust Phillip to finish the job. To make this point effectively, Toni should testify as to the details of several of the points that Phillip overlooked. Thus, if Toni provided Phillip with information concerning the purchase of several items of expensive equipment and Phillip forgot to claim depreciation, this would be important evidence of poor work. But Toni should be careful to make her points about tax law relatively brief and understandable. She won't gain by a long and boring rehash of her entire return. One good approach might be for Toni to submit pertinent sections of IRS publications or a privately published tax guide outlining the rules that require equipment to be depreciated.

Step 4. Toni should next present more detailed evidence that supports her claim that Phillip did poor work. The tax return as correctly prepared by the new accountant would be of some help, but it would be even better to have the second accountant come to court to testify about the details of Phillip's substandard work. Unfortunately for Toni, professionals are commonly reluctant to testify against one another, so this may be difficult to arrange. But Toni should at the very least be able to get a letter from the new accountant outlining the things that he found it necessary to do to change the return as prepared by Phillip.

Step 5. Toni should also present to the court her canceled checks, establishing the amounts paid Phillip for the last several years' returns, assuming, of course, that Phillip's previous bills were substantially less. For example, if Toni had been billed $1,700 and $1,900 in the two previous years, it would raise some questions as to whether Phillip's bill of $3,000 for the current year was reasonable.

Both Toni and Phillip should be prepared to answer questions. Especially in a case like this one, involving a technical field, the judge is almost sure to interrupt both Toni's and Phillip's presentations and ask for details. So in addition to preparing and practicing presenting their cases before a critical friend, both Phillip and Toni should be prepared to answer any questions and then smoothly return to presenting their cases.

What Happened?

Phillip was given a judgment for $1,800. The judge didn't explain his reasoning, but apparently felt that there was some right on each side and split the difference with a little edge to Phillip, probably because since Toni hired him in the first place and had worked with him for several years, she was on somewhat shaky ground claiming he was incompetent. This sort of compromise decision, where each side is given something, is common in Small Claims Court and again illustrates the wisdom of the parties' working out or mediating their own compromise. Even if Toni and Phillip had arrived at a solution where one or the other gave up a little more than the judge ordered, there would have been a savings in time and aggravation that probably would have more than made up the difference. ■

Judgment and Appeal

A. The Judgment

In most states, including California, the decision in your case will be mailed to the address on record with the clerk any time from a few days to a few weeks after your case is heard. The exception to this rule occurs when one side doesn't show up (or doesn't file an answer within the proper time, in states that require it) and the other wins by default. Default judgments are normally announced in the courtroom. The truth is that, in the vast majority of contested cases, the judge has already made up his mind at the time the case is heard, and notes down his decision before the parties leave the courtroom. Traditionally, decisions have been sent by mail because the court didn't want to deal with angry, unhappy losers, especially those few who might get violent. More recently, however, some judges have begun explaining their decisions in court, on the theory that both parties are entitled to know why a particular decision was reached. One progressive judge explained his policy in this regard as follows: "The only time I don't announce in court is when I have phoning or research to do or if I feel the losing party will be unnecessarily embarrassed in front of the audience."

Often when a judgment is entered against a person, she feels the judge would surely have made a different decision if he hadn't gotten mixed up, or overlooked some crucial fact, or had properly understood an argument. On the basis of my experience on the bench, I can tell you that, in the vast majority of Small Claims cases, there is little likelihood the judge would change his decision even if you had a chance to argue the whole case over. In any event, you don't. You have had your chance and the decision has gone against you. It won't help you to call the judge, or go to see him, or send him documents through the mail. (See Section D, below, for appeal rights.)

Now that a judgment has been entered, we need to expand our vocabulary slightly. The person who wins the case (gets the judgment) now becomes "the judgment creditor" and the loser is known as "the judgment debtor."

B. Time Payments

I have mentioned the fact that, in a great many states, including California, Connecticut, Michigan, New York and Minnesota, a judge may order that the loser be allowed to pay the winner over a period of time, rather than all at once. But the judge normally won't make this sort of order unless you request it. If you are in a state in which the judge announces her decision in court, this is not a problem, as you are present to ask for time payments if you lose. If you're in a state in which decisions are sent by mail, and if you have no real defense to a claim, or if you have a fairly good case but aren't sure which way the judge will go, be sure the judge knows that, if the judgment goes against you, you wish to pay in installments. You might put your request this way:

- "In closing my presentation, I would like to say that I believe I have a convincing case and should be awarded the judgment, but in the event that you rule for my opponent, I would like you to allow me time payments of no more than (whatever amount is convenient) per month."

    Or, if you have no real defense:

- "Your Honor, I request that you enter the judgment against me for no more than (an amount convenient to you) per month."

If you neglect to ask for time payments in court and wish to make this request after you receive the judgment, first contact the other party to see if she will voluntarily agree to accept her money on a schedule you can afford to pay. If she agrees, it is wise to write your agreement down and each sign it. If your opponent is an all-or-nothing sort of person and refuses payments, promptly contact the court clerk and ask that the case again be brought before the judge—not as to the facts, but only to set up a payment schedule you can live with. The clerk should arrange things for you, but if there is a problem, write a letter like this one to the judge:

47 West Adams St.
Brooklyn, NY
October 17, 199X

Honorable Felix Hamburg
Judge of the Small Claims Court
111 Center St.
New York, NY

Re: *Elliot v. Toller*
Index No. __

Dear Judge Hamburg:

I recently appeared before you in the case of *Elliot v. Toller* (Index No. _____). Mr. Elliot was awarded a judgment in the amount of $526. Paying this amount all at once would be nearly impossible because of (lack of employment, illness, or whatever). I can pay $25 per month.

Please change the order in this case to allow for a $25 per month payment. If it is necessary for me to make this request in court, please inform me of the time I should be present.

Sincerely,

John Toller

REQUEST TO PAY JUDGMENT IN INSTALLMENTS

Name and Address of Court: Ventura County Municipal Court
Small Claims Div.
800 So. Victoria Ave
Ventura, CA 93009

SMALL CLAIMS CASE NO. 1234

PLAINTIFF/DEMANDANTE (Name, address, and telephone number of each):

Don Gonzalez
P. O. Box 6489
Ventura CA 93006
805-654-2610
Telephone No.:

DEFENDANT/DEMANDADO (Name, address, and telephone number of each):

Luke Smith
10 N. Main St.
Ventura, CA 93006
805-654-2609
Telephone No.:

Telephone No.:   Telephone No.:

[ ] See attached sheet for additional plaintiffs and defendants.

REQUEST TO PAY JUDGMENT IN INSTALLMENTS

1. I request the court to allow me to make installment payments on the judgment entered against me in this case in the amount and manner stated below.
2. My request is based on this declaration, the court records, my completed financial declaration (Form EJ-165 – *obtain from court clerk*) attached to this declaration, and any other evidence that may be presented.
   NOTE: YOU MUST ATTACH A COMPLETED FINANCIAL DECLARATION WITH THIS REQUEST TO MAKE INSTALLMENT PAYMENTS.
3. Judgment was entered against me in this matter on *(date)*: 8/31/___   in the amount of *(specify)*: $1,004.91
4. Payment of the entire amount of the judgment at one time will be a hardship on me because *(specify)*:

   I am currently unemployed

5. I can and will make payments toward the judgment in the amount of *(specify)*: $ 40.00   per [ ] week [x] month.
6. I request the court to order that I make payments as specified in item 5 and that execution on the judgment be stayed as long as I make payments according to this schedule.

I declare under penalty of perjury under the laws of the State of California that the foregoing is true and correct.

Date: 10/12/___

....Luke Smith..........................
(TYPE OR PRINT NAME)

▶ *Luke Smith*
(SIGNATURE OF JUDGMENT DEBTOR)

NOTICE TO JUDGMENT CREDITOR

The judgment debtor has requested the court to allow payment of the judgment in installments. Complete the following and return this form to the court within 10 days. You will be notified of the court's order, or, if a hearing is necessary, the date of the hearing.

1. I am the judgment creditor, and I have read and considered the judgment debtor's request to make installment payments on the judgment.
2. a. [ ] I am willing to accept the payment schedule the judgment debtor has requested.
   b. [ ] I am willing to accept payments in the amount of *(specify)*: $ per [ ] week [ ] month.
   c. [ ] I am opposed to accepting installment payments because *(specify)*:

I declare under penalty of perjury under the laws of the State of California that the foregoing is true and correct.

Date:

....   ▶
(TYPE OR PRINT NAME)   (SIGNATURE OF JUDGMENT CREDITOR)

┌─────────────────────────────────────┐
│ SEE REVERSE FOR HEARING DATE, IF ANY. │
└─────────────────────────────────────┘
(Continued on reverse)

Form Approved by the
Judicial Council of California
SC-106 [New January 1, 1992]

REQUEST TO PAY JUDGMENT IN INSTALLMENTS
(Small Claims)

Code of Civil Procedure, § 116.620(b)

ORDER

1.
2.   Ventura County Municipal Court
      Small Claims Div.
3.   800 So. Victoria Ave
      Ventura, CA 93009   **SMALL CLAIMS CASE NO.** 1234
4.

5.   Don Gonzalez   Luke Smith
6.   P. O. Box 6489   10 N. Main St.
      Ventura, CA 93006   Ventura, CA 93006
7.   805-654-2610   805-654-2609
8.

9.

10.

11.

12.

13.   Judgment is to be paid $40.00 on the first day of each month
14.   until the entire amount of $1,004.91, plus interest figured at 8%
15.   per year is fully paid. Should the judgment debtor fail to make
16.   one or more payments, the judgment creditor may file an affidavit
17.   so stating with this court and this order shall thereby be va-
18.   cated by the court clerk—and the judgment creditor may proceed
19.   as if it had not been made.

20.

21.   DATED _____   _____
22.   JUDGE
23.

24.

25.

26.

27.

28.

C. The Satisfaction of Judgment

In all states, once a judgment is paid, whether in installments or a lump sum, a judgment creditor must file a "Satisfaction of Judgment" form with the court. If a judgment creditor who receives payment in full on a judgment fails to do this, the judgment debtor should send a written demand that this be done. A first-class letter is adequate. It's important to do this because otherwise the judgment will continue to appear on credit records as unpaid and may result in the judgment debtor being denied credit. If, after written demand, the judgment creditor still doesn't file his satisfaction within the required number of days of the request (usually between 15 and 30—check your local rules), and without just cause, many states provide that the judgment debtor is entitled to recover all actual damages he or she may sustain by reason of such failure (for example, denial of a credit application) and, in addition, in some states, a sum of money (California provides a $50 fine).

Here is a sample Satisfaction of Judgment form used in California. Again, it should be signed by the judgment creditor when the judgment is paid, and then filed with the court clerk. Don't forget to do this; otherwise, you may have to track down the other party later.

Sometimes people forget to get a Satisfaction of Judgment form signed when they pay a judgment, only to find they can't locate the judgment creditor later. If this happens and you need a Satisfaction of Judgment to clean up your credit record or for some other reason, you can normally get it if you present the court with proof the judgment was paid. The following documents will help you:

ACKNOWLEDGMENT OF SATISFACTION OF JUDGMENT

ATTORNEY OR PARTY WITHOUT ATTORNEY *(Name and Address)*:   TELEPHONE NO.:   FOR RECORDER'S OR SECRETARY OF STATE'S USE ONLY

ATTORNEY FOR *(Name)*:

NAME OF COURT:

STREET ADDRESS:

MAILING ADDRESS:

CITY AND ZIP CODE:

BRANCH NAME:

PLAINTIFF:

DEFENDANT:

CASE NUMBER:

ACKNOWLEDGMENT OF SATISFACTION OF JUDGMENT
☐ FULL   ☐ PARTIAL   ☐ MATURED INSTALLMENT

FOR COURT USE ONLY

1. Satisfaction of the judgment is acknowledged as follows *(see footnote* before completing)*:
   a. ☐ Full satisfaction
      (1) ☐ Judgment is satisfied in full.
      (2) ☐ The judgment creditor has accepted payment or performance other than that specified in the judgment in full satisfaction of the judgment.

   b. ☐ Partial satisfaction
      The amount received in partial satisfaction of the judgment is
      $

   c. ☐ Matured installment
      All matured installments under the installment judgment have been satisfied as of *(date)*:
2. Full name and address of judgment creditor:

3. Full name and address of assignee of record, if any:

4. Full name and address of judgment debtor being fully or partially released:

5. a. Judgment entered on *(date)*:
      ☐ (1) in judgment book volume no.:   (2) page no.:
   b. ☐ Renewal entered on *(date)*:
      ☐ (1) in judgment book volume no.:   (2) page no.:

6. ☐ An ☐ abstract of judgment ☐ certified copy of the judgment has been recorded as follows *(complete all information for each county where recorded)*:

COUNTY	DATE OF RECORDING	BOOK NUMBER	PAGE NUMBER

7. ☐ A notice of judgment lien has been filed in the office of the Secretary of State as file number *(specify)*:

NOTICE TO JUDGMENT DEBTOR: If this is an acknowledgment of full satisfaction of judgment, it will have to be recorded in each county shown in item 6 above, if any, in order to release the judgment lien, and will have to be filed in the office of the Secretary of State to terminate any judgment lien on personal property.

Date:

▶

_____
(SIGNATURE OF JUDGMENT CREDITOR OR ASSIGNEE OF CREDITOR OR ATTORNEY)

*The names of the judgment creditor and judgment debtor must be stated as shown in any Abstract of Judgment which was recorded and is being released by this satisfaction. A separate notary acknowledgment must be attached for each signature.

Form Approved by the
Judicial Council of California   **ACKNOWLEDGMENT OF SATISFACTION OF JUDGMENT**   CCP 724.060, 724.120,
EJ-100 (Rev. July 1, 1983)(Cor. 7/84)   724.250

1. A canceled check or money order written by the judgment debtor for the full amount of the judgment, or a cash receipt for the full amount of the judgment, signed by the judgment creditor after the date the court awarded judgment; and

2. A statement signed by the judgment debtor under penalty of perjury stating all of the following:

- The judgment creditor has been paid the full amount of the judgment and costs;
- The judgment creditor has been requested to file a Satisfaction of Judgment and refuses to do so or can't be located;
- The documents attached (such as the check or money order) constitute evidence of the judgment debtor's receipt of the payment.

Check with the clerk of your state for your local rules.

Sample Statement

My name is John Elliot. On January 11, 19___ , a judgment was awarded against me in Small Claims Court in Ithaca, New York (Case # 1234). On March 20, 19___ I paid Beatrice Small, the prevailing party, $1,200, the full amount of this judgment [or, if payments were made in installments—"I paid Beatrice Small, the prevailing party in this action, the final installment necessary to pay this judgment in full."]

I attach to this statement a canceled check [or other proof that the judgment was paid] for the full amount of the judgment endorsed by Beatrice Small.

Beatrice Small did not voluntarily file a Satisfaction of Judgment. When I tried to contact her, I learned that she had moved and had left no forwarding address.

Sincerely,

John Elliot

D. The Appeal

Unlike Small Claims Court itself, where rules and procedures are remarkably the same throughout the United States, the rules that cover appeals from Small Claims Court judgments vary greatly from one state to the next. A few, such as Connecticut, Hawaii, Michigan, North Dakota and South Dakota allow no appeal. New York allows an appeal of a judge's decision, but not an attorney-arbitrator's. California, Massachusetts and a few other states allow a losing defendant to appeal, but do not permit the person who brought the suit (the plaintiff) to do so (except that a losing plaintiff can appeal from counterclaims initiated by the defendant). In the Appendix you will find a very brief summary of the appeal procedures of every state.

Determining whether you are eligible to appeal is important, but it is only part of the information you need. It is just as important to determine what kind of appeal is permitted in your state. While it may be true, as Gertrude Stein suggested, that "rose is a rose is a rose," Small Claims appeals are not nearly so consistent. Some states allow an appeal only on questions of law, while others allow the whole case to be replayed from scratch. Let's pause for a moment and look at some of the differences.

⚠ You can't appeal if you didn't show up in Small Claims Court. Appeal rights are almost always restricted to those who showed up in Small Claims Court, argued their case and lost. If you defaulted (didn't show up), you normally can't appeal unless and until you get the default set aside. Normally, you must file paperwork to do this almost immediately, or the Small Claims judgment will become final and unappealable. (See Chapter 10, Section F, "If One Party Doesn't Show Up.")

1. New Trial on Appeal

In several states, including Pennsylvania and Texas, either party can appeal and have the case heard over from scratch. In other states, including California, Rhode Island and Massachusetts, normally only the defendant can appeal, but if she does, the whole case is also presented again by both sides, as if the first hearing hadn't occurred. When a whole new hearing is allowed on appeal (it's called a trial "de novo," in legalese), you simply argue the case over, presenting all necessary witnesses, documents and testimony. Starting from scratch is required because no records are normally kept at Small Claims Court hearings. However, in a few Small Claims Courts, judges now tape record hearings, and these recordings are available to the judge who considers the appeal, as part of the reargument of the case.

On appeal, both sides should give careful thought to how their presentation can be improved. This is particularly true if you are the person who lost. Ask yourself: Did the judge decide against me because I presented my case poorly or because I didn't support my statements with evidence? Or did the judge simply misapply the law? To answer these questions, you may have to do some additional legal research. (See Chapter 1, Section D, for some tips on how to do this.) Once you have decided how to improve your case, practice presenting it to an objective friend. When you are done, ask your friend which parts of your presentation were convincing and which need more work.

In some states, Small Claims appeals can be presented to the judge just as informally as was true in Small Claims Court. At the other extreme, however, some states' Small Claims Court appeal rules require that an appeal be conducted with all the pomp and circumstance of a regular trial court. Because procedures can differ even within the same state, I can't tell you exactly what type of hearing you will face. So again, it is important to take the time to check out exactly what type of appeal hearing rules you will encounter. For example, you may learn you'll need to be prepared to present your testimony while sitting in the witness box, or question your witnesses and introduce evidence using the formal lawyer style you have seen so often on TV.

What should you do if you see that your appeal will be conducted in a style you find intimidating?

- Read *Represent Yourself in Court,* by Paul Bergman and Sara Berman-Barrett (Nolo Press). This book beautifully explains how to conduct a contested civil trial in a formal courtroom setting, including how to present testimony and cross-examine witnesses. It should quickly increase your comfort level.

- Ask the judge, in advance, to conduct your appeal as informally as possible. You can do this on the day of your hearing, or better yet, by writing a brief, polite letter to the court ahead of time. Explain that, as a nonlawyer, you are thoroughly prepared to present the facts of your case, but that since you are unfamiliar with formal rules of evidence and procedure, you will appreciate it if your Small Claims appeal is conducted so that a citizen who has not spent three years at law school is given a fair opportunity to be heard.

- During your Small Claims appeal, if there is some procedure you don't understand, politely ask the judge for an explanation. If necessary, remind the judge that, as a taxpayer and a citizen, you are entitled to understand the rules and procedures that control the presentation of your case.

Don't assume the deck is stacked against you just because you lost in Small Claims Court. It is probably true that some judges have a bias toward the person who won the first time. Some may even believe that Small Claims Court appeals are not worth the time they take, and upholding the original judgment is a good way to discourage them. However, it's my experience that most judges will give you a fair hearing on appeal if you are well prepared and able to present a convincing case. So, if you believe you were victimized by a bad decision in Small Claims Court and your case involves enough money to make a further investment of time and energy worthwhile, by all means appeal.

2. Appeal on Questions of Law Only

In over 20 states, including Wisconsin and Vermont, appeals can be based only on questions of law, not on the facts of the case. (See Appendix for the other states.) This is the sort of appeal that the United States Supreme Court and the other formal appellate courts normally hear.

Example 1: Your Small Claims case involves your contention that a car mechanic botched fixing your car. After listening to both sides, the judge rules for the car mechanic, based on her conclusion that the repairs were made properly and something else was wrong with your car. You disagree, contending that the repairperson really did mess up the job. Too bad—you are not eligible to appeal, because this is a factual dispute.

Example 2: Assume you are a tenant suing for the return of a cleaning deposit withheld by the landlord. The appeals court agrees with you and awards you the amount of the deposit plus $500 in punitive damages. The landlord appeals, claiming that under the law of your state, the judge only has the power to award punitive damages in the amount of $250. Since this appeal claims a mistake was made in applying the law, it is proper and will be considered.

In most states, appeals made on the basis of a mistake of law must be backed up by a written outline of what the claimed mistakes are. This can put nonlawyers at a disadvantage because they are unfamiliar with legal research and legal writing techniques. Start by contacting the court clerk and requesting all forms and rules governing appeals. While you should take these seriously and do your best to comply, the good news is that most appellate judges will consider any well-reasoned written statement you submit claiming the Small Claims judge made a legal error.

Here is a brief example of appropriate paperwork:

Appeal from Small Claims Judgment #____, Based on Legal Error: Under the laws of the state of

_____.

A Small Claims judgment may be set aside if it is based on a legal error or mistake. In my personal injury case, the court incorrectly applied the statute of limitations, because it did not take into consideration the fact that I was a minor when the accident occurred.

My case is based on a personal injury I suffered on January 23, 1992, when I was 17 years and two months old. The Small Claims judge dismissed my case because it was not filed within one year after my injury, as is required by the statute of limitations. This was an incorrect application of the law.

It's true that under the terms of Code of Civil Procedure Sec. 340, a personal injury case must normally be filed within one year of the date of the injury, which in my case occurred on January 23, 1992. However, Sec. 352 of the Code of Civil Procedure also states: "If a person entitled to bring an action, mentioned in Chapter 3 of this title, be, at the time the cause of action occurred, ...under the age of majority...the time of such disability is not a part of the time limited for the commencement of the action."

Since I was still a minor until November 23, 1993 (at which point I became 18), under the terms of CCP Sec. 352, it was from this date (not from January 23, 1992) that the court should have begun counting the one-year statute of limitations for personal injury actions. Therefore, I was entitled to file my case until November 22, 1994. In fact, since I filed on June 27, 1994, I filed well within the allowed time.

In conclusion, I request that the judgment in this case be vacated and that I be granted a new Small Claims Court hearing.

E. Filing Your Appeal

If you haven't already done so, it is absolutely essential that you obtain and study a copy of your state's Small Claims appeal rules. They vary considerably, especially between those states where you can only appeal questions of law and those where you are entitled to a completely new trial.

1. File Your Appeal Promptly

In all states, appeals must be filed promptly, so wherever you are, don't delay. In California, New York and many other states, the defendant must file a notice of appeal within 30 days of the day the court clerk mails the judgment to the parties (or hands it over, if a decision is made in the courtroom). This means that if the decision was mailed, there will be less than 30 days to file an appeal from the day that the defendant receives the judgment. In a number of other states, including Massachusetts and Montana, appeals must be filed within 10 days, while Washington, D.C. requires that appeals be on file within three days.

Because many states start counting your time to appeal from the date the judgment was mailed, this date, which should appear on the judgment, is critical. If for some reason attributable to the magic of the U.S. Postal Service your judgment doesn't show up within the number of days in which you are allowed to appeal, call the Small Claims clerk immediately and request help in getting an extension of time to file your appeal.

Appeals must usually be filed using a form supplied by the Small Claims Court.

2. Appeal Fees

The appeal fee is often higher than the original filing fee; $20–$60 is typical. If you ultimately win your appeal (that is, get the original decision turned around in your favor), you can add these court costs to the judgment. In many states, the party filing an appeal must post a cash bond (or written guarantee by financially solvent adults) to cover the amount of the judgment if he loses. This is not required in California and some other states.

F. Arguing Your Appeal Without a Lawyer

You are entitled to have an attorney in formal court, where Small Claims Court appeals are heard. But since by definition your Small Claims case is not worth big bucks, you will probably decide it is not wise to hire one. Indeed, there should be little practical reason for an attorney, as you probably have an excellent grasp of the issues by this time.

But what if your opponent hires a lawyer? Aren't you at a disadvantage if you represent yourself? Not necessarily. As noted in Section D, above, in many states, the appeals court must follow informal rules, similar to those used in Small Claims Court, thus placing you on a relatively equal footing, even if your opponent has a lawyer. If you have prepared carefully, you may even have an advantage; you carry with you the honest conviction that you are right, while a lawyer arguing a Small Claims appeal always seems a bit pathetic. If, despite this common sense view of the situation, you still feel a little intimidated, the best cure is to go watch a few Small Claims appeals. Ask the court clerk when they are scheduled. Again, as noted above, since some states follow formal court rules for Small Claims appeals, you really do want to be prepared.

Jury Trial Note: A few states, including North Carolina and Virginia, permit jury trials on appeal. Most states don't. Check with your county clerk.

Discovery Note: Most states allow you to subpoena documents for your original hearing. (See Chapter 14, Section C, "Subpoenaing Documents.") Other formal discovery techniques, such as taking the deposition of your opponent and witnesses or requesting that your opponent answer a series of written questions, are normally prohibited in Small Claims Court. Unfortunately, in a few states, some of these discovery techniques are allowed for appeals. This is a mistake, since these techniques are expensive and time-consuming at the same time that they favor lawyers, who know all the tricks. We look forward to the day when these have been eliminated in all states.

G. Further Appeals

If a defendant loses the appeal, there is normally no right to file a second appeal. However, it is sometimes possible to file an "extraordinary writ" (a special request for review based on extraordinary circumstances) to a Court of Appeal claiming that for some reason either the Small Claims Court or first appeals court has made a serious legal mistake in their handling of the case (for example, had no power to consider the issues involved in your case). In some states, the lower court judge may have the power to recommend that the Court of Appeal hear your case. But it's important to understand that because of the relatively small amounts of money involved, extraordinary writs based on Small Claims judgments are almost never filed. And when they are, they are seldom granted. For these reasons, I do not cover this procedure here. ■

CHAPTER

24

Collecting Your Money

You won. You are entitled to the dollar amount of the judgment from the opposing party or parties. How are you going to get it? Your first job is to be patient for a short while longer. Here's why.

Appeals

If the other party appeared in court and fought the case, you must wait to see if she files an appeal. Depending on your state's rules, an appeal must normally be filed in 10 to 30 days.

Exception: In a few states, no appeals are allowed, and in several more, only a losing defendant can appeal. (See Appendix.) If the other party can't appeal, you can begin collection activities immediately.

Default Judgments

If you got your judgment because the defendant defaulted (that is, didn't show up), the defendant normally can't appeal until she first asks the court to set aside the default and allow her to defend the case. Most defendants who didn't show up in the first place don't bother to do this. Nevertheless, in some states, such as California, you must wait the time period in which the losing party is allowed to ask the court to set aside the default judgment. (See Chapter 10.) And even if waiting isn't required, it's always a good idea if you are in a state that allows defendants a certain number of days in which to petition the court to set aside the default judgment. The reason is simple: If you move to collect your judgment immediately, you may alert the defendant to try to set it aside.

Assume now that you do face a short waiting period before you can initiate official collections procedures, such as a wage attachment—is it a good idea to use this time to ask the losing party to pay up voluntarily? No. While it is not illegal to ask for your money during these waiting periods, it is unwise. If you make your request for money, you are likely to remind the defendant to take advantage of his right to appeal or set aside a default judgment. In short, if there is ever a time when you should "let sleeping dogs lie," this is it.

Once any waiting period is up, what should you do? Try asking politely for your money. This works in many cases, especially if you have sued a responsible person or business. If you don't have personal contact with the person who owes you money, try a note like the following:

P.O. Box 66
Springfield, IL
February 15, 19__

Mildred Edwards
11 Milvia Street
Springfield, IL

Dear Mrs. Edwards:

As you know, a judgment was entered against you in Small Claims Court on January 15 in the amount of $1,457.86. As the judgment creditor, I will appreciate your paying this amount within 10 days.

Thank you for your consideration.

Very truly yours,

David Osaki

If you receive no payment after sending your polite note, you will have to get serious about collecting your money or forget it. The emphasis in the previous sentence should be on the word "you." Much to many people's surprise, the court does not enforce its judgments and collect money for you—you have to do it yourself.

Some states permit the court to receive payments for you. Because they believe it encourages judgment debtors to pay what they owe, some Small Claims Courts, such as those in California, allow the debtor to pay the court clerk directly. The court then forwards the money to you. If you are interested, ask your clerk if a procedure like this is available.

However, don't get so carried away in your efforts that you harass the debtor or treat her unfairly or dishonestly! If you do, you could find yourself on the other end of a lawsuit.

A few of the ways to collect money from a debtor are relatively easy. I mentioned these briefly in Chapter 3. Hopefully, you gave some thought to collection before you brought your case. Should you only now realize your opponent doesn't have the money to buy a toothbrush, and never will, you are better off not wasting more time and money trying to get him to pay up, at least for the present. Remember, though—a judgment is valid for many years (between 10 and 20 years in most states) and can be renewed for an additional number of years if you can show you have tried to collect it but failed. In some situations, you may simply want to sit on your judgment, with the hope your judgment debtor will show a few signs of life in the future.

If the debtor owns real property, file a lien. Especially if a substantial amount of money is involved, it's a good idea to establish liens on the debtor's property (assuming this doesn't occur automatically), even if he's unlikely to buy or sell real property in the near future. (See Section A, below.)

Collection rules are getting tighter. A few states, such as New York, are putting teeth in their collection rules. In New York, if a judgment debtor who has the ability to do so doesn't pay three or more Small Claims Court judgments, a judgment creditor can get triple the judgment as damages, plus attorney fees. If you are in New York, contact the Small Claims Court clerk for details.

When the Debtor Pays By Check

Always make copies of checks written by the debtor to pay the judgment. Should you receive only partial payment and later want to collect the rest, you'll have information on where the debtor has been banking. If the debtor's check bounces, you may, depending on your state's law, be entitled to:

- sue in Small Claims Court (or in Municipal Court, if there is no Small Claims Court in your area), for the original amount of the bounced check plus damages. First, you must follow your state's detailed procedures, including usually sending a demand letter to the debtor (often by certified mail); or

- see if your county's district attorney's office will prosecute the debtor or refer the debtor to a bad check diversion program. These generally allow the person who wrote the bad check to avoid prosecution by making the check good and complying with other rules. Usually, you cannot seek damages if you enlist the district attorney's help—but you'll be spared the hassle of another lawsuit.

A. Create Property Liens

One important collection device used by judgment creditors is the property lien. In a little under half of the states, the entry of a court judgment automatically creates a lien on any real property the debtor owns in the county where the judgment was obtained. In the rest of the states, you must record the judgment with the county to create a lien on the debtor's real property. (In Alabama, Georgia, Massachusetts and Mississippi, the lien is on the debtor's real and personal property.) Also, in some states where you do not get a lien on personal property after the judgment is entered or recorded, you may be able to get a lien on the debtor's personal property by filing the judgment with the Secretary of State. See *Money Troubles: Legal Strategies to Cope With Your Debts,* by Robin Leonard (Nolo Press), for a comprehensive listing of different states' lien laws.

Once you have a lien on the judgment debtor's property, especially real property, there is a good chance you'll eventually be paid. It usually works like this: When the debtor sells or refinances her property, the buyer will see your lien on the property. In the case of a sale, you will normally be notified and paid out of the proceeds. If property is refinanced, the lender will normally insist on the existing liens being paid off.

Instead of waiting for the debtor to sell her property, you may be able to execute on the lien—that is, have the sheriff seize the property (typically a house) and arrange for a public sale from which you are paid out of the proceeds. This is unusual, however, because arranging a public sale is time-consuming and expensive. Furthermore, you may not get much money by selling property at this kind of sale, called a distress sale. Any mortgage holder, government taxing authority or other creditor who has placed a lien on the debtor's property before you is paid first. In addition, in most states, a portion of the debtor's equity is protected by "homestead laws." Only if the debtor has money over and above what he already owes on the real property and the amount of any homestead exemptions can you collect anything.

In many states, here's how to record your judgment against real property: First get an Abstract of Judgment from the Small Claims clerk's office. The clerk will prepare this paper for you. Then take the Abstract of Judgment to the county recorder's office in the county where the property is located, pay a fee and give the recorder the mailing address of the judgment debtor so he can be notified. Check with your Small Claims Court for the exact procedures.

Note: In some states, you have to specifically identify the property you're putting the lien on.

B. Levying on Wages, Bank Accounts, Business Assets, Real Property, etc.

If a polite letter doesn't work (ten days is plenty of time to wait), and you know the judgment debtor has the money, you will have to start acting like a collection agency. It is also possible to turn your debt over to a real collection agency, but this probably doesn't make too much sense, as the agency usually takes up to 50% of what it collects. Unless you are a regular customer, the agency probably won't treat your debt with much priority unless it believes it is easy to collect. If it is easy for the agency to collect, it probably won't be hard for you to do it yourself and save the fee.

If you know where the judgment debtor works, you are in good shape. In most states, you can get up to 25% of a person's net wages to satisfy a debt unless that person has a very low income, in which case the amount you can recover can be considerably less than 25%. Wage garnishments are not allowed in Texas and limited to 10% of persons' wages in New York. Some other states make it difficult to garnish the wages of a head of family in a situation where the family has a low income and needs all of its income to survive. The sheriff's or marshal's office in your area can supply you with rules in your state.

As mentioned, knowing where a judgment debtor banks can also be extremely valuable, as you can order a sheriff, marshal or constable to levy on a bank account and get whatever it contains at the time of the levy. Of course, a bank account levy will only work once at a given bank, as the debtor is pretty sure to move his account when he realizes you have access to it.

Rules restrict some types of bank account levies. Bank account levies are subject to your state's exempt property laws. In most states, approximately 75% of wages placed in a bank account are exempt from being taken to pay debts (100% if there has been a previous wage attachment involving the same money) for 30 days after payment. Social Security money and deposits from other public benefits, such as AFDC, unemployment insurance and veteran's benefits are totally exempt from attachment.

Stocks, bonds, mutual funds and other securities are normally not difficult to levy on if you know where they are held.

Other types of property are normally much more difficult to grab. Why? Because all states have a number of "exemption" laws that say that, even though a person owes money, certain types of her property can't be taken to satisfy the debt. Items protected typically include a portion or all equity in a family house, furniture, clothes and much more. (*Money Troubles: Legal Strategies to Cope With Your Debts,* by Robin Leonard (Nolo Press), includes a list of the exempt property laws of all 50 states.) Practically speaking, the only assets other than wages and bank accounts and securities that are normally worth going after to satisfy a Small Claims judgment are the receipts of an operating business (Section 4, below) and a motor vehicle (Section 5, below) in which the judgment debtor has an equity considerably in excess of the exemption amount in effect in your state. Theoretically, there are many other assets you could reach, but in most cases, they are not worth the time and expense involved, considering your judgment is for the Small Claims maximum, or less.

Place a lien on real property. As discussed in Section A, above, while it doesn't usually make sense to try to force a sale of a judgment debtor's house or other real property to collect a Small Claims judgment, placing a lien against real property is sensible—sooner or later the judgment debtor will sell or refinance, and chances are good your judgment will be paid, plus interest.

1. The Writ of Execution

Before you can levy on a person's wages or other property, you must get court permission, usually in a document called a Writ of Execution, Writ of Garnishment, Writ of Attachment or similar title. Some courts also require that you complete a short application for the writ. If you have a Small Claims judgment, you are entitled to this writ. In most states, you get your writ from the Small Claims Court clerk, who will help you fill it in. There is often a small fee, which is a recoverable cost. (See Section D, "Recovering Collection Costs and Interest," later in this chapter.)

2. The Sheriff (or Marshal or Constable)

Once you obtain a writ, the procedure to collect your money will be as follows in most states: Take or send the writ to the sheriff, marshal or constable in the county in which the assets are located. The Small Claims Court clerk will direct you. Do it right away, because the Writ of Execution expires within a certain period (often 60 to 180 days) if it is not served by the sheriff or marshal. If this time runs out, you will have to go back to the Small Claims Court clerk and get another writ issued. Give the sheriff, marshal or Small Claims clerk the following:

- The writ (original) and one to three or more copies, depending on the asset to be collected. Remember to keep a copy of the writ for your files.
- The required fees for collecting (this will vary as to the type of asset); call ahead to inquire.

Instructions on what type of asset to collect and where it is located. The sheriff, marshal, constable or Small Claims clerk may have a form they wish you to use when providing these instructions. Or the instructions might be a part of the writ form itself. Normally, however, they will accept a letter if it contains all the necessary information.

3. How to Levy on Wages and Bank Accounts

To seize a person's wages or bank account, you normally need to provide an official copy of the Writ of Execution to the sheriff, marshal or constable, and a letter of instruction like that shown below. If your state has a special wage garnishment form, use that—your Small Claims Court clerk advisor should know.

P.O. Box 66-D
Jackson, Wyoming 83001
March 1, 19__

Sheriff (Civil Division)
Mapleville, _____
Re: Carol Lamp vs. Frank Post
Small Claims Court No. 81-52

To Whom It May Concern:

Enclosed you will find the original and one copy of a Writ of Execution (Garnishment or Attachment) issued by the Small Claims Court in the amount of $__(fill in total due)__. I also enclose a check for your fee in the amount of $_____.

I hereby instruct you to levy on the wages of Frank Post, who works at the Graphite Oil Co., 1341 Chester St., Mapleville, _____. Please serve the Writ on or before March 15, 19__.

or

I hereby instruct you to levy on all monies in all accounts of Frank Post, located at the Bank of Trade, 11 City St., Mapleville, _____. If a bank account is in the name of defendant and someone else, you may have to post a bond, depending on your state's laws. Ask the court clerk or the sheriff or other levying officer for details.

Very truly yours,

Carol Lamp

---

4. Business Assets

In many states, it is possible to have someone from the sheriff's, marshal's or constable's office sent to the business of a person who owes you money to collect it from the cash on hand. You will want to ask your court clerk about your local rules. In many states, this can be done with a "till tap" or "keeper."

A till tap consists of a one-time removal of all cash receipts from the business. For a keeper, a deputy from the sheriff's, marshal's or constable's office goes to the place of business, takes all the money in the cash register, and then stays there for a set period of time (an "8-hour keeper," a "24-hour keeper," or a "48-hour keeper") to take more money as it comes in. Keepers' fees are high; a 48-hour keeper can cost as much as $400. It is also possible for the business's property to be seized and sold. But costs of doing so are often prohibitive.

Talk to the sheriff, marshal or constable in your area to get more details. He will want an original and copies of your writ, as well as instructions telling him where and when to go. Fees are recoverable from the judgment debtor if enough money comes in to cover them, plus the judgment.

5. Levying on Motor Vehicles (Including Planes, Boats and RVs)

Selling a person's motor vehicle tends to be difficult for several reasons, including the following:

- A portion of the equity in a car is exempt from your levy in many, but not all, states. For instance, Oregon is fairly typical in that it exempts equity worth $1,700 from attachment.

  Example: A judgment debtor in Oregon has a car worth $4,000 on which he owes $3,000 to a bank. This means his equity is $1,000—the bank owns the rest. As an equity of $1,700 is exempt under Oregon law, you would end up with nothing.

- You may not be able to instruct the sheriff to pick up the car from a garage or other private place unless you first go to court and obtain a judge's permission.

- The judgment debtor may not own the car she drives. It may be in someone else's name, belong to her employer, or she may owe a bank or finance company as much or more than the car is worth.

To find out if a judgment debtor owns the car he drives, go to the Department of Motor Vehicles. In most states, for a small fee, they will tell you who owns the car, including whether or not a bank or finance company is involved. Once you have this information, you can determine whether selling the car is likely to yield enough to pay off any loan you discover, provide the debtor with her exemption amount, cover the costs of sale and still leave enough to pay off all, or at least a substantial part, of your judgment. If you are convinced the vehicle is worth enough to cover these costs, as would be the case if it is relatively new and owned by the debtor free and clear, have the sheriff pick up the car and sell it. But remember, the sheriff fees to do this are relatively high (usually $400 or more), and must be paid in advance. Also, the sale price at a public auction will fetch far less than at a private sale. Your costs are recoverable when the vehicle is sold.

Call the sheriff, marshal or constable of the county in which the car is located to find out how much money he requires as a deposit with your writ and how many copies of the writ you need. Then write a letter such as this:

P.O. Box 66-D
Jackson, WY 83001
March 1, 19__

Sheriff (Civil Division)
Cheyenne, Wyoming
Re: Carol Lamp v. Frank Post
Small Claims Court
No. SC 81-52
To Whom It May Concern:

You are hereby instructed, under the authority of the enclosed Writ, to levy upon and sell all of the right, title and interest of Frank Post, judgment debtor, in the following motor vehicle:

[Type the description of the car as it appears on your D.M.V. report, including the license number.]

The vehicle is registered in the name(s) of Frank Post, and is regularly found at the following address(es):

[List home and work address of owner. Remember that the car might have to be parked in a public place.]

Enclosed is my check for $_____ to cover your costs of levy and sale.

Very truly yours,

Carol Lamp

Some states have no exemption for motor vehicles and some exempt a higher amount of equity. Check your state legal codes, call your local sheriff's or marshal's office, or consult *Money Troubles: Legal Strategies to Cope With Your Debts,* by Robin Leonard (Nolo Press), which contains an up-to-date list of all states' exemptions.

6. Stocks, Bonds and Other Securities

If the judgment debtor owns stock or other securities, your collection method will depend on how the ownership is physically represented.

If ownership is manifested in certificates held by the judgment debtor, you can levy against the certificates themselves as tangible personal property. However, you will first need to get a court order allowing you to reach property in a private home.

If, as is common, the certificates are held for the judgment debtor by a broker, you can initiate a third-party levy against the branch office of the stock brokerage firm. The sheriff, marshal or constable will require a writ, written instructions and fee to handle the levy.

Sometimes stock ownership is not manifested in certificates, but is recorded in the computers of the company issuing the securities. In this case, it is possible to make a third-party levy at a company's in-state headquarters. If the company's headquarters are out-of-state, you will need to obtain a court order assigning you the right to the securities.

7. Other Personal Property

As mentioned, normally it isn't worth the trouble to try to levy on small items of personal property, such as furniture or appliances, because they are commonly covered by one or another of the state exemption laws that provide certain possessions are exempt from being taken to satisfy debts. Even if property isn't exempt, you would need a court order to allow a levying officer access to property in a private home.

8. Pensions and Retirement Benefits

In many states, you can get at money in individual or self-employment retirement plans held in banks or savings institutions. You'll need to check your state laws to find out if retirement accounts are fair game. If you're entitled to go after this money, you can do so just as you do any other money kept in a bank. Of course, you need to know where the money is.

Private company retirement plans and state or local government retirement plans generally can't be touched until the money is paid over to the employee. Even then, the judgment debtor might claim those amounts as exempt.

Federal government pension and retirement benefits may not be garnished to satisfy any debts, except those for alimony and child support.

C. Finding Phantom Assets

As you now understand from reading the above sections, collecting on your Small Claims judgment isn't normally difficult if the judgment debtor has some money or property and you know where it is. But what do you do when you suspect that money or property exists, but have no idea how to find it? For example, you may know a person works, but not where, or that he has money in the bank, but not which one. Wouldn't it be nice to simply ask the judgment debtor a few questions he must answer?

Well, you often can. In a number of states, when a Small Claims Court judgment is entered against a person (or business) the loser (judgment debtor) must fill out a Statement of Assets form. This form must be sent by the judgment debtor to the person who won the case (the judgment creditor) within a required number of days after Notice of Entry of Judgment is mailed out by the clerk *unless* the judgment debtor pays off the judgment, appeals or makes a motion to set aside or vacate the judgment.

If a judgment debtor does not fill out this statement of assets form when required to do so (or if no such form exists), the judgment creditor can ask the court clerk to issue an order requiring the judgment debtor to appear in court in person to be questioned. In some states, this is called an Order of Examination or Judgment Debtor's Examination. This order, which must be properly served on the judgment debtor, requires the debtor to show up in court and provide the information personally. If the debtor fails to show up, the judge can issue a bench warrant for his arrest. Oh, and one hint—in many states, at the Order of Examination hearing, the judgment creditor can ask if the debtor has any cash in her possession. If so, this can be taken to satisfy at least a portion of the debt right on the spot.

D. Recovering Collection Costs and Interest

Costs (including the filing fee, costs of service, etc.) incurred prior to recovering a judgment should be included in the judgment total when it is entered by the judge. I discuss this in Chapter 15, Section C, "Don't Forget to Ask for Your Costs."

Here I am concerned with costs incurred after judgment. These are the costs that result when the judgment debtor doesn't pay voluntarily and you have to levy on his or her assets. This can be expensive and you will want to make the judgment debtor pay, if possible. Many costs of collecting a judgment are recoverable; a few are not. Generally speaking, you can recover your direct costs of collecting, which include such things as sheriff, marshal or constable fees, costs to get copies of required papers issued by the court (such as a Writ of Execution or Abstract of Judgment) and recording fees. Indirect costs such as babysitting costs, time off work, postage, photocopying, gasoline, etc., can't be recovered. Check with your clerk for rules.

You can also recover interest on the judgment. The interest rate depends on your state's laws; 8% to 12% per year is usual.

E. Renew Your Judgment

Judgments expire after a certain number of years—usually five to 20, depending on the state (see Chart). Fortunately, you are entitled to renew your judgment—and any liens based on it—if you do so before the expiration date. For information on how to renew a judgment, contact your Small Claims Court clerk's office.

TIME LIMIT TO COLLECT COURT JUDGMENT
(THESE PERIODS CAN BE RENEWED IN MOST STATES)

State	In-State Judgments	Out-of-State Judgment Registered in the State
Alabama	20 years	20 years
Alaska	10 years	10 years
Arizona	5 years	4 years or time allowed in state where judgment entered, whichever is less
Arkansas	10 years	10 years
California	10 years	10 years
Colorado	20 years	6 years
Connecticut	20 years (10 years if small claims court judgment)	20 years
Delaware	10 years	10 years
District of Columbia	3 years	time allowed in state where judgment entered
Florida	20 years	7 years
Georgia	7 years	5 years
Hawaii	10 years	6 years
Idaho	6 years	6 years
Illinois	20 years	5 years
Indiana	20 years	20 years
Iowa	20 years	20 years
Kansas	5 years	5 years
Kentucky	15 years	15 years
Louisiana	10 years	10 years
Maine	20 years	20 years
Maryland	12 years	12 years
Massachusetts	20 years	20 years
Michigan	10 years	10 years
Minnesota	10 years	10 years

State	In-State Judgments	Out-of-State Judgments Registered in the State
Mississippi	7 years	7 years
Missouri	10 years	10 years
Montana	10 years	10 years
Nebraska	5 years	5 years
Nevada	6 years	6 years
New Hampshire	20 years	20 years
New Jersey	20 years	20 years
New Mexico	14 years	14 years
New York	20 years	20 years
North Carolina	10 years	10 years
North Dakota	10 years	10 years
Ohio	21 years	15 years
Oklahoma	5 years	3 years
Oregon	10 years	10 years
Pennsylvania	6 years	6 years
Rhode Island	20 years	20 years
South Carolina	10 years	10 years
South Dakota	20 years	10 years
Tennessee	10 years	10 years
Texas	10 years	10 years
Utah	8 years	8 years
Vermont	8 years	8 years
Virginia	20 years	10 years
Washington	10 years	10 years
West Virginia	10 years	10 years
Wisconsin	20 years	20 years
Wyoming	5 years	5 years

Where Do We Go From Here?

It's easy to criticize America's legal system—almost everyone knows it's in trouble. The $1,000-a-day experts, with their degrees, titles and well-funded consulting companies, have studied the problem to death, with few positive results. And this is hardly surprising, since most of the experts involved in the studies, and in the resulting decisions, are lawyers who, at bottom, are unable to understand a problem of which they are so thoroughly a part.. Sometimes it almost seems that America's legal system was designed by the Chinese Emperor K'ang-hsi, who said " ...lawsuits would tend to increase to a frightening extent if people were not afraid of the tribunals and if they felt confident of always finding in them ready and perfect justice . . . I desire therefore that those who have recourse to the tribunals should be treated without pity and in such a manner that they shall be disgusted with law and tremble to appear before a magistrate."

But instead of my lecturing you about all the things that are wrong at the local courthouse, let's sit down at the kitchen table with a pot of tea and a bowl of raspberries and see if we can't design a better system for handling everyday disputes. After all, this republic was founded by ordinary people taking things into their own hands— they had to, because most of the governor-, judge- and lawyer-types were quite comfortable in England, thank you. And don't forget—we have already agreed that the present legal structure doesn't work, so we obviously have nothing to lose by making our own suggestions. Hey, leave a few raspberries for me, and why don't you jot down a few of your own ideas as we go along, so this becomes a two-way communication.

Before we get to specific suggestions for change, let's take a brief look at where things are now. As a society, we clearly have a fixation with trying to solve problems by suing one another. Nowhere in the world do people even come close to being as litigious as we are. The result of this love of lawsuits, or perhaps its cause—it's one of those chicken and egg problems—is the fact that whenever we get into any sort of spat with anyone, or even think we might get into one in the future, look for a lawyer. (And with close to one million in the U.S., it's not hard to find one.) It's gotten so bad that people who suffer an injury have been known to call their lawyer before their doctor. But there is an odd paradox here. At the same time that we tolerate vast numbers of lawyers eating at the top end of our societal trough, and are more and more likely to use them, public opinion polls tell us our respect for lawyers has fallen. Indeed, we rate their trustworthiness below that of used-car salespeople, undertakers and loan sharks. It's as if the less we respect lawyers, the more we use them. Perhaps we're afraid that if we don't sue first, someone will get the jump on us. (If you eat one more of those raspberries, I'll see you in court.)

Have you ever thought about how people solved their disputes in simpler societies? Let's pretend, for a moment, that we are members of a tribe of deer hunters in a preindustrial age. One fine fall morning, we both set out, bow in hand, you to the east and me to the west. Before long, you hit a high cliff and turn north. My way is blocked by a swift river, and I, too, turn north. Without our realizing it, our paths converge. Suddenly, a great stag jumps from the underbrush and we both pull back our bows and let fly. Our arrows pierce the deer's heart from opposite sides, seemingly at the same instant.

For a moment, we stand frozen, each surprised by the presence of the other. Then we realize what has happened and that we have a problem. To whom does the deer belong? We carry the deer back to the village, each unwilling to surrender it to the other. After the deer is gutted and hung, we speak to the chief of our group about our problem. He convenes a council of elders to meet late in the afternoon to consider it. Each of us has his say as to what happened. The deer carcass is examined. Anyone else who has knowledge of our dispute is invited to speak. Tribal customs (laws) are consulted, our credibility is weighed and a decision is made—in time for dinner.

Now, let's ask ourselves what would happen today if you and I simultaneously shot a deer (instead of each other) on the first day of hunting season and were unable to agree on whom it belonged to. Assuming we didn't fight it out on the spot but wanted the dispute resolved by "proper" legal procedures, lawyers would have to be consulted, court papers filed and responded to, a court appearance scheduled, words spoken in legalese and a formal court decision written and issued. All of this for a deer that would have long since rotted away unless it had been put in cold storage. If the deer had been frozen, the storage costs would have to be added to court costs and attorney fees, which, all together, would surely add up to a lot more than the value of the deer.

Seriously, what were the differences between the ways the two societies resolved the problem of who owned the deer? The so-called primitive one did a better job, but why? Obviously because their solution was in proportion to the problem, while today we make the dispute resolution process so cumbersome and expensive it usually dwarfs the dispute. The hunting society handled the disagreement quickly, cheaply, and, most importantly, in a way that allowed the disputing parties to participate in and understand what was going on. So the question becomes why can't our court system procedure achieve even one of these goals? In large measure, because lawyers have vested financial and psychic interests in the present cumbersome way of doing things and have neither the motivation nor the perspective to make changes.

But isn't this view a bit radical? Isn't there something uniquely valuable about the great sweep of the common law as it has evolved through the ages? Doesn't the majestic black-robed judge sitting on his throne mumbling age-old mantras somehow guarantee that God is in heaven, the republic safe and "justice will be done?" To all three questions, the best answer is, not necessarily. History is arbitrary—our dispute resolution mechanisms could have developed in a number of alternative ways. If our present system worked well, imposing it on the future would make sense. As, in fact, it hardly works at all, continuing it is silly. Those who get misty-eyed recounting the history, traditions and time-tested forms behind our present ways of resolving disputes are almost always people that benefit by its continuance. Consider, too, that in the United States, we have no pure legal tradition, having borrowed large hunks of our jurisprudence on a catch-as-catch-can basis from England, Spain, France, Holland and Germany, as well as various Native American cultures.

Okay, granted there have been legal systems that worked better than ours, and granted at least some change is overdue, what should we do? One significant reform would be to expand Small Claims Court. Like the system followed by the deer hunters, but unlike most of the rest of our legal system, Small Claims Court is simple, fast and cheap, and allows for the direct participation of the disputing parties. Never mind that up to now Small Claims Court has been tolerated as a way to keep lawyers' offices clear of penny-ante people with penny-ante disputes. It's there, it works and we can expand it to play a meaningful role in our lives.

As you know by now, Small Claims Court, as it is presently set up, has several disadvantages:

- *First:* The amount for which suit can be brought is ridiculously low.
- *Second:* In most instances, the court only has the power to make judgments that can be satisfied by the payment of money damages.
- *Third:* Many kinds of cases, such as divorces, adoptions, etc., aren't permitted in Small Claims Court at all.

- *Fourth:* Many states still allow lawyers to represent people in Small Claims Court, even though a recent study by the National Center for State Courts indicates that people win just as often without them.

Why not start our effort to improve things by doing away with these disadvantages? Let's raise the maximum amount for which suit can be brought to $15,000, or better yet, $20,000. I would like to suggest $25,000, but that's probably unrealistic given the high likelihood that it would result in vitriolic attorney opposition. But even an increase to $15,000 would be a significant reform, allowing tens of thousands of disputes to be removed from our formal legal system. One logical reason to pick $15,000 is that people can't afford lawyers to handle disputes for amounts below this.

Example: Randy the carpenter agrees to do $30,000 worth of rehabilitation to Al's home. When the work is completed, an argument develops about whether the work was done properly according to the agreement. Al pays Randy $15,000, leaving $15,000 in dispute. Randy goes to his lawyer and Al to his. Each has several preliminary conferences, after which the lawyers exchange several letters and telephone calls. Eventually, a lawsuit is filed and answered, a court date is obtained many months in the future and then changed several times, and finally a two-hour trial is held. Randy's lawyer bills him $4,480 (28 hours x $160 per hour) and Al's charges $4,725 (27 hours x $175 per hour), for a combined fee of $9,205. The dispute takes eleven months to be decided. In the end, Randy is awarded $10,000.

This is a typical case with a typical solution. Between them, the lawyers collected over half of the amount in dispute and took most of a year to arrive at a solution that very likely left both Randy and Al frustrated. Don't you think Randy and Al would have preferred presenting their case in Small Claims Court, where it would have been heard and decided in a month? Of course, either of them could have done worse arguing the case himself, but remember, when the legal fees are taken into consideration, the loser would have had to do a *lot* worse before he would have ended up in worse financial shape. Randy recovered $10,000 with a lawyer, but after subtracting the $4,480 lawyer fee, his net gain was only $5,520. Al ended up paying $14,725 ($10,000 for the judgment and $4,725 for his attorney). Thus, if a Small Claims Court judge had awarded Randy any amount from $5,521 to $14,724, both men would have done better than they did with lawyers. Of course, if this sort of case were permitted in Small Claims Court, there would be two big losers—the lawyers.

The second great barrier to bringing cases in Small Claims Court is the fact that, with minor exceptions, the court is limited to making money judgments. Think back for a moment to our problems with the twice-shot deer. How does the award of money make sense in this situation? In Small Claims Courts, the tribesman who didn't end up with the carcass would have had to sue the other for the fair market value of the deer. What nonsense—if we are going to have a dispute resolution procedure, why not permit a broad range of solutions, such as the deer being cut in half, or the deer going to one hunter and six ducks going to the other in compensation, or maybe even the deer going to the person who needed it most? Using an example more common at the end of the 20th century, why not allow a Small Claims Court judge to order that an apartment be cleaned, a garage repainted or a car properly fixed, instead of simply telling one person to pay X dollars to the other. One advantage of this sort of flexibility is that more judgments would be meaningful. Under our present system, tens of thousands of judgments can't be collected because the loser has no obvious source of income. We need to get away from the notion that people who are broke have neither rights nor responsibilities. To have a decent life, people need both.

Lawyers and judges often contend that it would be impossible to enforce nonmoney judgments. Perhaps some would be hard to keep track of. Certainly it might require some experimentation to find out which types of judgments are practical and which are not; however, since it is often impossible to collect a judgment under the present system, it can't hurt to try some alternatives.

The third barrier to bringing cases in Small Claim Court is the limitation on the types of cases that can be heard. Consequently, the next big change I propose, and the one that would truly make over our court system, involves expanding the types of cases that can be heard in Small Claims Court. Why not be brave and take the 20 most common legal problems and adopt simplified procedures enabling all of them to be handled by the people themselves, without lawyers? Why not open up our courthouses to the average person who, after all, pays the bills?

To accomplish this democratization of our dispute resolution procedures, it may be practical to divide Small Claims Court into several separate divisions, each responsible for a broad area of common concern. For example, there could be a landlord-tenant and a domestic relations division. Each division would have the authority to consider a broad range of problems and solutions falling within its area of concern. Today, if you have a claim against your landlord (or he against you) for money damages, you can use Small Claims Court only if the claim is under the dollar limit. If you want to have a roof fixed, a tenant evicted, or protect your privacy, etc., most Small Claims Courts can't help you, except possibly to award a money judgment for the intentional infliction of emotional distress. The Canadian province of British Columbia and a few East Coast cities have already put all landlord-tenant disputes into what amounts to a Small Claims Court format, easily and cheaply available to both landlord and tenant. Why can't this be done everywhere?

A domestic relations Small Claims Court could include simplified procedures to help people handle their own uncontested divorces, adoptions, name changes, guardianships, etc., safely and cheaply. And why not? Even with considerable hostility from lawyers and court personnel, almost 60 percent of the divorces in California are already handled without a lawyer—despite the fact that these people must deal with the absurd procedures inherent in going to formal court. I'm not advocating that sensible safeguards be dropped. For example, if a divorce involves children, you would want to have someone trained in the field carefully examine the parents' plans for custody, visitation and support to see if they are reasonable.

Without going into detail, I suggest that if we took lawyers out of our domestic relations courts, we would not only save millions of dollars and hours, but more importantly, we would lighten the heavy burden of hostility and anxiety that divorcing spouses must now bear. Our present system, in which parents and children become clients to a "hired gun" (the lawyer), is a bad one. By definition, the client role is weak and the gunfighter role strong. This imbalance commonly results in lawyers making critical decisions affecting their clients' lives—sometimes overtly, sometimes subtly. All too often, these decisions benefit the lawyer and his bank balance to the detriment of both clients' psyches and pocketbooks. The lawyer, after all, is paid more to fight, or at least to pretend to fight, than to compromise. I have seen dozens of situations in which lawyers have played on people's worst instincts (paranoia, greed, ego, one-upsmanship) to fan nasty little disagreements into flaming battles. Perhaps mercifully, the battles normally last only as long as the lawyers' bills are paid.

I could list a number of other areas of law that could be converted to a Small Claims approach (auto accidents, simple probates, perhaps even some criminal cases), but I am sure you get the point. We must take control of the decision-making processes that affect our lives. We must make ourselves welcome in our own courts and legislatures. We must stop looking at ourselves as clients who hear and obey and start taking responsibility for our own legal decisions.

Let's assume now that the obstacles can be overcome and the role of Small Claims Court will be greatly expanded. In the process of doing so, we will need to make a number of changes in the way the court now operates. It will be a good opportunity to throw out a number of existing procedures that owe more to history than to common sense. Here are a few specific ideas for changes:

1. Let's make Small Claims Court easily accessible. This means holding weekend and evening sessions. This is being done now experimentally in a few areas, but such sessions should be as routinely available everywhere else as they are in New York City. When court is held at 9 a.m. on weekdays, it often costs more in lost time from work for all the principals and witnesses to show up than the case is worth.

2. Let's get the judge out of the black robe and off of the throne. There is a part of all of us that loves the drama involved in seeing our magistrate sitting on high like the king of England, but I am convinced by my own brief experience as a "pro tem" judge that this pomp and circumstance is counterproductive. We would have a lot less confrontation and a lot more willingness to compromise if we got rid of some of the drama.

3. Let's ban lawyers and collection agencies in states where they are currently allowed.

4. While we're making changes, let's make a big one—let's put strict limits on the adversary system. It contributes a great deal to the posturing of the litigants and obfuscation of the dispute and very little to settling disputes efficiently. Or as the

distinguished legal scholar Roscoe Pound wrote, "The doctrine of contentious procedure...is peculiar to Anglo-American law...(it) disfigures our judicial administration at every point...(it) gives to the whole community a false notion of the purpose and end of law...Thus, the courts...are made agents or abettors of lawlessness."

We must move toward systems of mediation and arbitration in which, instead of a traditional judge, we have someone whose role is to facilitate the parties arriving at their own solution—imposing a decision only if they arrive at a hopeless impasse. Big business, big labor and, increasingly, even lawyers, are coming to realize that arbitration and mediation are good ways to solve problems. As is already done in Maine, Washington, D.C. and several other areas, let's require that before fighting it out in court, all parties to the dispute sit down at a table with a Small Claims Court mediator. This person, who would be trained for the job, would not necessarily be a lawyer. The mediator would help the parties search for areas of agreement and possible compromise, and, if this wasn't possible, at least help them define the area in dispute. Only if the dispute couldn't be resolved by the parties would the case be referred to a Small Claims Court judge who, after listening to each side, would decide it.

5. Appeal rules should also be changed. In many states, existing rules allow only the defendant to appeal, allow litigants to have lawyers on appeal and even allow the parties to start the whole case over. This is nuts. All too often, corporate defendants who have lawyers on retainer use the present system to frustrate consumers who have won in Small Claims Court. It is my belief that no appeal should be allowed in Small Claims Court—the amounts in question just aren't worth it. If appeals are allowed, they should be limited to obvious mistakes of law, and lawyers should be prohibited.

I don't mean to suggest the changes I propose in this short chapter are the only ones necessary. If we are going to put the majority of our routine legal work in Small Claims Courts, it will require turning our dispute resolution process on its head. Legal information must be stored and decoded so it is available to the average person. Clerks' offices and the other support systems surrounding our courts must be expanded and geared to serve the nonlawyer. Legal forms must be translated from "legalese" into English. Computer systems must be developed to bring legal information into our offices and living rooms.

Let's illustrate how things might change by looking at a case I recently saw argued in a Northern California Small Claims Court. One party to the dispute (let's call her Sally) arranged fishing charters for business and club groups. The other (let's call him Ben) owned several fishing boats. Sally often hired Ben's boats for her charters. Their relationship was of long standing and had been profitable to both. However, as the fishing charter business grew, both Sally and Ben began to enlarge their operations. Sally got a boat or two of her own and Ben began getting into the charter-booking business. Eventually, they stepped on one another's toes and their friendly relationship was replaced by tension and arguments. One day a blow-up occurred over some inconsequential detail, phones were slammed down and Sally and Ben each swore never to do business with the other again.

Before the day of the final fight, Sally had organized two charters on Ben's boat. These were to have taken place a week after the phones were slammed down. For reasons unconnected with the argument, the charters were canceled by the clubs that had organized them. Ben had about a week's notice of cancellation. He also had $600 in deposit Sally had paid him. He refused to refund the deposits. Sally sued him in Small Claims Court for $600.

Testimony in court made it clear that charters were commonly canceled and were often replaced by others booked at the last minute. Ben and Sally had signed a "Standard Marine Charter Agreement," which dealt with the issue of canceled charters because it was required by the Coast Guard, although they had never in the past paid attention to its terms. They had always worked out sensible adjustments on a situation-by-situation basis, depending on whether substitute charters were available and whether the club or business canceling had paid money upfront, etc.

When Ben and Sally first presented their arguments about the $600, it seemed they were not too far apart as to what would be a fair compromise. Unfortunately, the adversary nature of the court system encouraged each to overstate his (her) case and to dredge up all sorts of irrelevant side issues. "What about the times you overloaded my boat?" Ben demanded. "How about those holidays when you price-gouged me?" Sally replied. As the arguments went back and forth, each person got angrier and angrier and was less and less able to listen to the other.

The result was that after an hour of testimony, the judge was left with a confused mishmash of custom, habit, maritime charter contracts, promises made or not made, past performance, etc. No decision that he arrived at was likely to be accepted as fair by both Ben and Sally. Indeed, unless the judge gave one or the other everything he or she requested, both of them would surely feel cheated. That is not to say the hearing was all bad. Some good things did occur. The dispute was presented quickly and cheaply, and each person got to have his or her say and blow off some steam. All of these things would have been impossible in our formal court system. However, if Small Claims Court could be changed along the lines suggested above, a better result might have been reached.

Suppose that instead of a formal courtroom confrontation, Ben and Sally are first encouraged to talk the dispute out themselves. If this fails, then the next step is for the two of them to sit down in a noncourtroom setting with a court employee who is trained as a mediator and whose job is to help Ben and Sally arrive at a fair compromise—a compromise that will hopefully provide a foundation for Ben and Sally to continue to work together in the future. Only if compromise is impossible would there be recourse to a more formal court hearing. I am convinced that if this sort of three-tiered approach had been available, Ben and Sally would have worked out a compromise at the first or second stage. ■

Appendix

Small Claims Court Rules for the 50 States
(and the District of Columbia)

Please Read This

The following state-by-state Small Claims rules are for general reference only. They are not a substitute for getting a copy of your local Small Claims Court rules. Please do not make decisions based solely on the summary of state laws you read here. Our information is as sound as we can make it, but we might have inadvertently omitted or inaccurately stated a detail of particular importance to you. This can occur because laws have changed since we went to press or because the laws of many states vary from one county to the next and we haven't been able to include every local difference. So, whether you are a plaintiff or defendant, please call your Small Claims clerk for accurate up-to-date information.

ALABAMA

Small Claims Docket (District Court)
Statutes: Code of Alabama: Title 12, Chapter 12, Secs. 31, 70 and 71 and Alabama Small Claims Rules, Rules A to N; Ala. Rules of Judicial Administration Rule 17.
Dollar Limit: $3,000.
Where to Sue: County or district where any defendant resides, or injury or property damage occurred. A corporation "resides" wherever it is doing business.
Service of Process: Sheriff, adult approved by court or certified mail.
Transfer: No provision.
Attorneys: Allowed; required for assignees (collection agencies).
Appeals: Allowed by either party within 14 days to Circuit Court for new trial.
Evictions: No; must go on regular district court docket.
Notes: (1) The defendant must file a written answer within 14 days of service or will lose by default.
(2) Equitable relief is available.
(3) Director of Courts publishes guide to Alabama Small Claims rules.

ALASKA

Small Claims (District Court Judges and Magistrates)
Statutes: Alaska Statutes Title 22, Ch. 15, Sec. 040 District Court Rules of Civil Procedure, Rules 8 to 22.
Dollar Limit: $7,500.
Where to Sue: Court nearest to the defendant's residence or place of employment, district in which injury or property damage occurred or district where defendant does business.
Service of Process: Peace officer or registered or certified mail. Certified or registered mail service is binding on defendant who refuses to accept and sign for the letter. After such refusal, the clerk remails it regular first class, and service is assumed.

Transfer: Defendant (or plaintiff against whom a counterclaim has been filed) or judge may transfer case to regular District Court.

Attorneys or Legal Interns: Allowed; required for assignees (collection agencies).

Appeals: For claims over $50, allowed by either party, on law—not facts.

Evictions: No.

Notes: (1) The defendant must file a written answer within 20 days of service or will lose by default.

(2) The state cannot be sued in Small Claims Court.

ARIZONA

Justice of Peace (Small Claims Division) and Regular Justice Court

Statutes: Arizona Revised Statutes: Secs. 22-201 through 22-283 (Justice Court); Secs. 22-501 through 22-523 (Small Claims).

Dollar Limit: Small Claims Division, $2,500; regular Justice Court, $5,000.

Where to Sue: Precinct where any defendant resides, act or omission occurred, or obligation was to be performed. A corporation "resides" wherever it is doing business.

Service of Process: Sheriff, adult approved by court, or registered or certified mail with return receipt requested.

Transfer: To regular Justice Court if defendant in Small Claims Division counterclaims over $2,500 or objects at least ten days before hearing (for right of appeal and jury). For counterclaims over $5,000, transfer is allowed to Superior Court.

Attorneys: Allowed in Small Claims Division only if both parties agree in writing.

Appeals: Not allowed in Small Claims Division. Allowed in Justice Court.

Evictions: No in Small Claims Division; yes in Justice Court.

Notes: (1) Defendant must answer within 20 days in writing or will lose by default.

(2) Equitable relief is available.

(3) No right to jury trial in Small Claims Division. Allowed in Justice Court.

(4) Assignees (collection agencies) are not allowed to sue in Small Claims Division. Allowed in Justice Court.

ARKANSAS

Urban: Municipal Court (Small Claims Division);

Rural: Justice of the Peace

Statutes: Arkansas Statutes Annotated, Secs. 16-17-601 through 614; Sec. 16-17-704; Secs. 16-19-401 through 1108; Constitution, Amendment 64.

Dollar Limit: $5,000.

Where to Sue: County where a defendant resides, act or omission occurred, or obligation was to be performed. A corporation "resides" wherever it is doing business.

Service of Process: Sheriff, constable (Justice of the Peace Court only); certified mail (Small Claims only).

Transfer: In Small Claims, if the judge learns that any party is represented by an attorney, he or she must transfer to regular Municipal Court; no transfer provision in Justice of the Peace courts.

Attorneys: Not allowed (Small Claims); Allowed (Justice of the Peace).

Appeals: Allowed by either party within 30 days to Circuit Court for new trial.

Notes: (1) No assignees (collection agencies).

(2) Defendant must file written answer within 20 days of service if she's within the state, within 30 days if she's outside the state.

(3) No right of jury trial in Small Claims Division; allowed in Justice Court.

CALIFORNIA

Small Claims Division (Municipal or Justice Court)

Statutes: California Code of Civil Procedure Secs. 116.110 through 116.950.

Dollar Limit: $5,000, except that a plaintiff may not file a claim over $2,500 more than twice a year. $2,500 is also the limit for suits involving a surety company.

Where to Sue: Judicial district where any defendant resides (or resided when promise or obligation was made), act or omission occurred, or obligation was to be performed. A corporation "resides" wherever it is doing business.

Service of Process: Sheriff, disinterested adult, or certified or registered mail.

Transfer: If defendant counterclaims over $5,000, case will be heard in higher court if the Small Claims Court agrees to the transfer.

Attorneys: Not allowed, except representing themselves.

Appeals: Allowed by defendant (or plaintiff who lost on a counterclaim) within 30 days to Superior Court for new trial. Plaintiff may not appeal on her claim, but can make a motion to correct clerical errors or where a decision is based on a legal mistake.

Evictions: No.

Notes: (1) Assignees (collection agencies) cannot sue in Small Claims Court.

(2) No jury trials allowed.

(3) Equitable relief is available.

(4) Small Claims advisor available at no cost.

(5) List of interpreters may be available; call court. If a party does not speak and understand English, she may have assistance in court, other than an attorney.

(6) Judge may make a "conditional judgment" to order the performance or cessation of actions by a party.

COLORADO

County Court (Small Claims Division)

Statutes: Colorado Revised Statutes: Secs. 13-6-401 through 13-6-416, and Colorado Rules of Civil Procedure (County Courts), Rule 411, Rules of Civil Procedure (Small Claims Courts) Rules 501 through 521.

Dollar Limit: $5,000

Where to Sue: County in which any defendant resides, is regularly employed, is a student at an institution of higher education or has an office for the transaction of business.

Service of Process: Sheriff, disinterested adult, or certified mail.

Transfer: Allowed by defendant who has a counterclaim over $5,000.

Attorneys: Allowed only if attorney is plaintiff or defendant, or full- time employee or one of the following with respect to these types of plaintiffs or defendants: general partner (partnership), officer (corporation), active member (corporation or association). If an attorney does appear as permitted above, the other party may have one also.

Appeals: Allowed by either party within 15 days to District Court, on law—not facts. Parties may agree before or at trial that there will be no appeal.

Evictions: No.

Notes: (1) Assignees (collection agencies) cannot sue in Small Claims Court.

(2) No plaintiff may file more than two claims per month in Small Claims Court; no more than 18 claims per year allowed.

(3) No jury trials allowed.

CONNECTICUT

Small Claims (Superior Court)

Statutes: Connecticut General Statutes Annotated: Title 51, Secs. 15, 349; Title 52, Secs. 259, 549a through 549d.

Dollar Limit: $2,500.

Where to Sue: County or geographical area where the defendant resides or does business, or where act or omission occurred, or obligation occurred.

Service of Process: Peace officer, disinterested adult, registered mail or regular first-class mail.

Transfer: Allowed by defendant to regular Superior Court procedure, if he/she has a counter-claim over $2,500.

Attorneys: Allowed; required for corporations.

Appeals: Not allowed.

Evictions: No.

DELAWARE

Justice of the Peace (No Small Claims System)

Statutes: Delaware Code Annotated: Title 10, Secs. 9301 through 9640. Civil Rules, Justice of the Peace Courts.

Dollar Limit: $15,000.

Where to Sue: Anywhere in the state.

Service of Process: Sheriff, constable, or certified mail.

Transfer: No provision.

Attorneys: Allowed.

Appeals: Allowed by either party within 15 days to Superior Court for new trial (on claims over $5).

Evictions: Yes.

Notes: (1) Party can demand jury trial if right to trial provided by statute.

(2) Interest due on any cause of action may be added to the claim, even if adding it will make the amount exceed $15,000.

(3) *Counterclaims:* If defendant's counterclaim against Plaintiff exceeds $15,000, Plaintiff can still pursue the counterclaim in Small Claims Court. (There is no provision for transfer to another court.) If defendant wins her counterclaim, she then has two options: (1) the court will note the outcome on the record and defendant can prosecute the cause of action in higher court, or (2) defendant can waive the excess over $15,000 and take the $15,000 as her judgment.

DISTRICT OF COLUMBIA

Superior Court (Small Claims and Conciliation Branch)

Statutes: District of Columbia Code: Title 11, Secs. 1301 through 1323; Title 16, Secs. 3901 through 3910; Title 17, Secs. 301 through 307; and Superior Court Rules for Small Claims and Conciliation Branch.

Dollar Limit: $5,000.

Where to Sue: There is only one court in the District of Columbia.

Service of Process: U.S. Marshal, adult approved by court, or certified (with return receipt) or registered mail. Certified or registered mail is binding on defendant who refuses to accept letter.

Transfer: Transferable to regular Superior Court if justice requires, defendant's counterclaim affects interest in real property (land or housing), or either party demands a jury trial.

Attorneys or Certified Law Students: Allowed; required for corporations.

Appeals: To court of appeal by either party within three days.

Evictions: No.

Note: Mandatory mediation is required for contested cases.

FLORIDA

Small Claims Procedure (County Court)
Summary Procedure (County Court)
Statutes: Florida Rules of Court: Small Claims, Rules 7.010 through 7.341.
Dollar Limit: $2,500 (Small Claims Court); $15,000 (County Court).
Where to Sue: County where a defendant resides, act or omission occurred, or contract entered into. Corporation resides in its place of "customary business."
Service of Process: Peace officer, adult approved by court, or (for Florida residents only) registered mail, return receipt.
Transfer: Allowed to regular County Court procedure only if defendant counterclaims over $2,500.
Attorneys: Allowed; if attorneys involved, parties may use discovery. Court may require assignees (collection agencies) to have attorneys.
Appeals: Motion for new trial within 10 days after return of verdict or filing of judgment; Appealable to Circuit Court by either party within 30 days on law—not facts.
Evictions: Yes.
Notes: (1) Either party may demand jury trial; plaintiff must make demand when filing suit; defendant must make demand within five days after service or notice of suit or at pretrial conference.
(2) Defendant must file counterclaim in writing at least five days before appearance date.

GEORGIA

(Magistrate Court)
Statutes: Official Code of Georgia, Title 15-10-1 through 15-10-202.
Dollar Limit: $5,000.
Where to Sue: County where defendant resides.
Service of Process: Constable, official or person authorized by judge.
Transfer: To appropriate court if defendant's counterclaim over $5,000.
Attorneys: Allowed.
Appeals: To Superior Court of county for new trial.
Evictions: Yes.
Notes: (1) Courts may adopt local rules of procedure.
(2) No jury trials.
(3) Defendant must answer complaint (in writing or orally) within 30 days to avoid default.
(4) Equitable relief available.

HAWAII

Small Claims Division (District Court)
Statutes: Hawaii Revised Statutes, Title 34, Sec. 604-5; Secs. 633-27 through 633-36.
Dollar Limit: $3,500; no limit in landlord-tenant residential deposit cases. For return of leased/rented personal property, the property must not be worth more than $3,500. Counterclaims up to $20,000.
Where to Sue: Judicial district in which the defendant or a majority of defendants reside, or act or omission occurred, or where rental premises situated.
Service of Process: Sheriff, County Chief of Police, certified (return receipt) or registered mail, or by either party personally.
Transfer: If either party demands jury trial or the claim or counterclaim is over $5,000. Otherwise, only if plaintiff agrees.
Attorneys: Allowed (except in landlord-tenant deposit cases); also, with court permission, an attorney may represent another if he/she does not charge any fee.

Appeals: Not allowed.

Evictions: No.

Notes: (1) The state publishes a booklet on Small Claims Division procedures.

(2) Jury trials will be transferred to circuit court.

(3) Cases limited to: recover money, recover rented personal property, recover shopping carts, or recover damages sustained in repossessing carts.

(4) No punitive damages.

(5) Equitable relief available in landlord-tenant cases.

IDAHO

Small Claims Department of Magistrate's Division
(District Court)

Statutes: Idaho Code: Secs. 1-2301 through 1-2315.

Dollar Limit: $3,000.

Where to Sue: County where the defendant resides or where claim arose. A corporation "resides" wherever it is doing business.

Service of Process: Sheriff, disinterested adult, or certified or registered mail, return receipt.

Transfer: No provision.

Attorneys: Not allowed.

Appeals: Allowed by either party within 30 days to Attorney Magistrate for new trial.

Evictions: No.

Notes: (1) Assignees (collection agencies) cannot sue in Small Claims Court.

(2) No jury trials allowed.

ILLINOIS

Small Claims (Circuit Court)

Statutes: Illinois Compiled Statutes: Supreme Court Rules 281 through 289; Ch. 735, Secs. 5/1-104 and 5/2-416.

Dollar Limit: $5,000 (Small Claims); $2,500 (Cook County "Pro Se").

Where to Sue: County in which any defendant resides, act or omission occurred. A corporation "resides" where it is doing business.

Service of Process: Sheriff, court-approved adult, certified or registered mail, return receipt.

Transfer: If claim or counterclaim is over $5,000.

Attorneys: Allowed except in Cook County "Pro Se" branch. Defendant may have one.

Appeals: Allowed by either party within 30 days to Appellate Court, on law—not facts.

Evictions: No.

Notes: (1) Court may order installment payments by judgment debtor if unpaid over three years.

(2) Either party may demand a jury trial in small claims only. (If jury is demanded in Cook County, "Pro se" case is transferred to Small Claims.)

(3) Corporation may not appear as assignee.

INDIANA

Small Claims Court; Small Claims Docket
(Circuit Court, Superior Court and County Court)

Statutes: Indiana Statutes Annotated: Secs. 33-11.6-1-1 through 33-11.6-9-5 (Marion County Small Claims Court), 33-4-3-5 through 33-4-3-10 (Circuit Court), 33-5-2-2 through 33-5-2-7 (Superior Court), 33-10.5-1-4 (County Court).

Dollar Limit: $3,000 ($6,000 in Marion County).

Where to Sue: County in which any defendant resides or is employed, act or omission occurred,

or obligation was incurred or was to be performed by defendant.
Service of Process: Personal service first; if unable, then registered or certified mail.
Transfer: Defendant may transfer to regular docket by requesting jury trial at least three days prior to the trial date noted on notice of claim—only in Small Claims Court.
Attorneys: Allowed.
Appeals: From Small Claims docket of other courts, same as from regular circuit court.
Evictions: Yes, if total rent due does not exceed $6,000.
Note: Defendant may request jury trial within 10 days following service of complaint (Circuit) if can show questions of fact requiring a jury determination (in Circuit, Superior and County Courts).

IOWA

Small Claims Docket (District Court)
Statutes: Iowa Code Annotated: Secs. 631.1 through 631.16.
Dollar Limit: $4,000.
Where to Sue: County in which any defendant resides, act or omission occurred, or obligation was to be performed.
Service of Process: Peace officer, disinterested adult or (except in eviction suits) certified mail.
Transfer: At judge's discretion if defendant counterclaims over the dollar limit.
Attorneys: Allowed.
Appeals: Allowed by either party to District Court upon oral notice at end of hearing or if filed written notice within 20 days of judgment. No new evidence on appeal.
Evictions: Yes.
Notes: (1) The defendant must file a written answer within 20 days after service is made, or will lose by default; a form for this purpose accompanies the summons.
(2) Replevin (an action to recover a specific item of property) may be granted if value of property is $4,000 or less.
(3) The Small Claims Docket has jurisdiction over orders and motions relative to collecting judgments from personal property, including garnishments, where the amount involved does not exceed $4,000.

KANSAS

Small Claims (District Court)
Statutes: Kansas Statutes Annotated: Secs. 61-2701 through 61-2714.
Dollar Limit: $1,800
Where to Sue: County in which defendant lives or county where plaintiff resides if defendant served there, or defendant's place of doing business or employment.
Service of Process: Personal service by sheriff or adult approved by court, certified mail.
Transfer: If the defendant counterclaims over $1,800 but within the dollar limit of the regular district court, judge may decide claim or let defendant reserve right to bring claim in court of competent jurisdiction.
Attorneys: If one party uses an attorney (or is an attorney), all other parties shall have the opportunity to have an attorney.
Appeals: Allowed by either party within 10 days to District Court for new trial.
Evictions: No.
Notes: (1) Replevin (an action to recover a specific item of property) may be granted if value of property is $1,800 or less.
(2) No person may file more than 10 claims in same court during any calendar year.

KENTUCKY

Small Claims Division (District Court)

Statutes: Kentucky Revised Statutes: Secs. 24A.200 through 24A.360.

Dollar Limit: $1,500.

Where to Sue: Judicial district in which the defendant resides or does business, or if corporation, county of corporate headquarters.

Service of Process: Certified or registered mail first; if that fails, then by sheriff or constable.

Transfer: Allowed to regular District Court or Circuit Court if defendant's counterclaim over $1,500 or if defendant demands a jury trial, or if judge deems matter too complex for Small Claims.

Attorneys: Allowed.

Appeals: Allowed by either party within 10 days to Circuit Court, on law—not facts.

Evictions: Yes.

Notes: (1) Collection agents, or agencies or lenders of money at interest cannot sue in Small Claims Court.

(2) No person may file more than 25 claims in one calendar year in any district court.

(3) *Jury trials:* Plaintiff no, but if defendant makes a written request for jury trial within at least seven days before hearing date, case is transferred to regular court.

LOUISIANA

Rural (Justice of the Peace);

Urban (City Court: Small Claims Division)

Statutes: Louisiana Statutes Annotated: Sec. 13:5200 through 13:5211; Code of Civil Procedure, Articles 4831, 4911 through 4925. Code of Civil Procedure Article 42.

Dollar Limit: $2,000.

Where to Sue: Parish in which the defendant resides. A corporation or partnership may also be sued in a parish or district in which a business office is located.

Service of Process: Certified mail with return receipt, or sheriff or constable, if certified mail is marked "unclaimed" or "refused."

Transfer: Small claims may be transferred to City Court procedure for any reason if defendant files written request within time allowed for filing answer to complaint; transfer by counterclaim ("reconventional demand") over the dollar limit. In Justice of the Peace Court, if demand asserted in amended or supplemental pleading exceeds jurisdictional amount, transfer to court of appropriate jurisdiction.

Attorneys: Allowed.

Appeals: Allowed by either party in Justice of the Peace Courts within 15 days to District Court for new trial. No appeal from Small Claims Division of City Court.

Evictions: Yes, regardless of the amount of monthly or yearly rent or rent for the unexpired term.

Notes: (1) Equitable relief is available in either court.

(2) Judge may award installment payments.

(3) Default taken in Justice of the Peace Court if answer not filed within 10 days of service.

(4) No class actions, summary proceedings, or executory proceedings allowed.

(5) Party may request arbitration.

MAINE

Small Claims (District Court)

Statutes: Maine Rules of Small Claims Procedure, Maine Revised Statutes Annotated: Title 14, Secs. 1901, 7481 through 7486.

Dollar Limit: $4,500

Where to Sue: District Court "division" in which the defendant resides or has place of business or where the transaction occurred or where registered agent resides if corporation.

Service of Process: Registered or certified mail, or personally.

Transfer: Allowed.

Appeals: Allowed by either party within 10 days to Superior Court.

Evictions: Yes.

Notes: (1) Equitable relief available but limited to orders to return, reform, refund, repair or rescind.

(2) Jury trial not allowed.

(3) Judges have power to refer cases to mediation. Mediators are available in all Maine courts, and handle a high percentage of contested cases.

MARYLAND

Small Claims Action (District Court)

Statutes: Annotated Code of Maryland: Courts and Judicial Proceedings Secs. 4-405, 6-403; Rules of Civil Procedure, District Court Rule 3-701; Rules-Appeals from District Courts Rule 1314e and 1312a.

Dollar Limit: $2,500.

Where to Sue: County in which any defendant resides, is employed, or does business, or where injury to person or property occurred. Corporation may be sued where it maintains principal office.

Service of Process: Sheriff or nonparty, personally or by certified mail. If refused, clerk remails and service is presumed.

Transfer: To regular civil docket if counterclaim exceeds $2,500 or if defendant demands jury trial.

Attorneys: Allowed.

Appeals: Allowed by either party within 30 days to Circuit Court for new trial.

Evictions: Yes, as long as the rent claimed does not exceed $2,500, exclusive of interest and costs.

MASSACHUSETTS

Small Claims Division (Boston—Municipal Court;
elsewhere—District Court)

Statutes: Massachusetts General Laws Annotated: Ch. 214, Secs. 1A, 2; Ch. 218, Secs. 21 through 25, Ch. 93A, Sec. 9 (consumer complaints).

Dollar Limit: $2,000; no limit for action for property damage caused by a motor vehicle.

Where to Sue: Judicial district in which the plaintiff or defendant resides, is employed, or does business. Actions against landlords can also be brought in the district in which the property is located.

Service of Process: Sheriff, constable, or certified mail.

Transfer: Allowed only at court's discretion to regular civil docket.

Attorneys: Allowed.

Appeals: Allowed by defendant within 10 days to Superior Court for new trial ($100 bond required). Jury allowed on appeal.

Evictions: No.

Notes: (a) Generally:
    (1) Equitable relief is available.
    (2) Mediation is available at request of either party and with agreement of both parties.
  (b) For consumer complaints:
    (1) Plaintiff must make demand 30 days before filing suit.
    (2) Attorney's fees available.
    (3) Triple damages available.

MICHIGAN

Small Claims Division (District Court)

Statutes: Michigan Compiled Laws Annotated: Secs. 600.8401 through 600.8427.

Dollar Limit: $1,750.

Where to Sue: County where defendant resides or where act or omission occurred.

Service of Process: Personal service, or court clerk's certified mail with return receipt.

Transfer: Either party may transfer to regular District Court procedure. Defendant's counterclaim over $1,750 will also cause transfer.

Attorneys: Not allowed, except on own behalf.

Appeals: Not allowed, except that if action is heard by District Court magistrate, parties can appeal to Small Claims Division for new trial within seven days.

Evictions: No.

Notes: (1) Assignees (collection agencies) cannot sue in Small Claims Court.

(2) No jury trial.

(3) Time payments allowed.

(4) Instruction sheet available from court.

(5) May not file more than five claims in one week.

MINNESOTA

Conciliation Court (County Court)

Statutes: Minnesota Statutes Annotated Section 491A.01, District Court Rules 501 through 525.

Dollar Limit: $7,500 [$4,000 in cases involving a commercial plaintiff.]

Where to Sue: County in which any defendant resides or automobile accident occurred. A corporation may be sued in any county in which it has "an office, resident agent, or business place."

Service of Process: Mail or personal service by clerk [certified mail if claim is over $2,500.]

Transfer: To County Court on jury demand or defendant's counterclaim above jurisdictional limit.

Attorneys: Not allowed except with court's approval.

Appeals: To County Court for new trial or jury trial.

Evictions: No.

Notes: (1) If defendant counterclaims over jurisdictional limit and files in another court, clerk will strike the Small Claims case from calendar.

(2) Defendant must file counterclaim within five days of the trial date.

(3) *Student Loans:* As long as an educational institution has administrative offices in the county in which the conciliation court is located, it may bring actions to recover student loans even though the defendant is not a resident of that county, as long as (a) the student loans were originally awarded in that county; (b) overdue notice was sent by first-class mail to the last known address of borrower; (c) the notice states that a conciliation court action may be commenced in the county where the loan was awarded.

MISSISSIPPI

Justice Court

Statutes: Mississippi Annotated Code: Secs. 9-11-9 (amount), 9-11-27, 11-9-103 through 11-9-143, 11-51-85.

Dollar Limit: $2,500.

Where to Sue: District in which any defendant resides; if nonresident, where act or omission occurred, or obligation entered into. A corporation "resides" where its registered office is located.

Service of Process: Sheriff, constable, or disinterested adult (only in "emergency" with court's permission).

Transfer: No provision.

Attorneys: Allowed.

Appeals: Allowed by either party within 10 days to Circuit Court for new trial.

Evictions: No.

Notes: (1) Either party may demand a jury trial.

(2) Equitable remedy to recover a specific item of property (*replevin*) is allowed.

(3) Some help to collect judgments is available.

MISSOURI

Small Claims Court (Circuit Court)

Statutes: Annotated Missouri Statutes: Secs. 482.300 through 482.365. Missouri Rules of Court: Rules of Practice and Procedure in Small Claims Court, Rules 140.01 through 155.

Dollar Limit: $3,000.

Where to Sue: County in which any defendant resides, or act or omission occurred; county in which plaintiff resides and at least one defendant may be found. A corporation "resides" wherever an office or agent is located. Suit against corporation must be brought where defendant resides or the subject of the claim arose.

Service of Process: Certified mail, return receipt. If impossible, sheriff will serve.

Transfers: Allowed to regular Circuit Court if defendant counterclaims over $3,000, unless all parties agree to stay in Small Claims Court.

Attorneys: Allowed.

Appeals: Allowed by either party within 10 days for new trial before regular Circuit Court judge.

Evictions: No.

Notes: (1) Assignees (collection agencies) cannot sue in Small Claim Court.

(2) Only six claims allowed per plaintiff per 12 months.

(3) Jury trials not allowed.

(4) Each county may promulgate local rules.

(5) *Counterclaims:* Any time up to 10 days after service of process and before the hearing date, defendant may file a counterclaim against plaintiff.

MONTANA

Small Claims Court (Justice Court and District Court)

Statutes: Montana Code Annotated: Title 3, Chapter 12, Secs. 101 through 106 (District Court); Title 25, Chapter 34, Secs. 101 through 404; Title 25, Chapter 35, Secs. 501 through 807 (Justice Court); Title 3, Chapter 10, Sec. 1004.

Dollar Limit: $3,000.

Where to Sue: County or judicial district in which any defendant can be served.

Service of Process: Sheriff, constable. (Justice Court only—disinterested adult).

Transfer: Allowed by defendant to Justice Court if request filed within 10 days of receipt of complaint.

Attorneys: Not allowed, unless all parties present have attorneys.

Appeals: Allowed by either party within 30 days (District Court) for new trial. Within 10 days (Justice Court) on law, not facts.

Evictions: No.

Notes: (1) Small Claims must be based on contract, express or implied.

(2) Assignees (collection agencies) cannot sue in Small Claims Court.

(3) Maximum 10 claims per year.

(4) Defendant may request jury trial unless he counterclaims.

(5) Defendant's counterclaim (up to $2,500) arising out of the same transaction or occurrence must be served on plaintiff at least 72 hours before the hearing date.

NEBRASKA

Small Claims Court (County or Municipal Court)
Statutes: Revised Statutes of Nebraska: Secs. 25-2801 through 25-2807; 25-2728 through 25-2738 (appeals).
Dollar Limit: $2,100.
Where to Sue: County in which any defendant resides (or works, or can be found, if plaintiff lives there), or injury or property damage occurred. A corporation "resides" wherever it regularly does business through an office or agent.
Service of Process: Sheriff or certified mail, sent by clerk.
Transfer: Transferable to regular civil court on defendant's request or counterclaim over $2,100.
Attorneys: Not allowed.
Appeals: Allowed by either party within 30 days to District Court for new trial but no jury permitted. Attorneys allowed.
Evictions: No.
Notes: (1) Jury trials not available.
(2) Equitable relief available.
(3) Assignees (collection agencies) cannot sue in Small Claims Court.
(4) Plaintiff may not bring more than two claims in a week nor more than 10 in one year.
(5) *Transfers:* Defendant may request a transfer to the regular docket in order to have a jury trial by giving notice to the court at least two days before the hearing date.

NEVADA

Small Claims (Justice Court)
Statutes: Nevada Revised Statutes: Title 6, Secs. 73.010 through 73.060; and Justice Court Rules of Civil Procedure, Chapter XII, Rules 88 through 100.
Dollar Limit: $3,500.
Where to Sue: City or township in which defendant resides, does business, or is employed.
Service of Process: Personal service by sheriff or constable, licensed process server, adult approved by court, Justice of the Peace, or registered or certified mail (mailed by court clerk), return receipt.
Transfer: No provision.
Attorneys: Allowed.
Appeals: Allowed by either party within 20 days to District Court, on law—not facts. New trial at court's discretion.
Evictions: No.
Note: Recovery of money only.

NEW HAMPSHIRE

Small Claims Actions (District or Municipal Court)
Statutes: New Hampshire Revised Statutes Annotated: Vol. 4C, Secs. 503:1 through 503:10; Rules of District and Municipal Court, Rules 4.1 through 4.28, 1.11.
Dollar Limit: $2,500.
Where to Sue: Town or district in which defendant resides or plaintiff resides, or act or omission occurred.
Service of Process: Certified mail sent by court or other court-approved method, return receipt.
Transfer: To Superior Court if claim plus counterclaim exceeds $2,500 or if case exceeds $500

and either party requests jury trial.

Attorneys: Allowed.

Appeals: Allowed by either party to Supreme Court, on law—not facts. Must be made within 30 days.

Evictions: No.

Note: Claims may not involve title (ownership) to real estate.

NEW JERSEY

Small Claims Section
(Special Civil Part of Law Division of Superior Court)

Statutes: New Jersey Rules of Court: Superior Court Rules, Law Division Special Civil Part Rule 6:1 through 6:12.

Dollar Limit: $2,000 in Small Claims; $10,000 in Regular Special Civil Court.

Where to Sue: County in which any defendant resides. A corporation "resides" wherever it is actually doing business; if defendants do not reside in New Jersey, county where act or omission occurred.

Service of Process: Officers of the Special Civil Part, adult approved by court, or certified mail.

Transfer: Allowed to Civil Part if defendant counterclaims over $5,000 or demands jury trial.

Attorneys: Allowed.

Appeals: Allowed by either party within 45 days to Appellate Division of Superior Court, on law—not facts.

Evictions: No.

Notes: (1) The court will not hear cases involving personal injury or property damage except those resulting from auto accidents.

(2) Assignees (collection agencies) cannot sue in Small Claims Court.

(3) *Landlord-Tenant:* Small Claims Court has jurisdiction over landlord-tenant actions where the matter in dispute is the return of all or part of the security deposit.

NEW MEXICO

Metropolitan Court (Urban); Magistrate's Court (Rural)

Statutes: New Mexico Statutes: Annotated Secs 34-8A-1 through 12; 35-3-3 through 6; 35-8-1 and 2; 35-10-1 through 6; 35-13-2; Rules of Civil Procedure for the Metropolitan and Magistrate Courts.

Dollar Limit: $5,000 (Magistrate's Court); $5,000 (Metropolitan Court).

Where to Sue: County in which the defendant resides, may be found, or act or omission occurred.

Service of Process: By mail, and if no response, personal service by sheriff or disinterested adult.

Transfer: No provision.

Attorneys: Allowed.

Appeals: Allowed by either party within 15 days to District Court.

Evictions: Yes.

Notes: (1) Jury trial at either party's request; plaintiff must make jury trial request in the complaint and defendant must make request in the answer.

(2) Voluntary mediation program in Bernalillo County.

(3) No libel, slander or malicious prosecution.

(4) Small Claims Court also has jurisdiction over contested parking violations or operation of vehicle regulations.

NEW YORK

Small Claims [New York City Civil Court, Civil Courts outside of New York City, District Court in Nassau and Suffolk Counties (except 1st District), Justice Courts in rural areas.] See below for New York City Commercial Small Claims Court.

Statutes: Consolidated Laws of New York Annotated: Uniform Justice Court Act Secs. 1801 through 1814; NYC Civil Court Act Secs. 1801 through 1814; Uniform City Court Act Secs. 1801 through 1814; Uniform Rules for the NY State Trial Courts, Secs. 208.41 and 208.41-a.

Dollar Limit: $3,000.

Where to Sue: Political subdivision in which the defendant resides, is employed, or has a business office.

Service of Process: Certified mail (binding on defendant who refuses mail) or ordinary first class mail. If after 21 days not returned as undeliverable, then notice presumed.

Transfer: Allowed by court's discretion.

Attorneys: Allowed. Most large corporations must be represented by an attorney. Corporation defendant can defend self.

Appeals: Allowed from the decision of a judge (but not an arbitrator) within 30 days to County Court, by defendant within 30 days to County Court or Appellate Division, on law—not facts. Plaintiffs can appeal only on the ground that "substantial justice" was not done.

Evictions: No.

Notes: (1) Arbitration is available. Arbitrator's ruling unappealable.

(2) Assignees, corporations and partnerships cannot sue in Small Claims Court (exceptions: municipal corporations, public benefit corporations, school districts, school district public libraries).

(3) No counterclaim permitted in Small Claims action unless within the dollar limit.

(4) Section 1812 of the NYC Civil Court Act, Uniform City Court Act and the Uniform Justice Court Acts provide treble damages against judgment debtor who is sued in second action to enforce judgment, and who has unreasonably failed to pay within 30 days of first judgment *and* who has failed to pay at least in two small claims judgments recorded against him or her. Additional sanction against defaulting defendant whose liability arises from his or her business activities. Court will notify appropriate licensing and public certifying agencies or attorney general.

New York City Commercial Small Claims Court [NYC Civil Court Act, 1801-A to 1814-A] and Uniform City Court Act, 1801-A to 1814-A.

• only corporations, partnerships and associations can sue, they must sue for money only, and the jurisdictional amount is $3,000

• plaintiff must "reside" in NY

• defendant must reside, be employed, or have an office for transacting business in the county where suit is brought

• plaintiff can bring no more than five claims per month

• no assignees (collection agencies).

NORTH CAROLINA

Small Claims Actions (District Court)

Statutes: General Statutes of North Carolina: Chapter 7A, Secs. 210 through 232. Chapter 42, Sec. 26 through 36:2 (ejectments).

Dollar Limit: $3,000.

Where to Sue: County in which the defendant resides. A corporation "resides" where it "maintains a place of business."

Service of Process: Sheriff, registered or certified mail, adult approved by court. For evictions, sheriff may mail using ordinary first-class and then telephone or visit to arrange time to personally serve.

Transfer: No provision unless question of land title.

Attorneys: Allowed.

Appeals: Allowed by either party within 10 days to District Court for new trial. Jury trial allowed if request within 10 days of appeal's notice.

Evictions: Yes.

Notes: (1) Rules of evidence apply.

(2) Counterclaim that would make amount in controversy exceed $3,000 not allowed.

NORTH DAKOTA

Small Claims Court (County Court)

Statutes: North Dakota Century Code Annotated: Secs. 27-08.1-01 through 27-08.1-08.

Dollar Limit: $5,000.

Where to Sue: County where the defendant resides. If defendant is a corporation or partnership, where it has a place of business or where the subject of the claim arose.

Service of Process: Disinterested adult or certified mail.

Transfer: Defendant may transfer case to regular civil court procedure.

Attorneys: Allowed.

Appeals: Not allowed.

Evictions: No.

Notes: (1) No jury trial.

(2) Plaintiff may not discontinue once small claims process invoked; if plaintiff seeks to discontinue, then dismissal with prejudice (i.e., no right to refile).

OHIO

Small Claims (Municipal and County Courts); County Court

Statutes: Ohio Revised Code Annotated: Title 19, Secs. 1925.01 through 1925.17, 1901, 1907; Rules of Civil Procedure (generally applicable).

Dollar Limit: $3,000 in small claims (municipal); $5,000 in small claims (County Court); $15,000 in regular County Court with simplified mediation procedure.

Where to Sue: County in which the defendant resides, has place of business, or obligation occurred. Actions involving notes can be brought only where obligation was incurred.

Service of Process: Sheriff, certified mail by clerk, return receipt.

Transfer: Allowed from Small Claims to regular Civil Court procedure upon defendant's counterclaim over $3,000, upon request, or motion of court.

Attorneys: Allowed.

Appeals: To Court of Appeals within 30 days.

Evictions: No.

Notes: (1) Each plaintiff is limited to 24 claims per year.

(2) Municipal Court cases limited to recovery of personal property, taxes and money.

(3) No jury trials, except in County Court.

(4) No assignees except to recover taxes if appointed by authorized employee of state political subdivision.

OKLAHOMA

Small Claims (District Court)

Statutes: Oklahoma Statutes Annotated: Title 12, Secs. 1751 through 1773, 134, 139, 141.

Dollar Limit: $4,500.

Where to Sue: County in which the defendant resides, or obligation was entered into. In automobile or boat accident cases, where the accident occurred. A corporation may be sued in a county in which it is "situated" (i.e., has an office) or where the act or omission occurred.

Service of Process: Certified mail by clerk, return receipt. Plaintiff may request Sheriff or other disinterested adult.

Transfer: Allowed to regular District Court on a defendant's request or counterclaim over $4,500 unless both parties agree in writing to stay in Small Claims Court. Defendant must make a transfer request at least 48 hours prior to the time ordered for her appearance and answer.

Attorneys: Allowed, but can't charge more than 10% of judgment in uncontested cases.

Appeals: Allowed by either party within 30 days to Oklahoma Supreme Court, on law only—not facts.

Evictions: No.

Notes: (1) A jury trial may be demanded by either party.

(2) Suits to recover personal property are allowed.

(3) Small claims judgment becomes a lien on judgment debtor's real property.

(4) Assignees (collection agencies) not allowed to sue in Small Claims Court.

(5) Defendant must file any counterclaim at least 72 hours before appearance date.

(6) No suits for libel or slander.

OREGON

Small Claims Department (District or Justice Court)

Statutes: Oregon Revised Statutes: Secs. 46.405 through 46.560, 55.011 through 55.140.

Dollar Limit: $2,500.

Where to Sue: County where defendant resides or can be found; tort cases may be filed in county where injury occurred and contract cases may be filed in county where contract was to be performed.

Service of Process: Certified mail, return receipt, sheriff, adult approved by court.

Transfer: To regular docket or other appropriate court if counterclaim is more than $2,500 and defendant requests transfer; or, in District Court if defendant demands jury trial.

Attorneys: Not allowed without judge's consent.

Appeals: From District Court, no appeal. From Justice Court, allowed by defendant (or plaintiff, on counterclaim) within 10 days to Circuit Court for new trial.

Evictions: No.

Notes: (1) The defendant must respond (settle claim, request hearing in writing or request jury trial) within 14 days or will lose by default.

(2) If greater than $200 claim, defendant may seek jury trial.

PENNSYLVANIA

Philadelphia—Philadelphia Municipal Court;

Everywhere else—District or Justice Court

Statutes: Pennsylvania Statutes Annotated: Title 42, Judiciary and Judicial Procedure, Secs. 1123, 1511 through 1516; Rules of Civil Procedure Governing District or Justice Court, Rules 201 through 325; Philadelphia Municipal Court Rules of Civil Practice, Rules 101 through 144.

Dollar Limit: $5,000 (Municipal Court); $8,000 (District or Justice Court).

Where to Sue: Where defendant can be served or, if corporation or partnership, where it regularly conducts business or has principal place of business, or where act or omission occurred.

Service of Process: Sheriff, constable, disinterested adult or registered or certified mail.

Transfer: If defendant counterclaims over dollar limit, he may bring suit in Court of Common Pleas within 30 days (Municipal Court); No provision (District or Justice Court).

Attorneys: Allowed.
Appeals: Allowed by either party within 30 days to Court of Common Pleas for new trial.
Evictions: Allowed.
Notes: (1) Either party can request a jury trial and case will be transferred.
(2) Judge may make award of installment payments.
(3) In Philadelphia, if claiming more than $2,000 for injury to self or property, will have to submit a verified (signed under oath) statement of claim.

RHODE ISLAND

Small Claims (District Court)
Statutes: General Laws of Rhode Island: Title 10, Chapter 16, Secs. 1 through 16; Title 9, Chapter 12, Sec. 10 (appeals).
Dollar Limit: $1,500.
Where to Sue: District where either party resides, unless plaintiff is corporation, then only where defendant resides.
Service of Process: Certified or registered mail first; if that fails, then by sheriff, constable, deputy, or adult approved by court. Certified or registered mail is binding on defendant who refuses letter.
Transfer: Allowed to regular District Court procedure on defendant's counterclaim over $1,500, provided the Small Claims judge decides that the counterclaim has merit.
Attorneys: Allowed; required for corporations, except close corporations.
Appeals: Allowed by defendant to Superior Court for new trial. Defendant right to appeal unavailable if plaintiff is consumer and defendant is manufacturer/seller whose failure to file answer in Small Claims Court results in default.
Evictions: No.
Notes: (1) Actions for contracts (including sale of personal property) and damages resulting from a retail sale or delivery of services to a member of the general public.
(2) Judge may order judgment to be paid in installments.

SOUTH CAROLINA

Magistrate's Court (No Small Claims Procedure)
Statutes: Code of Laws of South Carolina: Title 22, Chapter 3, Secs. 10 through 320; Title 15, Chapter 7, Sec. 30; Rules of Civil Procedure 3, 82; and Title 18, Chapter 7, Sec. 20.
Dollar Limit: $2,500.
Where to Sue: County or township where defendant resides. An insurance company "resides" where it is doing business.
Service of Process: Sheriff or disinterested adult.
Transfer: Check with clerk of court. Counterclaims over $5,000 must be transferred to the docket of common pleas.
Attorneys: Allowed.
Appeals: To County or Circuit Court, on law—not facts. Party may make motion for new trial within five days, and may appeal within 25 days after motion denied.
Evictions: Yes.
Notes: (1) Either party may request jury trial.
(2) Defendant must answer within 20 days of service.

SOUTH DAKOTA

Small Claims Procedure (Circuit or Magistrate's Court)
Statutes: South Dakota Compiled Laws Annotated: Title 15, Chapter 39, Secs. 45 through 78.
Dollar Limit: $4,000.

Where to Sue: County in which any defendant resides, or injury or property damage occurred. A corporation "resides" at its principal place of business.

Service of Process: Certified or registered mail first, return receipt; service this way is binding on defendant who refused to accept and sign for the letter. If undeliverable, then service must be made by sheriff, or disinterested adult, county resident.

Transfer: Allowed at judge's discretion on defendant's demand for jury trial (must include affidavit saying jury needed because facts are complex).

Attorneys: Allowed.

Appeals: Not allowed.

Evictions: No.

TENNESSEE

Court of General Sessions (No Specific Small Claims Procedure)

Statutes: Tennessee Code Annotated: Title 16, Chapter 15, Secs. 501 through 713; Title 19, Chapters 1 through 3.

Dollar Limit: $15,000; $25,000 in counties where population is over 700,000; $25,000 in a suit to recover personal property.

Where to Sue: District nearest to defendant's residence. For debt collection, where defendant is nonresident, suit can be bought where plaintiff resides. Eviction suits brought where property is located.

Service of Process: Sheriff, deputy sheriff, constable, or certified mail.

Transfer: No provision.

Attorneys: Allowed.

Appeals: Allowed by either party to Circuit Court for new trial.

Evictions: Yes.

Note: Tennessee has no actual Small Claims system, but sessions are normally conducted with relatively informal "equitable" rules.

TEXAS

Small Claims Court (Justice Court)

Statutes: Texas Government Code Secs. 28.001 through 28.055. Rules of Civil Procedure for Justice Courts, Rule 523-591.

Dollar Limit: $5,000.

Where to Sue: Precinct in which the defendant resides or obligation was to be performed. Corporations and associations may be sued where they have representatives.

Service of Process: Sheriff, constable, certified mail.

Transfer: The defendant may file a written motion to transfer as provided by the rules governing justice courts.

Attorneys: Allowed.

Appeals: Allowed by either party within 10 days to County Court for new trial (only for cases where amount in controversy exceeds $20).

Evictions: No.

Notes: (1) No assignees (collection agencies) or lenders of money at interest may sue in Small Claims Court.

(2) A jury trial may be demanded by either party.

(3) *Default judgments:* If a default judgment is entered against either defendant or plaintiff, that person has 10 days to file a written motion to show good cause for setting aside dismissal or default judgment for failure to appear.

UTAH

Small Claims (Circuit or Justice Court)

Statutes: Utah Code Annotated: Secs. 78-6-1 through 78-6-15.

Dollar Limit: $5,000.

Where to Sue: County in which the defendant resides or act or omission occurred. Corporation can be sued where has office or place of business.

Service of Process: Sheriff or disinterested adult.

Transfer: No provision.

Attorneys: Allowed.

Appeals: Either party may appeal for a new trial by filing within 10 days of notice of entry of judgment. The District Court will try the appeal in accordance with Small Claims Court procedures, except that a record of the trial will be maintained.

Evictions: No.

Notes: (1) Assignees (collection agencies) cannot sue in Small Claims Court.

(2) Either party may demand jury trial.

(3) Utah has evening hour sessions.

(4) Defendant must counterclaim at least two days before trial.

VERMONT

Small Claims Procedure (District Court)

Statutes: Vermont Statutes Annotated: Title 12, Secs. 405, 5531 through 5538; Vermont Rules of Civil Procedure 80.3.

Dollar Limit: $3,500.

Where to Sue: Territorial unit in which any defendant or plaintiff resides, or act or omission occurred.

Service of Process: Sheriff, constable, disinterested adult (with court's permission), or certified mail, return receipt.

Transfer: Not allowed.

Attorneys: Allowed.

Appeals: Allowed by either party within 30 days to Superior Court on law only—not facts.

Evictions: No.

Notes: (1) Defendant must give written answer within 20 days of service or will lose by default.

(2) Counterclaims over $3,500 allowed; however, recovery will be limited to $3,500.

(3) Defendant may request jury trial.

VIRGINIA

Small Claims Court (District Court) in all larger counties; otherwise regular District Court

Statutes: Code of Virginia: Secs. 16.1-76 through 16.1-118.1; 16.1-122.1 through 16.1-122.7.

Dollar Limit: $1,000 up to $10,000 in regular district court (check with County Court clerk). $10,000 in District Court.

Where to Sue: District in which any defendant resides, is employed, or regularly conducts business, where act or omission occurred, or where property is located.

Service of Process: Sheriff or adult approved by court.

Transfer: Allowed.

Attorneys: Not allowed unless bringing their own suit.

Appeals: Allowed by either party within 10 days (on cases over $50) to Circuit Court for new trial; either party may request jury trial.

Evictions: Yes.

Note: No jury trials allowed.

WASHINGTON

Small Claims Department (District Court)
Statutes: Revised Code of Washington Annotated: Title 3, Sec. 66.040, Title 12, Secs. 40.010 through 40.120; Washington Court Rules Part V (Justice Court Civil Rules), Rule 73.
Dollar Limit: $2,500.
Where to Sue: County where any defendant resides. Corporation resides where it transacts business or has an office.
Service of Process: Sheriff or deputy, constable, disinterested adult, or certified or registered mail.
Transfer: Allowed if corporate plaintiff is represented by lawyer and defendant requests transfer to regular civil docket.
Attorneys or Paralegals: Not allowed without judge's consent, unless the case was transferred from regular civil court.
Appeals: No appeal by a party who requested Small Claims Court if the claim was under $1,000. Otherwise, within 14 days to Superior Court for new trial.
Evictions: No.
Notes: (1) Defendant with counterclaim over $2,500 must sue on it separately.
(2) May sue only to recover money.
(3) Court may order judgment payment plan if the debtor is present in court.

WEST VIRGINIA

Magistrate's Court
Statutes: West Virginia Code: Chapter 50, Secs. 2-1 through 6-3, Chapter 56, Sec. 1-1, Rules of Civil Procedure for Magistrate's Courts, Rules 1-21.
Dollar Limit: $5,000.
Where to Sue: County in which any defendant resides or can be served; also where act or omission occurred. West Virginia corporations reside at principal office; other corporations where they do business.
Service of Process: Sheriff or disinterested adult (clerk prepares summons and forwards to sheriff).
Transfer: Allowed if all parties agree to remove to Circuit court, or by any party for claims over $300. Also allowed at magistrate's discretion if defendant requests transfer in her answer or within a reasonable time.
Attorneys: Allowed.
Appeals: Allowed by either party within 20 days to Circuit Court for new trial.
Evictions: Yes.
Notes: (1) Defendant must give written answer in 20 days (30 days if service was made on attorney authorized to accept service for defendant) or lose by default. Time limit is five days for eviction action.
(2) Jury trial may be demanded by either party if claim over $20 or possession of real estate involved.
(3) The deposition (recorded questions and answers) of a witness unable to attend may be taken.

WISCONSIN

Small Claims (Circuit Court)
Statutes: Wisconsin Statutes Annotated: Secs. 799.01 through 799.45, 421.401.
Dollar Limit: $5000. No limit on eviction suits.
Where to Sue: County where claim arose or in which any defendant resides or does substantial business. If defendant is a state agency or official, Dane County. If a claim arose from consumer

transaction, county where consumer sought or acquired the property, services, money or credit that is the subject of the claim, or where the consumer signed the contract.

Service of Process: Except for evictions, summons mailed by court clerk, return receipt requested. For evictions, personal service required.

Transfer: Allowed to regular County Court procedure on defendant's counterclaim over $5,000.

Attorneys: Allowed.

Appeals: Allowed by either party within 45 days to Court of Appeals, on law—not facts. No appeal from default judgment. Appeal in eviction action must be initiated within 15 days of judgment.

Evictions: Yes.

Note: (1) Either party may request jury trial.

(2) A motion for a new trial must be made within 20 days of judgment.

WYOMING

County Court or Justice of the Peace Court

Statutes: Wyoming Statutes Annotated: Code of Civil Procedure Secs. 1-21-201 through 1-21-205; 5-5-101 through 5-5-175; Rules of Civil Procedure for Justice of the Peace Courts, Rules 1 through 8.

Dollar Limit: $4,000. County Court, $7,000.

Where to Sue: County in which the defendant resides or can be served for personal injury in county where accident occurred. If defendant is Wyoming corporation, in county where corporation is situated or has principal office or place of business; for nonresident corporation, where cause of action arose or plaintiff resides.

Service of Process: Sheriff or deputy, deputized process server, certified or registered mail, court-approved adult. Court can serve, within county, by registered mail.

Transfer: Allowed.

Attorneys: Allowed. If one party gets one, the other may, if desired, have a continuance to obtain counsel.

Appeals: Allowed by either party within 10 days to District Court on law only—not facts.

Evictions: Yes.

Notes: (1) Either party may demand jury trial.

(2) Arbitration is available in some circumstances.

INDEX

prior to judgment, recovery of, 15/8, 24/13
See also Judgment, collection
Counsel table, in courtroom, 13/7
Counterclaim
  definition, 1/7
  See also "Claim of Defendant" form
County governments. *See* Public agencies
County Recorder's office, definition, 1/8
Court clerk, in courtroom, 13/6-7
Court costs, 10/1, 10/8
Court date. *See* Hearing date
Courthouse, locating, 13/6
Court jurisdiction, 1/8, 8/1, 9/1-8, 12/2
Court papers, 10/2-7
  and stating case, 2/1-2
  See also specific forms
Court reporter, in courtroom, 13/7
Courtroom layout and procedure, 13/6-8, 14/3,
  15/2-4
Court times, 13/6
Creditors. *See* Debt cases
Cross complaint. *See* "Claim of Defendant" form

D

D.B.A. ("Doing business as"), 7/2-3, 8/3-4
Damage cases. *See specific types of cases*
  (Clothing damage, etc.)
Damage deposits. *See* Deposits, rental
Damages
  from breach of contract, 2/8, 4/5-7
  and intentional harm, 2/13-14
  by minor, 8/6-7
  mitigation of, 4/5-6
  for pain and suffering, 2/16, 4/10, 4/11-13
  punitive, 2/13-14, 4/13, 20/3
Death of defendant, 8/8
Debt cases, 2/4, 2/7, 18/1-11
  from defendant's viewpoint, 18/7-11
  defenses, 18/9-10
  from plaintiff's viewpoint, 18/3-7
  and Small Claims Court, 18/1-3
  statute of limitations, 18/5
Debts, nonpayment. *See* Debt cases
"Declaration for Subpoena Duces Tecum" form,
  sample, 14/8
Declaration of Nonmilitary Service, 11/11
Defamation cases, 21/7-8
Default judgment, 10/10-13, 12/3, 15/1-2

appeal of, 10/13, 15/2, 23/10
and collection of judgment, 24/2-4
definition, 1/7
and military personnel, 11/11
setting aside, 10/11-12, 15/2
Defendant's Claim. *See* "Claim of Defendant"
  form
Defendant, 12/1-8
  checklist, 1/5
  death of, 8/8
  definition, 1/7
  failure to appear in court, 10/10-13
  multiple, 8/2, 8/4-5, 9/6, 17/4
  out-of-state, 12/2
  presentation of case, 15/5
  See also specific types of cases
Defense, lack of, 12/3-4
Delay of case. *See* Continuance
Demand letter, 6/2-3, 6/8-15, 16/4-5, 18/4-5,
  19/6
  samples, 6/14-15, 16/4, 17/10-11, 19/6
Department of Consumer Affairs, 17/8
Department of Motor Vehicles
  and motor vehicle accidents, 8/6, 19/2, 24/11
  and recovery of costs, 15/8
  and used car dealers, 17/8
Deposits, rental, 2/4, 20/3-7
Diagrams. *See* Drawing and diagrams
Discovery techniques, for appeal, 23/14
Dismissed case
  definition, 1/7
  vacating, 10/15
Dispute resolution. *See* Arbitration; Mediation
Disqualification of judge, 13/9
District attorney, and consumer fraud, 17/8
Districts. *See* Public agencies
Doctrine of strict liability. *See* Liability
Documentation, 10/2, 13/8, 13/10-11, 18/6
  costs for obtaining, 15/8
  and default judgment, 15/2
  in landlord-tenant cases, 20/5
  in motor vehicle purchase cases, 17/5, 17/8
  in motor vehicle repair cases, 16/6
  and record keeping, 2/2
  See also Evidence
Documents, subpoenaing, 14/6-9
Dog-bite cases, 4/11, 21/4-5
Drawings and diagrams, in courtroom, 15/3,
  16/6, 19/4

CATALOG

...more from Nolo Press

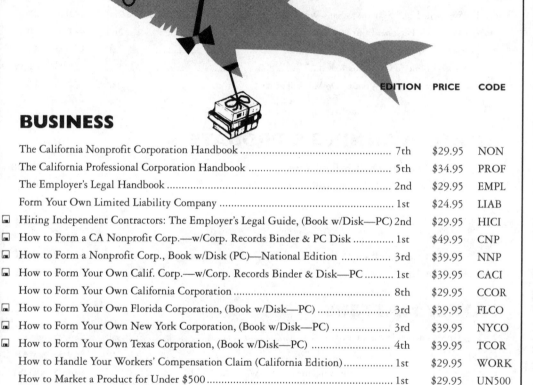

☐ Book with disk
⬤ Book with CD-ROM

	EDITION	PRICE	CODE

Starting and Running a Successful Newsletter or Magazine .... 1st $24.95 MAG
▣ Taking Care of Your Corporation, Vol. 1, (Book w/Disk—PC) .... 1st $29.95 CORK
▣ Taking Care of Your Corporation, Vol. 2, (Book w/Disk—PC) 1st $39.95 CORK2
Tax Savvy for Small Business .... 2nd $26.95 SAVVY
Trademark: How to Name Your Business & Product .... 2nd $29.95 TRD
Your Rights in the Workplace .... 3rd $19.95 YRW

CONSUMER

Fed Up With the Legal System: What's Wrong & How to Fix It .... 2nd $9.95 LEG
How to Win Your Personal Injury Claim .... 2nd $24.95 PICL
Nolo's Everyday Law Book .... 1st $21.95 EVL
Nolo's Pocket Guide to California Law .... 5th $11.95 CLAW
Trouble-Free Travel...And What to Do When Things Go Wrong .... 1st $14.95 TRAV

ESTATE PLANNING & PROBATE

8 Ways to Avoid Probate (Quick & Legal Series) 1st $15.95 PRO8
How to Probate an Estate (California Edition) .... 9th $34.95 PAE
Make Your Own Living Trust .... 2nd $21.95 LITR
▣ Nolo's Will Book, (Book w/Disk—PC) .... 3rd $29.95 SWIL
Plan Your Estate .... 3rd $24.95 NEST
The Quick and Legal Will Book .... 1st $15.95 QUIC
Nolo's Law Form Kit: Wills .... 1st $14.95 KWL

FAMILY MATTERS

A Legal Guide for Lesbian and Gay Couples .... 9th $24.95 LG
California Marriage Law .... 12th $19.95 MARR
Child Custody: Building Parenting Agreements that Work .... 2nd $24.95 CUST
Divorce & Money: How to Make the Best Financial Decisions During Divorce .... 3rd $26.95 DIMO
Get A Life: You Don't Need a Million to Retire Well .... 1st $18.95 LIFE
The Guardianship Book (California Edition) .... 2nd $24.95 GB
How to Adopt Your Stepchild in California .... 4th $22.95 ADOP
How to Do Your Own Divorce in California .... 21st $24.95 CDIV
How to Do Your Own Divorce in Texas .... 6th $19.95 TDIV
How to Raise or Lower Child Support in California .... 3rd $18.95 CHLD
The Living Together Kit .... 8th $24.95 LTK

▣ Book with disk
● Book with CD-ROM

	EDITION	PRICE	CODE
Nolo's Law Form Kit: Hiring Childcare & Household Help	1st	$14.95	KCHLO
Nolo's Pocket Guide to Family Law	4th	$14.95	FLD
Practical Divorce Solutions	1st	$14.95	PDS
Smart Ways to Save Money During and After Divorce	1st	$14.95	SAVMO

GOING TO COURT

	EDITION	PRICE	CODE
Collect Your Court Judgment (California Edition)	3rd	$24.95	JUDG
How to Seal Your Juvenile & Criminal Records (California Edition)	6th	$24.95	CRIM
How to Sue For Up to 25,000...and Win!	2nd	$29.95	MUNI
Everybody's Guide to Small Claims Court in California	12th	$18.95	CSCC
Everybody's Guide to Small Claims Court (National Edition)	6th	$18.95	NSCC
Fight Your Ticket ... and Win! (California Edition)	6th	$19.95	FYT
How to Change Your Name (California Edition)	6th	$24.95	NAME
Mad at Your Lawyer	1st	$21.95	MAD
Represent Yourself in Court: How to Prepare & Try a Winning Case	1st	$29.95	RYC

HOMEOWNERS, LANDLORDS & TENANTS

	EDITION	PRICE	CODE
The Deeds Book (California Edition)	4th	$16.95	DEED
Dog Law	3rd	$14.95	DOG
Every Landlord's Legal Guide (National Edition)	1st	$34.95	ELLI
For Sale by Owner (California Edition)	2nd	$24.95	FSBO
Homestead Your House (California Edition)	8th	$9.95	HOME
How to Buy a House in California	4th	$24.95	BHCA
The Landlord's Law Book, Vol. 1: Rights & Responsibilities (California Edition)	5th	$34.95	LBRT
The Landlord's Law Book, Vol. 2: Evictions (California Edition)	6th	$34.95	LBEV
Leases & Rental Agreements (Quick & Legal Series)	1st	$18.95	LEAR
Neighbor Law: Fences, Trees, Boundaries & Noise	2nd	$16.95	NEI
Safe Homes, Safe Neighborhoods: Stopping Crime Where You Live	1st	$14.95	SAFE
Tenants' Rights (California Edition)	13th	$19.95	CTEN

HUMOR

	EDITION	PRICE	CODE
29 Reasons Not to Go to Law School	4th	$9.95	29R
Poetic Justice	1st	$9.95	PJ

Book with disk
Book with CD-ROM

	EDITION	PRICE	CODE

IMMIGRATION

MONEY MATTERS

PATENTS AND COPYRIGHTS

RESEARCH & REFERENCE

SENIORS

⊡ Book with disk

◉ Book with CD-ROM

	EDITION	PRICE	CODE

SOFTWARE
Call for special direct discounts on Software

	EDITION	PRICE	CODE
California Incorporator 2.0—DOS	2.0	$79.95	INCI
Living Trust Maker 2.0—Macintosh	2.0	$79.95	LTM2
Living Trust Maker 2.0—Windows	2.0	$79.95	LTWI2
Small Business Legal Pro Deluxe CD—Windows/Macintosh CD-ROM	2.0	$79.95	SBCD
Nolo's Partnership Maker 1.0—DOS	1.0	$79.95	PAGI1
Personal RecordKeeper 4.0—Macintosh	4.0	$49.95	RKM4
Personal RecordKeeper 4.0—Windows	4.0	$49.95	RKP4
Patent It Yourself 1.0—Windows	1.0	$229.95	PYP12
WillMaker 6.0—Macintosh	6.0	$49.95	WM6B
WillMaker 6.0—Windows	6.0	$49.95	WIW6B

Special Upgrade Offer
Get 25% off the latest edition off your Nolo book

It's important to have the most current legal information. Because laws and legal procedures change often, we update our books regularly. To help keep you up-to-date we are extending this special upgrade offer. Cut out and mail the title portion of the cover of your old Nolo book and we'll give you 25% off the retail price of the NEW EDITION of that book when you purchase directly from us. For more information call us at 1-800-992-6656. This offer is to individuals only.

Book with disk
Book with CD-ROM

ORDER FORM

Code	Quantity	Title		Unit price	Total
			Subtotal		
			California residents add Sales Tax		
			Basic Shipping ($6.00 for 1 item; $7.00 for 2 or more)		
			UPS RUSH delivery $7.50–any size order*		
			TOTAL		

Name

Address

(UPS to street address, Priority Mail to P.O. boxes) * Delivered in 3 business days from receipt of S.F. Bay Area use regular shipping. order.

FOR FASTER SERVICE, USE YOUR CREDIT CARD & OUR TOLL-FREE NUMBERS

Order 24 hours a day   1-800-992-6656
Fax your order   1-800-645-0895
e-mail   cs@nolo.com
General Information   1-510-549-1976
Customer Service   1-800-728-3555, Mon.-Fri. 9am-5pm, PST

METHOD OF PAYMENT

☐ Check enclosed

☐ VISA   ☐ MasterCard   ☐ Discover Card   ☐ American Express

Account #   Expiration Date

Authorizing Signature

Daytime Phone

PRICES SUBJECT TO CHANGE.

VISIT OUR STORES   VISIT US ONLINE

You'll find our complete line of books and software, all at a discount.

BERKELEY   **SAN JOSE**
950 Parker Street   111 N. Market Street, #115
Berkeley, CA 94710   San Jose, CA 95113
1-510-704-2248   1-408-271-7240

on the Internet

www.nolo.com

NOLO PRESS 950 PARKER ST., BERKELEY, CA 94710

ake 1 minute & Get a 1-year

NOLO *News* subscription free!*

With our quarterly magazine, the **NOLO** *News*, you'll

Learn about important legal changes that affect you

Find out first about new Nolo products

Keep current with practical articles on everyday law

Get answers to your legal questions in
Ask Auntie Nolo's advice column

Save money with special Subscriber Only discounts

Tickle your funny bone with our famous
Lawyer Joke column.

only takes one minute to reserve your free 1-year
bscription or to extend your **NOLO** *News*
bscription.

*U.S. ADDRESSES ONLY.
ONE YEAR INTERNATIONAL SUBSCRIPTIONS: CANADA & MEXICO $10.00;
ALL OTHER FOREIGN ADDRESSES $20.00.

call 1-800-992-6656

fax 1-800-645-0895

e-mail NOLOSUB@NOLOPRESS.com

or mail us this postage-paid registration card

R E G I S T R A T I O N   C A R D

NAME _____ DATE _____

ADDRESS _____

_____ PHONE NUMBER _____

CITY _____ STATE _____ ZIP _____

WHERE DID YOU HEAR ABOUT THIS BOOK? _____

WHERE DID YOU PURCHASE THIS PRODUCT? _____

DID YOU CONSULT A LAWYER? (PLEASE CIRCLE ONE)   YES   NO   NOT APPLICABLE

DID YOU FIND THIS BOOK HELPFUL?   (VERY)   5   4   3   2   1   (NOT AT ALL)

SUGGESTIONS FOR IMPROVING THIS PRODUCT _____

_____

WAS IT EASY TO USE?   (VERY EASY)   5   4   3   2   1   (VERY DIFFICULT)

DO YOU OWN A COMPUTER? IF SO, WHICH FORMAT? (PLEASE CIRCLE ONE)   WINDOWS   DOS   MAC

We occasionally make our mailing list available to carefully selected companies whose
products may be of interest to you. If you do not wish to receive mailings from these companies,
please check this box ❑

NSCC 7.0

"Nolo helps lay people perform legal tasks without the aid—or fees—of lawyers."**—USA Today**

[Nolo] books are ..."written in plain language, free of legal mumbo jumbo, and spiced with witty personal observations."**—Associated Press**

"...Nolo publications...guide people simply through the how, when, where and why of law."**—Washington Post**

"Increasingly, people who are not lawyers are performing tasks usually regarded as legal work... And consumers, using books like Nolo's, do routine legal work themselves."**—Washington Post**

"...All of [Nolo's] books are easy-to-understand, are updated regularly, provide pull-out forms...and are often quite moving in their sense of compassion for the struggles of the lay reader."**—San Francisco Chronicle**